BRITISH BY-ELECTIONS

British By-Elections

The Volatile Electorate

PIPPA NORRIS

CLARENDON PRESS · OXFORD

1990

Oxford University Press, Walton Street, Oxford OX2 6DP

Oxford New York Toronto
Delhi Bombay Calcutta Madras Karachi
Petaling Jaya Singapore Hong Kong Tokyo
Nairobi Dar es Salaam Cape Town
Melbourne Auckland

and associated companies in
Berlin Ibadan

Oxford is a trade mark of Oxford University Press

Published in the United States
by Oxford University Press, New York

British Library Cataloguing in Publication Data

Norris, Pippa, 1953–
British by-elections: the volatile electorate.
1. Great Britain. Parliament. House of Commons. Members.
By-elections, history
I. Title
324.941
ISBN 0–19–827330–4

Library of Congress Cataloging in Publication Data
Norris, Pippa.
British by-elections: the volatile electorate/Pippa Norris.
p. cm.
Includes bibliographical references.
1. Elections—Great Britain. 2. Voting—Great Britain. 3. Public
opinion—Great Britain. I. Title.
JN956.N667 1990 90–31230   324.941'085—dc20
ISBN 0–19–827330–4

Typeset by BP Integraphics, Bath, Avon
Printed and bound in
Great Britain by Bookcraft (Bath) Ltd,
Midsomer Norton, Avon

Preface

THIS book would not have been possible without the help of many colleagues. In particular the author would like to acknowledge the invaluable contribution made by Vincent Hanna who initiated and encouraged the project. Research for this book has the advantage of access to a series of surveys of by-election and marginal constituencies, designed by the author and commissioned by BBC 'Newsnight' from 1985 to 1987. The author is grateful to the BBC for supporting the project and to everyone who helped in the early stages by assisting with constituency surveys, including John Curtice, Roger Eatwell, Brendan Evans, Ian Gordon, Mark Hagger, Roger Iles, Clive Payne, Linda Anderson, and David Woodhead, along with all other colleagues and students who contributed towards the fieldwork.

I am also indebted to those who commented on early versions of the manuscript, or who provided general encouragement at various states, including Joni Lovenduski, William Miller, Hugh Berrington, David Butler, Ivor Crewe, Patrick Dunleavy, and Richard Rose. Comparative material in Chapter 13 draws on work developed with Frank Feigert and research on candidates in Chapter 8 was developed with Joni Lovenduski. The *European Journal of Political Research* and *Electoral Studies* published early reports on parts of the research. Additional information about opinion polls was provided by Bob Wybrow at Gallup, Brian Gosschalk at MORI, Bob Waller at Harris and Nick Sparrow at NOP. Denise Ralph helped with the data-coding and survey administration. Newcastle Polytechnic provided sabbatical leave, and the author is grateful to colleagues at the Center for European Studies, Harvard University and the Institute for Research on Women and Gender, Columbia University who generously provided facilities to complete the book. Henry Hardy at Oxford University Press supported the project. Thanks are due to all with the usual caveat that, of course, any mistakes in the book remain the responsibility of the author.

Edinburgh University   P. N.
1989

Contents

Figures

Tables

Abbreviations

Ab.	Abstained
BE	By-election
Corr.	Correlation
DK	Don't know
GE	General election
GLC	Greater London Council
ILEA	Inner London Education Authority
LSDP	Liberal-Social Democrat Party
MORI	Market and Opinion Research International
N.	Number of cases
NALGO	National and Local Government Officers' Association
NOP	National Opinion Polls
ORC	Opinion Research Centre
PC	Plaid Cymru
Ref.	Refused to answer
SDP	Social Democrat Party
SEG	Socio-economic group
SNP	Scottish Nationalist Party
TSRU	Telephone Survey Research Unit

Introduction

WHEN I first became interested in British Parliamentary by-elections I was struck by something of a paradox. In the press contests in Glasgow Hillhead, Bermondsey, and Greenwich generated headline news. On television 'by-election specials' broadcast the results until the early hours of the morning. During the mid-eighties the Social Democrats and Liberals mobilized about a thousand activists from all parts of the country into key contests. National party leaders and managers invested time and money in constituency campaigns. In short, by-elections were treated seriously by journalists and politicians alike.

Yet despite popular interest by-elections were largely neglected in the academic literature on British elections and voting behaviour. There were passing references to these contests but few detailed studies (with the notable exceptions of Cook and Ramsden, 1973 and Mughan 1986*a, b,* 1988). Political science has tended to dismiss by-elections as trivial 'media-events'. The reasons which attract journalistic interest have tended to deter serious analysis. This book aims to remedy the neglect by comparing a range of post-war contests to consider how voters react in by-elections, why support shifts during the campaign, and what this tells us more generally about the nature of electoral behaviour in recent decades.

Conventional explanations of by-elections fall into two main categories. One pervasive view, the 'Campaign-Specific' thesis, sees by-elections as idiosyncratic contests reflecting the strengths and weaknesses of individual candidates and local party organizations in particular constituencies. As such we should beware of attaching too much significance to the results, or interpreting the outcome in terms of national trends, for each contest is *sui generis.* Yet others suggest that a series of by-elections falls into a systematic pattern which provides an indication of current party strength in the country. As such by-elections can be treated as equivalent to public opinion polls, only considered more reliable as these contests involve 'real' rather than hypothetical votes (the 'Referendum' thesis). In this view by-elections are analogous to a referendum on the government's record, with the results reflecting electoral support for the party in government. Which perspective is most persuasive?

THE CAMPAIGN-SPECIFIC THESIS

For some the most satisfactory explanation of by-elections rests on the distinctive combination of factors in each specific campaign: divisions within the local party, a weak grassroots organization, the ideology or personality of selected candidates, the unpopularity of certain government actions, the circumstances causing the by-election, the publication of certain polls, the political character of the local council, media publicity, the perceived closeness of the race, or individual events within the campaign (see for example the accounts in chapters 2–10 in Cook and Ramsden 1973; Studlar 1984; Pollock 1941). On these grounds it can be argued with some plausibility that the results would have been very different without the constituency polls in the Greenwich by-election, the adoption of Peter Tatchell as a far-left Labour candidate at Bermondsey, or the personal stature of Roy Jenkins at Glasgow Hillhead. After the event politicians representing the losing parties invariably tend to downplay the wider significance of the results. Each is dismissed as a 'little local difficulty'. As Balfour remarked after a defeat:

I do not for one instance [*sic*] admit that by-elections are a test, or ought to be regarded as a test, of public feeling. They are, of course, a test of the feelings of a particular constituency at the time the by-election takes place. They are not, and they cannot be made, the index and test of what the feeling of the people of the country is as a whole. (Quoted in Pollock 1941: 528.)

If campaign-specific factors dominate it follows that commentators should be cautious about drawing wider inferences from particular results about British public opinion, support for the parties in the country as a whole, or, still less, the prospects for a subsequent general election. 'By-elections can never be regarded as offering a direct mirror of how the voting would go in a general election' (Butler 1973: 9). 'Individual by-elections are poor guides to the future course of politics ... Politicians who dismiss bad by-election results as irrelevant are probably correct' (Craig 1987: vii).

THE REFERENDUM THESIS

Yet others believe that, although local circumstances play a part, by-elections can be explained most satisfactorily by certain systematic features of these contests, notably the trend towards greater by-election instability, the dramatic third party victories, and the significant erosion of government support. In this view Greenwich and Orpington were not singular events but represent recurrent trends in electoral behaviour.

One of the most striking developments has been the gradual trend towards unstable by-elections evident from the mid sixties onwards. In the immediate post-war years few seats changed hands but during the last decade about a third of all by-elections were lost by the incumbent party. This increased volatility is closely associated with the rise of multi-party politics, but cannot be wholly attributed to this development, as Labour and the Conservatives have been the main beneficiaries in some seats. We will consider these developments in the light of explanations based on theories of partisan dealignment and realignment.

The second remarkable feature of these contests is shown by the classic third party by-election victories, epitomized by Orpington, Bermondsey, Greenwich, and Glasgow Govan. It is these contests which provide the answer to a journalist's prayer: the drama of the underdog candidate coming from behind to triumph over the established laws of electoral physics. Yet traditional theories of voting behaviour have not established why third parties can sometimes manage these famous victories, and yet sometimes fail. In the mid eighties why Brecon and Radnor but not Tyne Bridge; why Ryedale but not Knowsley North? How could third parties suddenly mobilize support in some contests, even in seats with majorities of 30 to 40 per cent, while failing to achieve similar breakthroughs in general elections, or even subsequent by-elections? We will explore this puzzle, as a key to understanding the nature of third party support, in the context of theories of tactical voting.

The last characteristic feature of by-elections, which has attracted most theoretical interest, is the significant erosion of government support evident in most contests. This tendency is strongest in the mid-term period of any administration, in a broadly cyclical pattern popularly known as the 'mid-term blues', with some governments managing to stage a revival in the run-up to the subsequent general election. Why should the government consistently lose votes? The conventional explanation often heard is that voters treat by-elections as a referendum on government performance. As such by-elections provide voters with the opportunity to protest against the government in power, to 'send a message to No. 10', in the full knowledge that they can return to the party in government in a general election.

The underlying assumption of the referendum thesis is that the British electorate is relatively unmoved by local forces so that a by-election will accurately reflect trends in public opinion across the country. This pervasive viewpoint underpins much of the journalistic interest in these contests; hence it has become commonplace for the media to project the likely composition of the House of Commons based on particular by-election results. Politicians frequently quote favourable results as indicators of party popularity, only these are considered more reliable than opinion polls as they involve 'real votes' during an actual campaign rather than questions about how the electorate would behave in a hypothetical general election. As one commentator remarked about Canadian by-elections: 'while no particular significance can be placed on the result of a single by-election, a series of by-elections can be relied upon to reflect national opinion trends, and, consequently, barring any sudden reversal of opinion, to forecast within broad limits the strength of government party support at the next general election' (Scarrow 1961: 23).

The assumption that by-election results reflect general public reactions to the government's record is a widespread view in the press; for example the government's loss of Ryedale in May 1986 was largely explained as the public's verdict on the Westland affair and the American bombing of Libya. In the mid seventies the loss of Walsall North, Birmingham Stechford, and Ashfield was commonly attributed to the economic performance of the Labour administration, facing high inflation, problems with the balance of payments, and industrial unrest. In 1989 Labour's victory in the Vale of Glamorgan was widely explained by the unpopularity of the Conservative administration's proposed health service reforms.

Academic support for the referendum thesis has been provided in studies by Taylor and Payne (1973), Oakeshott (1973), and Mughan (1986*a, b,* 1988), based on an analysis of post-war constituency results. Taylor and Payne argue that a 'rational choice' model provides a plausible explanation of the behaviour of the electorate in by-elections. The authors conclude that by-elections allow voters to register their approval or disapproval of government policy, either by switching or abstention. By-election results are therefore strongly related to the changing cycle of government popularity (Taylor and Payne 1973). Matthew Oakeshott has argued that by-election results reflect the electorate's view of the government's performance, specifically on the economy. He suggests that strong anti-government swings in by-elections have been associated with deteriorating conditions in the economy, such as the rate of unemployment, the growth of retail prices, changes in real personal income, and increases in taxation (Oakeshott 1973).

In recent years the most thorough examination of by-elections based on constituency results has been provided by Anthony Mughan. In seeking to explain the government's loss of votes in mid-term elections Mughan concludes that public approval of the government's record in office is the strongest direct influence on its by-election support. Therefore there are grounds for interpreting these contests, at least in part, as a referendum on the economic and political performance of the party in office (Mughan 1988; see also Mughan 1986*a, b*; Studlar and Sigelman 1987; Lewis 1943; King 1968). Yet Mughan's complete model, the most rigorous recent test of this theory, accounts for only a limited amount of variance (22 per cent) in the by-election vote for the governing party. Therefore, Mughan acknowledges (1988: 51), in this model the majority of variance remains unexplained: 'Clearly much else besides a government's economic and political record determines their mid-term electoral performance.'

As these authors recognize, the referendum argument may sound plausible but much of the evidence supporting the theory can be questioned. In the absence of survey data about individual voters these studies rely upon constituency results. This source suffers from certain limitations; it is well known that correlation does not necessarily imply causation. The association between government popularity in opinion polls and in by-elections may be spurious as a result of a third factor; for example the treatment of the parties in the media may lead to a sudden surge in support for the Scottish Nationalists (SNP) in by-elections and opinion polls. There are problems about the direction of causality: the national standing of the parties may affect local by-election results but by-election victories due to local factors (such as the strong performance of a candidate like Rosie Barnes in Greenwich), may have a significant impact on the national popularity of the parties (Clarke, Stewart, and Zuk 1986). We can only have full confidence in the referendum model if trends in constituency results are confirmed at the level of the individual voter.

Further, previous models have focused exclusively upon government support without seeking to explain the by-election vote for the opposition parties. Yet this is inadequate under the conditions of multi-party politics where the swing between opposition parties, from the Liberals to the Scottish Nationalists, or from Labour to the Social Democratic Party, may prove decisive. Thus the referendum thesis makes certain important assumptions about the nature of voting behaviour which need to be systematically re-examined. We will therefore consider the nature and conditions of government support in the light of theories of retrospective voting.

METHODS AND DATA

This book utilizes two primary sources of information. For the analysis of trends over time, we will compare 359 constituency by-election results from 1945 to 1987. This allows us to investigate such questions as whether levels of voting turn-out relate to the marginality of seats, whether the extent of minor party support has increased over time and whether there are cycles in government popularity. Constituency results also allow cross-cultural comparisons with by-elections in such countries as Canada and Australia.

Nevertheless constituency-level results provide limited information, so the analysis is supplemented by a series of thirty-seven constituency surveys commissioned by BBC 'Newsnight'. The surveys were carried out from 1985 to 1987 in Tyne Bridge, Fulham, Ryedale, West Derbyshire, Knowsley North, Greenwich, and Truro. These disparate by-elections, from the routine and predictable inner-city opposition seat of Tyne Bridge to the more controversial and volatile contests in Greenwich, proved ideal for testing theories under different conditions. The constituencies were socially and politically diverse, from the vast rural acres of Ryedale to the urban estates of Knowsley North, from the affluence of professional parts of Fulham to the solid unemployment of Tyne Bridge. In Fulham, Ryedale, and West Derbyshire the government was defending the seat, while Greenwich, Tyne Bridge and Knowsley North were Labour seats and the Liberals found themselves in the rare position of being the incumbent in the Truro by-election.

With hindsight it was apparent that the research design of the surveys suffered from several shortcomings; items on government performance, prospective issues and candidate evaluations were not included in all surveys. Design limitations left out many items which with hindsight would have been desirable. As might be expected from a collaborative enterprise, there was often a conflict of interest between journalistic and academic needs. The final survey represented a compromise, an attempt to go beyond the standard items in commercial polls without the resources to generate a detailed academic survey such as the British Election Study. The surveys met the prime needs of journalism; BBC 'Newsnight' coverage of by-elections was widely respected and the record of the final polls proved to be highly accurate. But in the analysis stage it became clear that many aspects of the explanatory model could not be fully confirmed on the basis of the available material. Despite their limitations the BBC 'Newsnight' polls provide the most comprehensive survey data on by-elections currently available.

DEVELOPMENT OF THE BOOK

The book falls into two main parts reflecting the differences between the campaign-specific and the referendum perspectives. Part I starts by outlining the basic legal context of by-elections and their functions for Parliament, parties, and the electoral system (Chapter 1). The book goes on to document chronological developments since the war (Chapters 2 to 5), notably how by-elections have been transformed from relatively quiet and predictable two-party contests in the fifties to the more dynamic campaigns characteristic of the eighties. The book compares campaigns within a few months of each other, in Knowsley North and Greenwich, as detailed case-studies to examine the conditions producing electoral volatility (Chapters 6 and 7). Certain general trends can be drawn out of this account, notably the periodic rise and fall of Liberal and nationalist support, but Part I is essentially concerned with exploring the detailed circumstances which affect particular campaigns.

Part II is concerned with systematic trends. Chapter 8 considers increased by-election volatility in terms of theories of partisan dealignment and realignment. Chapter 9 develops a general model of by-elections, based on retrospective evaluations of government performance, and explores the empirical support for this theory. Chapters 10 and 11 consider the influences shaping the campaign, including the role of party organizations, the selection of candidates, media coverage, and opinion polls. To explain the rise of multi-party politics Chapter 12 develops a typology of voters, distinguishing core, tacticals, floaters, and abstainers. The concluding chapter compares British by-elections with those in Australia and Canada, to see whether there are similar patterns of electoral behaviour (Chapter 13). It is hoped that this study will contribute towards understanding by-elections for their own sake, as intrinsically interesting phenomena, as well as throwing further light on the general nature of the volatile electorate.

PART I

Developments in By-Elections, 1945–1987

1

Causes and Functions of By-Elections

THE primary purpose of Parliamentary by-elections is to replace members in constituencies which fall vacant between general elections, but these contests can serve a range of other functions with an impact on Parliament, political parties, and election campaigns. By-elections can have significant consequences for the recruitment of new blood to the House. There have been almost 400 contests since the war and during some Parliaments there has been as much as a 10 per cent turnover of members through by-elections. By-elections have allowed parties to bring back leading front-benchers defeated in the previous general election, such as Harold Macmillan in 1945, Anthony Barber in 1965, and Shirley Williams in 1981. This route into Parliament has become more significant in recent years given the increased safeness of incumbent MPs (Curtice and Steed 1986).

By-elections may serve other important needs. By-elections have been seen as vital tests of party support; in the early eighties the fledgeling strength of the Liberal–Social Democratic Alliance was judged in the light of the string of by-election victories from Warrington to Crosby, while in the late eighties the resurgence of two-party politics was proclaimed following Labour's victory in the Vale of Glamorgan. The result in mid-Staffordshire in 1990 reinforced the crisis in support for Mrs Thatcher's leadership. Key contests have had considerable impact on subsequent events—and indeed on subsequent by-elections. Victories can substantially boost national party popularity in the monthly opinion polls while a poor performance can lead to the demoralization of party activists, leadership splits, and internal party recriminations.

By-elections have proved crucial for the Parliamentary strength of minor parties increasing the credibility of challenges to the established two-party system. Third party gains can allow the initial breakthrough in a constituency which a member can sometimes translate into long-standing support. By-elections provide a public platform in the full glare of national television for fringe parties which stand no chance of winning the seat.

Lastly by-elections may have important consequences for election campaigns. These contests can function as dry-runs for the general election campaign, allowing parties to experiment in a single constituency with innovations in campaign strategies and tactics. Parties can test reaction among the electorate to the presentation of new policy proposals or campaign themes. Where a by-election is seen to revolve around a central issue the result may serve to modify government policy. Contests provide an ideal training-ground for election agents, grassroots activists, and party organizers. The media have been able to try out innovations in electoral coverage including the first television reporting during a campaign in the 1958 Rochdale by-election. By-election results may influence the Prime Minister's decision concerning the precise timing of a general election. The loss of a single seat rarely brings down the government, although it cost the 1974–79 Labour government their majority status in Parliament (Butler and Kavanagh 1985). Therefore significant political consequences may flow from these contests beyond the impact on individual constituencies.

THE LEGAL CONTEXT

Once a vacancy arises for a constituency any Member of Parliament may move the writ to fill the vacancy, although by convention this is usually done by the Chief Whip of the party which previously held the seat (see Craig 1987). If a majority of the House agrees the Speaker must issue the writ. The Party Whips may delay calling a by-election if there are problems with the choice of candidates, to avoid calling a by-election immediately before a general election or to secure more advantageous timing. In 1962 the Conservatives delayed calling Orpington for six months, with disastrous consequences for the party. There is no statutory limit to the time a seat may be left vacant, although in 1973 the Speaker's Conference on Electoral Law suggested that the motion for a by-election writ should normally be moved within three months of the vacancy arising, or within four months in exceptional circumstances.

In recent years MPs have sometimes tried to move the writ as a filibuster tactic, as the procedure takes formal precedence over any other Parliamentary business. In 1989 the Labour MP Dennis Skinner moved the writ for the Tory Vale of Glamorgan to prevent debate on a Private Member's bill on abortion. A few months later the Scottish Nationalist Jim Sillars tried unsuccessfully to move the writ for Glasgow Central to delay the Chancellor's speech on the Budget. Once the writ is moved the timetable for a by-election is laid down in Schedule 1, Part 1 (Rules 1 and 2) of the Representation of the People Act, 1983 (as amended 1985). The writ is issued on the first day of the campaign, with polling following on the Thursday at least two weeks, and not more than three weeks, later (see Craig 1987).

This book focuses on 359 British Parliamentary by-elections from the start of modern party politics in 1945 to the end of Mrs Thatcher's second administration in June 1987. In the United Kingdom there were almost 400 by-elections during this period (see Table 1.1). In accordance with previous practice, however, certain excep-

Table 1.1. *Number of Parliamentary by-elections, UK 1945–1987*

	UK	N. Ireland	Great Britain
1945–50	52	2	47[a]
1950–51	16	2	14
1951–55	48	4	44
1955–59	52	3	49
1959–64	62	1	61
1964–66	13	0	13
1966–70	38	1	37
1970–74	30	0	30
1974–74	1	0	1
1974–79	30	0	30
1979–83	20	3	17
1983–87	31	15	16
TOTAL	393	31	359

Note: a. Excluding university and unopposed contests.
Source: Calculated from Craig (1987). It should be noted that subsequent tables calculated from constituency results are also based on this source.

tional cases are excluded: contests in Northern Ireland because of the distinctive nature of party competition in these constituencies; uncontested by-elections; those with major boundary changes; and by-elections in university seats.

CAUSES OF BY-ELECTIONS

In the post-war period the most common cause of Parliamentary by-elections has been the death of the sitting member, accounting for half of all contests (see Table 1.2). Another third resulted from resignations, usually for non-political reasons such as ill-health or

Table 1.2 *Causes of by-elections, 1945–1987*

	Death	Resignation	Elevation[a]	Other[b]	Total	%British Parlt. seats
1945–50	20	18	7	2	47	7.5
1950–51	7	1	6	0	14	2.3
1951–55	17	15	10	2	44	7.2
1955–59	24	11	12	2	49	7.9
1959–64	26	21	11	3	61	9.9
1964–66	5	3	5	0	13	2.1
1966–70	27	10	0	0	37	5.9
1970–74	17	10	1	1	30	4.8
1974–74	0	1	0	0	1	0.2
1974–79	17	10	3	0	30	4.8
1979–83	12	3	1	1	17	2.7
1983–87	11	4	1	0	16	2.5
TOTAL	183	107	57	11	359	4.8
%	51	30	16	3	100	

Notes: a. Elevation to the Peerage including Life Peerages.
   b. 'Other' includes succession to the Peerage, expulsion from the House of Commons, and elections declared void following petitions.

a career transfer. In a few notable cases members resigned to seek an electoral mandate under a new party or independent banner, notably Dick Taverne's short-lived success as a Democratic Labour candidate in the Lincoln by-election in 1973 and Bruce Douglas-Mann's attempt to be returned as a Social Democrat for Mitcham and Morden in 1982. The most dramatic use of this tactic caused the fifteen by-elections following the mass resignation of Irish Unionist MPs under the leadership of the Reverend Ian Paisley and James Molyneaux in protest against the Anglo-Irish agreement in January 1986. Campaigning on a single issue, in an attempt to demonstrate public opposition to the agreement, all Ulster Unionists, Ulster Democratic Unionists, and Ulster Popular Unionists were eventually returned, although the tactic failed to influence government policy.

The number of by-elections has declined significantly over the years; there were sixty-one by-elections during the 1959–64 Conservative administration but only sixteen during Mrs Thatcher's second administration (1983–87) (see Fig. 1.1). This trend can be

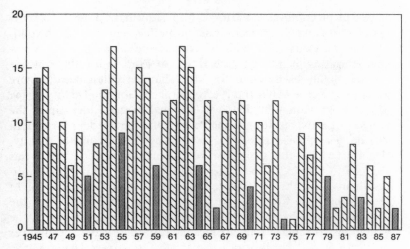

Fig. 1.1   Number of by-elections per year, GB, 1945–1987

attributed to changes in electoral practices and in party management. There has been a fall in the number of by-elections occasioned by the acceptance of an office of profit under the Crown, bankruptcy, lunacy, an election petition, expulsion from the House of Commons, sitting or voting in the House of Commons without taking the oath of allegiance, disqualification from having been elected to the Commons, or being elected member for more than one constituency (Craig 1987). In the nineteenth century certain government Ministers had to offer themselves for re-election upon appointment but this was changed with the Re-Election of Ministers Amendment Act, 1926. Successful petitions for electoral offences have also declined. In 1947 the Labour MP for Gravesend was expelled for contempt of the House of Commons, while a by-election was called in Norfolk South in 1954 when the Conservative MP was imprisoned for forging documents. The most controversial recent case produced the 1961 and 1963 by-elections in Bristol South-East due to the disqualification of Tony Benn on his elevation to the peerage, which resulted in the 1963 Peerage Act. There have been no recent by-elections due to cases of corruption, election petitions, bankruptcy or disqualification.

The second reason for the decline is that since the mid-sixties administrations have sought where possible to avoid by-elections caused by promotions to the upper house, given the potential embarrassment for the government inherent in these contests. In the mid-fifties about a quarter of all by-elections were caused by the government elevating members to the House of Lords but today this has become highly exceptional. In Mrs Thatcher's first decade there was just one case. After the 1983 general election the Deputy Prime Minister, William Whitelaw, was elevated to the leadership of the House of Lords, resulting in the Penrith and the Border by-election. The danger of this strategy was shown by the outcome of this by-election, where the Conservative majority of over 15,421 was reduced to just 552. Later when Lord Whitelaw retired due to ill-health in 1988, there was speculation that the government might seek to reinforce Conservative support in the Lords but, given the expected risks of a by-election no members were elevated from the Commons to replace him. In recent years there have been fewer by-elections due to ill-health and death, as party managers have encouraged older members to stand down at general elections, to avoid potentially difficult contests. We therefore need to turn to trends to see how by-elections have been transformed from the stable contests characteristic of the post-war years to more volatile contests common in the eighties.

2

By-Elections, 1945–1966

WE can identify four major periods of by-election results: the immediate post-war decade (1945–55) was dominated by two-party politics, characterized by routine contests, highly stable results, and minimal attention in the press. Liberal support was reduced to the lowest point this century and the Nationalists were similarly quiescent. The following decade, from the mid-fifties to mid-sixties, was marked by the first signs of increased electoral volatility, symbolized by Orpington, with slightly more seats changing hands (1955–66). In subsequent chapters we will cover the development of multi-party politics from the mid-sixties (1966–79), with unexpected gains for the Scottish Nationalists, Plaid Cymru, and the Liberals. During the first two terms of the Thatcher administration (1979–87), by-elections were transformed by the rise of the Liberal–Social Democratic Alliance, changes in campaign techniques, and saturation coverage in the media. In Mrs Thatcher's third term the sharp decline in support for Paddy Ashdown's Social and Liberal Democrats and David Owen's SDP, coupled with the fluctuating fortunes of the Greens and the Scottish Nationalists, created an uncertain future for the centre ground of British politics.

TWO-PARTY POLITICS IN THE POST-WAR DECADE

We have become accustomed to thinking of by-elections as fairly dramatic contests which often generate national media interest but during the post-war decade there were over a hundred British by-elections which tended to be characterized by routine campaigns, predictable results, and minimal press coverage. The pattern of steady-state contests reflected the stability of the two-party dominance in general elections with most core Labour and Conservative voters remaining loyal throughout successive elections. What hope for the Liberals and Nationalists when from 1945 to 1970 the two major parties won, on average, 92% of the vote and hence 98% of all Parliamentary seats? Where there were fluctuations in the vote, these were highly uniform across the whole country. The job of the professional election pundit was certainly easier, if less exciting, than in later decades. In Crewe's words: 'To know the swing in Cornwall was to know, within a percentage or two, the swing in the Highlands; to know the results of the first three constituencies to declare on election night, was to know not only which party had won—but by how many seats' (1985).

In the immediate post-war years, given the massive shift of votes in the 1945 landslide Labour victory, it is surprising that so few seats reverted to the Tories in subsequent by-elections (see Table 2.1). At this time Labour even increased its share of the vote

Table 2.1.   *Changes of seat in by-elections, 1945–1966*

Govt.		Total No.	Changes of seats No.	%
Lab.	1945–50	47	0	0
Lab.	1950–51	14	0	0
Con.	1951–55	44	1	2
Con.	1955–59	49	7	14
Con.	1959–64	61	8	13
Lab.	1964–66	13	2	15
TOTAL		228	18	8

Note: This excludes exceptional cases such as uncontested by-elections in university seats.

in about a quarter of all by-elections, a remarkable achievement by the Attlee government in the light of subsequent trends in government support. By the late forties the Conservatives started to make more consistent voting gains in contests although these were largely due to switches from Liberals rather than from Labour. As an indication of the exceptional voting stability during the post-war decade the average ('Butler') swing in by-elections was 1.3% from Labour to Conservative (for a summary of voting change see Table 2.2). In terms of votes out of a hundred contests only a handful could be classified as highly volatile, such as Glasgow Bridgeton in 1946, Glasgow Gorbals in 1948, Bristol West in 1951, and Inverness in 1954. As a result in the post-war by-elections Labour and the Liberals took no seats and the Conservatives made only minor gains—

Table 2.2.   *Summary of by-elections, 1945–1955 (% vote; change)*

Govt.		Con.		Lab.		Lib.	
Lab.	1945–50	42	(+5)	51	(−3)	13	(−2)
Lab.	1950–51	49	(+7)	50	(−2)	10	(−8)
Con.	1951–55	50	(−1)	47	(−1)	10	(+2)

Note: The figures represent the change in the mean share of the Liberal vote from the previous general election to the by-election irrespective of whether the Liberals fought the seat in the previous general election.

from Independents in Combined English and Combined Scottish University seats, from the Independent Labour Party (ILP) in Glasgow, Camlachie, and from Labour in the ultra-marginal Sunderland South.[1]

MINOR PARTIES 1945–1955

The Liberals were exceptionally weak during these years; they contested only a quarter of all by-elections and when they did stand their support often proved negligible. In over a hundred campaigns the Liberals only managed a relatively strong performance (with over 25% of the vote) in three. For the Liberals, as one commentator noted: 'During this period, by-elections were an embarrassment' (Steed 1983: 79). This reflected their performance in general elections. The 1950 election proved a disaster for the Liberals; two-thirds of the party's candidates lost their deposit and the Parliamentary party was reduced to nine MPs. The number of votes per Liberal candidate declined even on the 1945 result. 'To win only 9 seats with 475 candidates, and to lose 319 deposits—this was defeat on a scale which it would be hard to parallel' (Nicholas 1951: 299). Within a year and a half, before they could recover in terms of party morale, funds, and candidates, the Labour government called another election. In the 1951 and 1955 general elections the Liberals received their worst results, reduced to only six MPs with less than

[1] Because of their special circumstances, all these by-elections except Sunderland South are excluded in subsequent tables which calculate changes of seats and votes. Throughout this comparison excludes by-elections held in Northern Ireland because of differences there in the party system.

3% of the national vote (see Fig. 3.3). Five of the elected Liberal MPs were unopposed by Conservative candidates. In the 1951 election only forty-three Liberal candidates saved their deposits, and nine of these had been given clear runs against the Conservatives in local electoral pacts (for details of the electoral truce see Rasmussen 1965: 102–13). In more than three out of every four seats the two main parties had the field to themselves. As Butler concluded: 'The contest in 1951 marked a return to an overwhelmingly two-party pattern of politics' (1952).

In addition in the early fifties party membership sank to its lowest point of just over 76,000. In local elections the Liberals fared equally badly, reduced across the country to just fifty-six borough councillors (1.5%) in 1955. No significant council remained in Liberal control during this period and there were no Liberal representatives in major cities such as Liverpool and Birmingham. It seemed to many observers at the time as though the Liberal Party was electorally bankrupt and might even disappear altogether from the political scene. As William Wallace noted: 'Between 1950 and 1954 the Liberal Party came very close to extinction ... the Liberal Party of 1955 must to a dispassionate observer have looked rather like an interesting historical relic than a live political party' (1983: 43–4).

Nationalist parties were similarly quiescent with a minimal share of the vote. In a by-election in April 1945 Dr Robert McIntyre won Motherwell for the SNP, but this was due to a wartime truce where the local Conservatives agreed not to contest the seat, and McIntyre was only in Parliament for a month before being unseated in the general election. In the late forties Scottish nationalists devoted their energies to the Scottish Convention, an extra-Parliamentary body, and this period saw perhaps the lowest point in the fortunes of the SNP (Brand 1978). In the 1950 general election there were eight candidates representing the various branches of Scottish Nationalism, gaining on average 1,573 votes each. Nationalist activity by the Convention, notably the mass petition in 1949 to demand a Parliament for Scotland, took attention away from the Scottish Nationalist Party. It was seen as more credible to work through the major parties and sign the Covenant to achieve Home Rule than to vote for the SNP (Kellas 1984: 130–2). By the end of the decade the Scottish Nationalists were reduced to fewer than 1,000 members and the party was kept alive by only a few active branches (Mullin 1979; Brand 1978: 249–56).

Given the predictability of the outcome it is perhaps not surprising that in the early fifties voting participation in by-elections tended to be relatively low. On average turn-out dropped by 9% from 1945 to 1950 and by 16% from 1950 to 1951. In such contests as Ogmore, Glamorganshire in 1946, Hayes and Harlington in 1953, and Ilford North in 1954 fewer than half of those who voted in the previous general election turned out for the by-election. From 1952 to 1955 one in four of those who voted in the general election stayed at home for the following by-election. Nearly all the campaigns were low-stimulus, routine contests, which generated little public excitement. The quality press would give a few passing references to the campaign, noting the reason for the vacancy, the candidates who were standing, and the final result, but rarely devoted much attention to the contest.

BY-ELECTIONS FROM 1955 TO 1966

The decade between the general elections of 1955 and 1966 can be seen as a period of transition in by-election campaigns. Most contests remained low-stimulus events but there were occasional electoral surprises.[2] The first harbinger of change was Torquay in 1955, where Peter Bessell managed to raise the Liberal vote from 14% to 24%, followed by promising Liberal performances in Herefordshire and Gainsborough. During the early by-elections under the Eden administration there was little change in Conservative support but the government started to experience a significant and consistent loss of votes from mid-1957, following the Suez crisis and the resignation of Anthony Eden. This gave the Labour Party the opportunity of their first by-election gains since the war, taking Lewisham North from the Conservatives in February 1957. A few weeks later Labour repeated their triumph with Lady Megan Lloyd George, who trounced the Liberals in Carmarthen, a seat which had been held by R. Hopkins Morris since 1945. This was followed by consecutive Labour victories in Rochdale and Glasgow Kelv-

---

[2] Excluding by-elections in Mid-Ulster in 1956 and changes in Liverpool Garston in 1957 and Ealing South in 1958, where the transition was from Independent Conservative to Conservative.

ingrove in 1958. On the surface this series of Labour victories seemed impressive but all these seats were marginals, changing hands with relatively small swings of the vote. The Labour revival proved short-lived; Macmillan managed to restore confidence in the government in the run-up to the September 1959 general election, with no further loss of by-election seats. The stability of by-election results proved an accurate harbinger of the 1959 campaign.

THE FIRST LIBERAL REVIVAL 1956–1958

In the post-war era we can identify four main periods of Liberal resurgence: 1956–8, 1962–3, 1972–4 and (in the Alliance) 1981–7. Each stage has reached a slightly higher plateau of support before falling back. Throughout the late fifties the Liberals showed an increasingly strong performance, contesting more seats and achieving on average about one in four by-election votes (see Table 2.3). The basis for the revival can be attributed to a number of factors which coalesced in the spring and summer of 1956. In the early fifties the party had been bitterly split between the radical individualists, committed to free trade and a minimal role for the state, and the Radical Reform Group who were part of the tradition of social liberalism developed by William Beveridge. In 1956 these divisions resolved themselves with the departure of some of the leading individualists, the realignment of the Reform Group within the party and the election as leader of Jo Grimond, the MP for Orkney and Shetland. The new leader revitalized the party, redefining the aims as a realignment on the centre-left. This was reinforced by the Suez crisis, where the Liberal Party came out in opposition to military intervention. British and French military action against the Egyptian seizure of the Suez Canal had shattered the Conservative government. The aftermath of Suez brought an influx of new recruits to the party.

The party also changed its tactics, concentrating more efforts on by-elections with a new campaign team. The party developed a special by-election central fund to channel resources to local associations (Rasmussen 1965: 100). Evidence that this strategy paid electoral dividends was provided by the solid Liberal performance in contests like Herefordshire and Gainsborough in 1956 and Edinburgh South in 1957. In Dorset North (1957) the Liberals achieved

a third of the vote, forcing Labour into third place. In the same
year this was followed by stronger performances in Gloucester and
Ipswich, and in 1958 in Rochdale where the Liberals moved into
second place with 35% of the vote with their candidate, Ludovic
Kennedy the television presenter. Then at last in March 1958 the
Liberals managed to achieve a real victory. Mark Bonham Carter,
the grandson of Asquith, triumphed over the Tories in Devon Torrington. The outcome increased the Liberal share of the vote to 38%
in a seat which they had not even contested in the previous general
election. For the first time in almost thirty years the Liberals had
won a by-election. According to Gallup there was an immediate
rise in their position in the national polls, from 12% in January
1958 to a peak of 19% in May, before a gradual decline again by
the end of the year (see Fig. 2.1). In by-elections which they contested

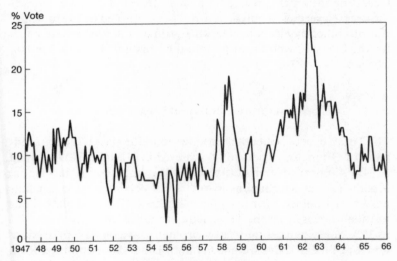

FIG. 2.1.   Liberal Party popularity, 1947–1966

in favourable areas the Liberal impetus was maintained in the run-up
to the 1959 election with more than a quarter of the vote in Somerset
Weston-Super-Mare, Argyll, East Aberdeenshire, Southend West,
and Kirkcudbrightshire and Galloway Wigtownshire.

For the Liberals this series of results confirmed that survival was

assured and a significant breakthrough for their party might even
be possible. As the Liberal Executive told the annual assembly in
September: 'this year marked, if not the revival of the Liberal Party,
the period in which the revival has become apparent to the general
public and has attracted the attention of the other parties and of
the press' (quoted in Rasmussen 1965, 26). By-elections increased
Liberal credibility by offering tangible evidence of electoral success.
The government managed to recover, however, in the run-up to
the 1959 general election. The public opinion polls indicated that
the crucial swing back to the Conservatives began in the summer
of 1958, with the general increase in prosperity, a decline in unemployment, and stable prices; and the party's fortunes steadily
improved thereafter (Butler and Rose 1960: 198). The Liberals
enjoyed some modest success in the 1959 general election, doubling
the number of candidates fielded from 101 in 1955 to 216, and slightly
increasing their average vote by 1.8% to 16.9% in contested constituencies. Nevertheless only six Liberal MPs returned to Westminster.
As with other by-elections, Devon Torrington proved a false dawn
for the Liberals, who failed to hold the constituency in the general
election.

THE SECOND LIBERAL REVIVAL 1962–1963

The Tories experienced no more losses until the classic Liberal land-
mark of Orpington, where in March 1962 Eric Lubbock overturned
a 34% Conservative majority, renewing hopes of a substantial
Liberal revival. Orpington proved a classic victory: the Liberals
more than doubled their vote, from 21% to 53% of the poll; Labour
lost their deposit and the Tory share of the poll dropped from 57%
to 35%. Some commentators saw Orpington as a one-off affair, since
no more Liberal gains were made until David Steel captured Roxburghshire, Selkirkshire, and Peeblesshire three years later. Many
attributed the result to particular features of the campaign such
as the attractiveness of Eric Lubbock as a candidate compared with
Peter Goldman, the influence of anti-Semitism, the effectiveness of
the Liberal party organization, localism, and the current unpopularity of the Macmillan government.

But other commentators interpreted Orpington as part of a more
general trend. There were indicators of Liberal strength before Orp-

ington. In the preceding year, although not gaining seats, the Liberals had achieved a similar increase in their share of the vote in the Worcester, Paisley, and Moss Side by-elections. In local elections for counties, borough, and urban district councils the Liberals made scattered gains in 1960, before making a consistent series of net gains; 192 in 1961, 567 in 1962, before falling back to 169 in 1963 (Wallace 1983). In Gallup national polls the Liberals had been achieving promising results, averaging about 14% throughout 1961, compared with 10% in 1960 (see Fig. 2.1). Although Orpington was not replicated for some years it was not just a 'one-off'; in many ways it provides the prototype of a classic Liberal victory such as a Ryedale or a Liverpool Edge Hill.

The crucial feature of the Orpington campaign was that it fulfilled all the conditions necessary for tactical voting, discussed in detail in subsequent chapters. It was a government seat at a time when the Conservatives were increasingly unpopular according to Gallup national opinion polls. Extensive press coverage created considerable public interest in the campaign. Early canvass returns and opinion polls showed that there was a large proportion of undecided voters in the constituency. The Liberals started from a good base since in the previous general election they were equal second with Labour. Locally they gained credibility by demonstrating that they could win in the 1961 UDC elections. The impression that they were a serious force to be contended with was reinforced by the results of another by-election in Blackpool North the day before Orpington went to the polls, where the Liberals beat Labour to second place. Lastly an eve-of-poll survey by NOP, widely publicized by Lubbock's agent, showed a probable Liberal win.

As a result the Labour campaign seems to have collapsed, as Ken Young (1973) suggests, above all because Labour was seen as having no chance of winning. Since the Liberals were thought to be most likely to displace the Tories, it seems probable that for tactical reasons Labour voters shifted towards the Liberal camp. Without survey evidence this cannot be confirmed but, as we shall discuss later, Orpington fits the criteria for tactical voting which have led to other remarkable Liberal and Nationalist victories. As a type Orpington was far from unique.

In the short term the publicity surrounding Orpington lent the Liberals electoral credibility and political momentum. In the aftermath of Orpington the Liberals improved their position in the national opinion polls, ahead of the major parties in one NOP poll, and registering a post-war peak of 20–25% from April to October 1962 in Gallup national polls (see Fig. 2.1). At the same time the Liberals experienced a substantial increase in membership, from 250,000 in 1961–2 to 350,000 in 1963 (Wallace 1983). The Liberals continued to achieve a fairly strong share of the votes in by-elections such as Derbyshire West and Leicester North East. But in terms of seats it was the Labour Party which benefited from the unpopular- ity of the government with a series of victories, gaining Dorset South and Woodside in 1962, Luton in 1963, and Lanarkshire Rutherglen in 1964.[3] In Dorset South Labour were returned by default, with the Conservative vote split over the issue of Britain's entry into the Common Market, and the Independent Conservative attracted enough support to save his deposit.

By-election results reflected the position of the parties in the national opinion polls. Since mid-1961 Labour had led the Con- servatives in both Gallup and NOP, but for nearly a year Labour's standing hardly rose while Conservative support was eroded by the Liberals. Then in late 1962 Liberal support declined and Labour moved forward again (Butler and King 1965: 20). Government sup- port weakened following the Vassall and Profumo affairs, divisions about Britain's proposed entry to the Common Market, the resigna- tion of Macmillan owing to ill-health, and the emergence of Sir Alec Douglas-Home as leader. The economy experienced difficulties throughout 1962, with increased unemployment, problems with the balance of payments, low productivity, and an unpopular 'pay pause'. Meanwhile Harold Wilson took over the leadership of the Labour Party, following Gaitskell's illness in January 1963. Under Wilson's management the party was reinvigorated, presenting a more contemporary and classless image, concerned with the urgent need to modernize British industry, science, and technology. Throughout 1963 and 1964 the by-election omens for Labour were particularly encouraging, with the Liberals falling back from their earlier revival, and the Tory government consistently losing votes. In the twelve-month run-up to the general election in September 1964 the party increased their share of support in twelve of the thirteen by-elections, on average by 6.4%, their best annual perform-

---

[3] Excluding Tony Benn's campaign in Bristol South-East in 1963 because of the special circumstances of the by-elections.

ance since the war. In the general election Wilson managed to break the Conservative hegemony of the 1950s, although with a Parliamentary majority over all other parties of only four seats.

From September 1964 to January 1966 there were only thirteen by-elections, with no strong swings of the vote, although there were two by-election defeats. Three months after Harold Wilson's 1964 victory the government lost Leyton, a supposedly safe seat, to the Tories. This result was widely attributed to special circumstances, notably Labour forcing the contest in an attempt to get Patrick Gordon Walker, the former Foreign Secretary, back into the Cabinet. In March the Tories lost Roxburghshire, Selkirkshire, and Peebleshirè, where the Liberals had expected to do well since the seat was already highly marginal, to the vigorous and energetic campaign fought by David Steel.

Table 2.3. *Summary of by-elections, 1955–1966 (% vote; change in parentheses)*

Govt.	Con.		Lab.		Lib.[a]	
Con. 1955–59	44	(−9)	46	(+1)	25	(+13)
Con. 1959–64	35	(−14)	43	(−2)	24	(+17)
Lab. 1964–66	45	(+2)	38	(−2)	18	(0)

Note: a. This represents the mean share of the vote for the Liberals where they contested by-elections irrespective of whether they fought the seat in the previous general election.

To summarize trends, there was slightly greater electoral volatility in the early sixties compared with the post-war decade, but changes in seats remained exceptional: from 1955 to 1965 out of 123 British by-elections only seventeen seats changed hands. The change of vote was also relatively stable, (see Table 2.3); the Liberals gained votes but this was largely due to Liberal intervention in seats which they had not contested in the previous general election. Once we control for this factor the Liberals' gains are fairly modest. In the following decades the rise of multi-party politics led to a significant change with increasing indications of electoral instability.

3
By-Elections, 1966–1979

FROM the start of Harold Wilson's second term of office the government started losing by-election seats in rapid succession. The years of this administration proved a watershed in British by-election history: out of 37 contests the government was defeated in almost half. The Labour government, returned to office in April 1966 with a comfortable majority of 97, ran into serious trouble within four months. In early 1966 the government faced increasing economic problems with speculation against sterling, the mounting balance of payment deficit, and the seamen's union on strike. To tackle the economic problems the government introduced a series of unpopular measures: the wages freeze in July 1966 to bring down inflationary pressures, the devaluation of the pound in November 1967, and reductions in public expenditure on defence, education and health. As Fig. 3.1 shows, the immediate impact on public opinion was clear: a 20% Labour lead in the opinion polls in May 1966 was transformed into a 20% Conservative lead by May 1968 (see Butler and Pinto-Duschinsky 1971). Public dissatisfaction was reflected in the series of by-elections during the second Wilson administration.

THE FIRST NATIONALIST REVIVAL, 1966–1969

In the post-war decades we can identify three major periods of nationalist revival: 1966–9, 1972–5 and (for the SNP) 1987 to the present. In 1966 Plaid Cymru were the first to benefit from government unpopularity in Carmarthen where, just four months after the general election, its President, Gwynfor Evans, managed to take the seat from Labour. This breakthrough symbolized the start of the revival of the Welsh Nationalists: 'A credibility gap had been breached, the electorate no longer deemed a nationalist vote an empty protest' (Williams 1982). The victory led to a marked increase in Plaid Cymru membership, in branch formations and a transforma-

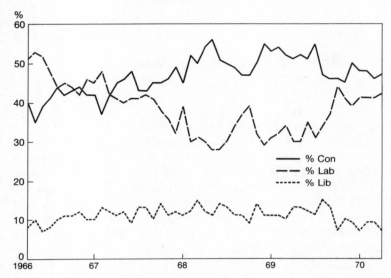

Fig. 3.1. Party popularity, 1966–1970

tion of party morale: 'It is impossible to over-estimate the psychological lift given to the party by the Carmarthen success' (Balsom 1979: 135). Although Plaid Cymru had only a single MP, the victory had symbolic and practical consequences. Carmarthen changed Plaid Cymru from a cultural-political pressure group into a party with Parliamentary representation. Gwynfor Evans was able to exploit his position at Westminster to establish Plaid Cymru as a strong voice for Wales. Plaid Cymru continued to perform strongly in Rhondda West in March 1967, although traditionally considered one of the safest Labour seats.

Following their by-election success both Plaid Cymru and the Scottish Nationalists made an all-out effort in the 1970 general election to contest seats across Wales and Scotland on the platform of national independence. But Plaid Cymru's advance was not to hold in the general election, where 25 of its 36 candidates lost their deposits. Gwynfor Evans lost Carmarthen in the general election although the party achieved 11.5% of the votes cast in Wales, and a comfortable second place in Merioneth, Caernarvon, Rhondda East, Aberdare, and Caerphilly (Kellas 1984). The result represented stronger support for the party although it was judged a disappointing outcome when compared with conventional expectations set by by-elections where the Nationalists had averaged one-third of the votes cast.

From 1967 to 1969 there were parallel trends north of the border. In Glasgow Pollok (March 1967) the Scottish Nationalist candidate, George Leslie, polled 28% of the vote, a remarkable result in the Strathclyde region where the SNP had enjoyed little previous support. In November the SNP followed this with Winifred Ewing's overwhelming victory in Hamilton, Lanarkshire, with 46% of the vote. The result caused a shock to the established party system since this had been seen as the second safest Labour seat in Scotland, which the Nationalists had not even contested in the previous general election. With an attractive candidate, a colourful campaign, and an enthusiastic and well-organized team of volunteers the SNP cut the Labour vote from 71% to 41%, forcing the Tories into third place. 'It had a tremendous impact on Scottish public opinion ... This election really marks the arrival of the SNP for the majority of the Scottish electorate as a party with a serious political future' (Brand 1978: 262). Following Hamilton the Scottish Nationalists experienced a surge of support in local elections. In Scottish municipal elections in May 1968 the SNP won 30% of the vote, gaining 100 seats, and as a result holding the balance of power in Glasgow (Kellas 1984). The SNP had experienced a period of particularly strong growth in 1966–7, with almost 200 new branches being established throughout Scotland. By 1969 there were 486 branches across Scotland (Kellas 1984). Mass membership multiplied dramatically, from 42,000 in 1966, to 80,000 in 1967 and about 120,000 in 1968 (Kellas 1984: 142).

The by-election gains for the Nationalists were impressive, establishing their credibility as an electoral force, giving them their first Parliamentary representatives, and laying the foundation for their revival in the early seventies. As Dennis Balsom noted, by-election breakthroughs may have significant consequences for nationalist parties, providing a stimulant which breaks traditional party loyalties and strengthens local party organizations, even if the seat reverts to the major parties in the following general election (Balsom 1979; see also W. L. Miller 1981). Nevertheless in 1969 the party started to experience a downturn in its fortunes, with members leaving, for reasons which have not been clearly established. Possibly the party had lost control and become over-extended through rapid expansion. The performance of the inexperienced SNP councillors on Glasgow Corporation attracted considerable criticism (Brand 1978: 263). It was also difficult to maintain momentum through by-elections; after Hamilton the party had to wait two years before the next suitable contest, at Glasgow Gorbals in October 1969, where they came second with 25% of the vote. By the time of Ayrshire and Bute, in March 1970, the SNP were returned behind Labour and the Tories, with 20% of the vote.

Despite this slight downturn in support, in the May 1970 general election the SNP increased the number of candidates they fielded, from 23 in 1966 to 65 in 1970, ambitiously contesting almost every Scottish seat. As a result they doubled their overall share of the vote in Scotland, from 5% in 1966 to 11.4% in 1970, with strong performances in eleven north-east and Highland seats. Nevertheless this result has to be qualified: only Donald Stewart in the Western Isles was returned to Parliament, Hamilton reverted back to Labour, the party lost its deposit in 42 seats, and the share of the vote per SNP candidate declined slightly from 1966. On balance probably this can be judged a gradual advance in the overall strength of the SNP, which developed a national presence across all of Scotland, although in the aftermath of Hamilton activists had expected more radical progress.

THE LIBERAL PARTY

The Liberals had mixed fortunes throughout the late sixties. The momentum from the first period of Liberal revival, from 1958 to 1962, had slackened. In by-elections, as in general elections, their performance confirmed that the Liberals tend to do better under periods of Conservative rule. In Carmarthen, where they might have expected to do well, they were displaced as the party of protest by Plaid Cymru. The Liberals took some comfort from Wallace Lawler's triumph in the by-election in Birmingham Ladywood in 1969, where he had built up a local base which enabled him to increase the Liberal share of the vote by 30%. But this was an exceptional result: in local Gallup polls about a third of the Liberal voters attributed their support to the candidate rather than the party. Overall the Liberal performance in these years can only be described as patchy. In the late sixties, as one commentator observed: 'Aside from its youth wing and from pockets of new activity, the Party as a whole drifted slowly downhill. Its most striking failure was its inability to tap the discontent with the Labour government during the mid-term period' (Wallace 1983: 63). From 1966 to 1970 the Liberals contested three out of four by-election seats but they only increased their average share of the vote by 4%.

Although the Nationalist breakthroughs attracted intense publicity for sheer numbers, it was the Conservatives who were the main by-election victors during this period. The Tories broke established by-election records, winning a dozen seats from Labour compared with only three equivalent gains in the previous twenty years (see Fig. 3.2). On 28 March 1968 three Labour seats fell to the Tories on the same day: Acton, Dudley, and Meriden, followed three months later by the loss of Oldham West and Nelson and Colne. Some of the by-election seats were conventionally seen as marginal, such as Cambridge in 1967 and Northamptonshire in 1969, but Labour had enjoyed solid majorities (over 25%) in others such as Walthamstow East and Swindon in 1969. On average the Labour vote was down by 17% from 1966–70, the worst by-election performance of any party since the war, serving as an accurate portent for Wilson's defeat in the 1970 general election.

Many contemporary observers attributed Labour's performance to the unpopularity of the Wilson administration, including disillusionment with the government's economic performance following the devaluation of the pound, rising levels of unemployment, and increased rates of inflation (McKie 1973). The pattern of by-election results was consistent with other measures of government popularity, such as their low standing in Gallup opinion polls during these years. In Wilson's second term the government lost 15 seats in 37 by-elections, or one in four.

But in a longer-term perspective it can be argued that the trends towards increasingly volatile by-election results, which started in the mid-sixties, cannot be explained as simply a reaction to an exceptionally unpopular Labour government since volatility persisted under the Heath, Callaghan, and Thatcher administrations. In the light of these trends it can be suggested that the Labour Party's losses reflect a long-term shift in the nature of by-elections, towards high-stimulus campaigns with a more changeable electorate, as much as an immediate reaction to particular political circumstances.

When Labour entered the 1970 campaign they had every expec-

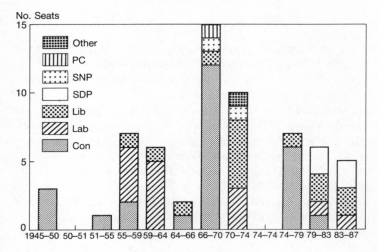

FIG. 3.2. By-election gains, 1945–1987

tation of a comfortable return to office. Despite periods of unpopularity in the late sixties, by May 1970 commentators widely believed that Labour had recovered, according to evidence from the national opinion polls and spring local elections. In their final campaign polls all companies except ORC estimated Labour to be in the lead. The first results on election night, in Guildford, Cheltenham, Salford, and Wolverhampton, correctly indicated that Harold Wilson was heading for an unexpected defeat. Against the odds the Conservatives won a comfortable Parliamentary majority with 330 seats, and a 4.8% two-party national swing of the vote. Labour were not the only disappointed party: the Liberal vote was down almost everywhere and judged against contemporary expectations the Nationalist result was widely seen as poor. In the longer term, with the benefits of hindsight, the performance of the minor parties could be seen as not entirely unexpected. The revival of the Nationalists and Liberals in the post-war years was characterized by ebbs and flow, with each plateau tending to be slightly higher than the past, rather than a process of continuous and steady growth.

THE THIRD LIBERAL REVIVAL 1972–1974

In the first few years of the Heath administration the government faced a series of intractable problems concerning inflation, economic growth, the balance of payments, a series of industrial disputes, and controversy about Britain's entry into the European Community. Despite this in the first two years by-elections were fairly stable, although in 1971 Labour won Worcestershire Bromsgrove from the Tories and significantly increased support in Hayes and Harlington. The Liberals contested only half the by-elections in this period, with minimal impact, and displayed a similarly weak performance in the national opinion polls and local elections. The party's leadership seemed ineffective with Jeremy Thorpe distracted by the personal tragedy of the loss of his wife; party activists demoralized by the 1970 result; internal party divisions concerning the radicalism of the Young Liberals and the strategy of community politics. But in late 1972 the pattern was to shift significantly to the benefit of the minor parties.

The third period of Liberal revival started with Cyril Smith's return for Rochdale in October 1972, although many attributed this to particular circumstances, notably the widespread appeal of the popular local candidate. Two months later Rochdale was followed by an even more remarkable Liberal gain in Sutton and Cheam, a middle-class suburban constituency which had previously returned a solid Conservative majority of 30%. In this seat Grahame Tope, a prominent member of the new radicals in the party, actively campaigned on a platform of community politics to increase the Liberal share of the vote from 15% to 54%. In March 1973 there were strong Liberal performances in Durham Chester-le-Street and Manchester Exchange. In July 1973 this was followed by the triple successive triumphs against the Tories in the Isle of Ely (Clement Freud), Berwick-upon-Tweed (Alan Beith) and in Ripon, Yorkshire (David Austick). 'It was a revival greater in degree and scale than anything seen for a generation' (Cook 1976: 154). Within twelve months the Liberals had managed almost to double their Parliamentary representation, from six to eleven MPs. Support in Gallup's national polls surged ahead, with the Liberal share of the vote increasing from 10% during 1972 to 18–19% during the following two years (see Fig. 3.3).

Commentators at the time found it difficult to explain the particu-

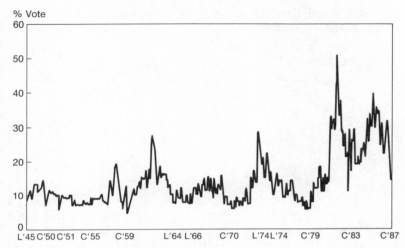

% Vote

FIG. 3.3.   Liberal Party popularity, 1966–1979

lar circumstances which triggered the second Liberal revival. The government was unpopular, but in the past this usually served to benefit the main opposition party. There were deep internal strains within the Labour Party over entry into the European Community and the extent of public ownership, which may explain why they failed to profit from the government's troubles (Butler and Kavanagh 1974: 258). In part it was fortunate for the Liberals that certain by-elections fell in favourable territory: Rochdale and Ripon had a strong tradition of Liberalism. Community politics proved an effective strategy for building up local support, with the focus on grassroots activity and regular leafleting. Through community politics ordinary people would be encouraged to work together for local improvements and were thereby drawn into Liberal activism. The idea was developed around 1968 by radical Young Liberals, using the American Civil Rights movement as their model, but the practice was soon widely adopted throughout the party. Previously much Liberal support had come from traditional rural constituencies and the Celtic areas, but this technique provided a strong local council base in central urban areas such as Leeds, Liverpool, Eastbourne, and Birmingham. By 1973 the Liberals were the largest party on

Liverpool and Eastbourne councils and the second largest party on five other local authorities.

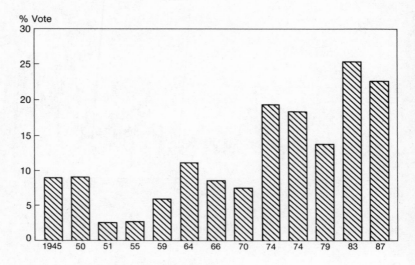

% Vote

FIG. 3.4.   Liberal general election results

There was another by-election which, with hindsight, had significant implications for the future development of centre parties. In 1973 the Lincoln by-election attracted considerable attention, with Dick Taverne resigning from the Labour Party to fight as an independent Social Democratic Labour candidate opposed to the party's leftward drift. Taverne was eventually returned with a majority of over 13,000, which was widely interpreted as evidence for a growing desire for a new 'centre' party. Taverne held his seat in the February 1974 election although the victory was short-lived; he went down to defeat against Labour in the October 1974 general election.

The record of by-elections, local elections, and opinion polls seemed to indicate that, after occasional false dawns, the Liberal bandwagon was at last picking up genuine momentum. This was confirmed by the February 1974 general election results, where the Liberals more than doubled their share of the vote from 7.5% in 1970 to 19.3%, their best result since the 1920s (see Fig. 3.4). Significantly, from 1970 to 1974 not only did they increase the number of candidates fielded, from 332 to 517, but they also almost doubled the share of the vote per candidate (from 6,376 to 11,720). The Liberal Parliamentary party expanded to fourteen MPs, with Alan Beith in Berwick, Clement Freud in Ely, and Cyril Smith in Rochdale consolidating their by-election gains. Although Sutton and Cheam as well as Ripon reverted to the Tories, the Liberals won Cardiganshire and Colne Valley from Labour, Bodmin and the Isle of Wight from the Conservatives, along with the new seat of Hazel Grove. The Liberals did remarkably well everywhere in terms of electoral support, with more than 6 million votes, although they were strongest in the south and south-west. In the October 1974 general election the Liberals fell back slightly from their peak, fielding 619 candidates to contest almost every British seat but losing three-quarters of a million votes, so that their overall share declined to 18.3%. This was a good result set in the context of their post-war record, but at the time the effects of the electoral system proved profoundly disappointing for the Liberal leadership.

THE SECOND NATIONALIST REVIVAL 1972–1975

The Scottish Nationalists found that support fell back during 1969 to 1972, with members deserting, although few branches disappeared completely (Brand 1978: 263–4). Some dismissed the party as a spent force, but during the lean years the party developed a stronger core of activists. At the time of the energy crisis the discovery of North Sea oil, with its implications for an independent Scottish economy, gave the SNP an ideal issue which they could exploit. The SNP was also helped by the publication in November 1973 of the Kilbrandon Commission's recommendation for some sort of devolved Scottish Assembly. It was difficult for the Nationalists to use by-election campaigns to maintain popular momentum, as during the Heath administration there were only four Scottish and one Welsh contests. Nevertheless Plaid Cymru took a third of the vote in Merthyr Tydfil in 1972, an area where they had been relatively weak. The SNP also managed to win a third of the vote in Stirling and Falkirk Burghs in 1971 and also achieved a near-win, coming within 2% of victory, in Dundee East in January 1973. The SNP finally triumphed with Margo MacDonald in Glasgow Govan in August 1973, where their vote quadrupled from 10% to 41.9%.

Therefore the by-election results since 1972 could be seen to signal the second period of nationalist revival. The groundswell of support for the SNP was evident in the February 1974 general election, where the party's share of the Scottish vote jumped from 11.5% to 21.9%. The Parliamentary party grew from two to seven MPs: as well as holding the Western Isles the SNP won three Conservative seats in the north-east and one in Argyll, and gained Dundee East and East Stirlingshire from Labour, although they narrowly failed to retain Govan. In the October 1974 general election they maintained their momentum, achieving their highest level of support to date: 30% of the Scottish vote, resulting in eleven MPs. It should be noted that this was a pattern distinctive to Scotland, since in the same election support for Plaid Cymru remained stable and Liberal support fell. The SNP came second in forty-two other seats and in terms of votes the Conservatives were reduced to being the third party in Scotland. At the same time mass membership in the SNP had expanded to about 85,000. 'The SNP had never been so sure of itself or so confident of the future' (MacIver 1982: 126).

THE 1974–1979 LABOUR GOVERNMENT

Overall by-elections and opinion polls during the Heath years had proved remarkably turbulent; from 1970 to February 1974 out of thirty by-elections one-third had changed hands. In the mid-seventies during the Callaghan administration the special circumstances of the Lib.–Lab. pact led to a slightly different pattern, indeed this is the only period in recent years when the Liberals consistently achieved a worse performance in by-elections than in the previous general election. The Liberals lost votes in every by-election with two exceptions: Newcastle Central in 1976, where Liberal support increased by 17% to put them in second place, and David Alton's substantial gain in Liverpool Edge Hill in 1979, with the highest Liberal share of the vote (64%) achieved in any post-war by-election.

As for the Nationalists, the indications from Scottish opinion polls, which started on a regular basis in 1974, were that SNP support fluctuated in the mid-seventies, before a fairly steady slide in party fortunes from late 1977 to 1979. There were only three by-elections during this period: in April 1978 the Scottish Nationalists maintained their support with a third of the vote in Glasgow Garscadden, but failed to repeat their triumph in Hamilton a few months later. In October 1978 they achieved a poor performance (8.8% of the vote) in Berwick and East Lothian, which reflected their general decline in the opinion polls. The party had been demoralized by the defeat of devolution in the March 1979 referendum, where in Scotland only 52% of those who turned out voted in favour, and was divided by personality disputes. In the 1979 general election the party managed to retain only two of its eleven parliamentary seats, and less than two-thirds of its October 1974 vote. In Wales devolution was defeated even more heavily in the 1979 referendum, but Plaid Cymru suffered a less calamitous fall in electoral support, retaining their two northern strongholds, Caernarvon and Merionethshire.

Overall the Conservatives were the main beneficiaries during the Wilson/Callaghan administrations, gaining five seats even against substantial Labour majorities such as Ashfield (41%) and Walsall North (33%). The Ashfield result was seen as particularly surprising as most contemporary commentators regarded it as one of Labour's safest seats. As *The Times* predicted the day before the poll: 'In Ashfield, a constituency remarkable for the steadiness of its voting habits, a Labour defeat is barely credible.'[1] In contrast the Grimsby contest on the same day, caused by the death of Anthony Crosland, was regarded as more vulnerable, with a Labour majority of 15%. The results confounded expectations with Austin Mitchell holding on to Grimsby but Ashfield lost, with a 21% swing against the government. Possibly the circumstances generating the by-elections, one caused by a death evoking sympathy, one by a gratuitous resignation, played a part in the result. These years also saw increased support for extremist minor parties, particularly the campaigns in Birmingham Ladywood, Ilford North, and Birmingham Stechford, which were contested by National Front and Socialist Worker candidates, with violent clashes between supporters.

SUMMARY

The results of by-elections since the mid-sixties show the emergence of certain consistent trends (for a summary see Table 3.1). From 1956 to 1958 the Liberals doubled their share of the vote in by-

[1] *The Times*, 27 Apr. 1977.

Table 3.1. *Summary of by-elections, 1966–1979 (% vote; change in parentheses)*

Govt.	Con.		Lab.		Lib.[a]	
Lab. 1966–70	46	(+7)	35.	(−17)	14	(+4)
Con. 1970–74	32	(−11)	43	(−4)	22	(+12)
Lab. 1974–79	42	(+10)	38	(−9)	12	(−5)

Note: a. This represents the mean share of the Liberal vote where they contested by-elections irrespective of whether they fought the seat in the previous general election.

elections, reflecting increased popular support and the greater number of candidates fielded. The second Liberal revival reached its peak around 1962, before falling back under the early years of Wilson's government. The third Liberal revival started with the by-elections of 1972–3, reaching its crest in the February 1974 general election, before once more declining in a cyclical pattern.

To a lesser extent the Nationalists experienced a similar roller-coaster of short-term gains which failed to consolidate into a long-term base (see Table 3.2). There have been three major periods of Nationalist revival: 1966–9, 1972–4, and (for the SNP) 1987 to the present (see Kellas 1973; W. L. Miller 1981; Brand 1978; Denver

Table 3.2. *Nationalist by-election (BE) and general election (GE) results*

	Scottish Nationalists				Plaid Cymru			
	% vote BE[a]		% Scottish vote GE		% Vote BE[a]		% Welsh vote GE	
1966–70	—	(0)	5.0	(23)	39.7	(3)	4.3	(20)
1970–74	35.6	(3)	11.4	(65)	37.0	(1)	11.5	(36)
1974–74	—		21.9	(70)	—	(0)	10.7	(36)
1974–79	29.2	(3)	30.4	(71)	—	(0)	10.8	(36)
1979–83	17.0	(4)	17.3	(71)	8.7	(1)	8.1	(36)
1983–87	—	(0)	11.8	(72)	6.0	(2)	7.8	(36)

Notes: Figures in parentheses represent the number of seats contested.

a. Changes of votes where Nationalists contested both the previous general election and the by-election.

1985; Drucker and Brown 1980). Overall the SNP fought about half of the post-war by-elections in Scotland, increasing their share

Table 3.3. *Changes in the Nationalist vote*

		No.	GE vote	BE vote	Change
SNP Withdrawals	(GE only)	2	4.4	—	−4.4
SNP Consistents	(GE & BE)	12	15.1	21.8	+6.8
SNP Interventions	(BE only)	14	—	17.3	+17.3
PC Withdrawals	(GE only)	0	—	—	—
PC Consistents	(GE & BE)	12	8.1	20.8	+12.8
PC Interventions	(BE only)	4	—	6.6	+6.6

Table 3.4. *Changes of seat in by-elections, 1966–1979*

Govt.		Total BE No.	Change of seat[a] No.	%
Lab.	1966–70	37	15	41
Con.	1970–74	30	10	33
Lab.	1974–79	31	7	23
TOTAL	1966–79	98	32	33

Note: a. Excluding exceptional cases.

of support by about 7% where they contested both the by-election and the previous general election, and gaining about 17% of the vote where they intervened only in the by-election (see Table 3.3). In the post-war years Plaid Cymru contested eighteen by-elections, more than doubling their share of the vote (12.8%) from the general to the by-election. The strongest performances by Plaid Cymru were all in the mid sixties: Caerphilly in 1966, Rhondda in 1967, and Carmarthen in 1968.

The problem for third parties has not been to make gains but to convert temporary defectors into permanent loyalists. Compared with earlier years two-party politics was replaced by more complex patterns of multi-party contests, with sharper switches of voting support, higher levels of participation and more unexpected results. Overall about a third of all the by-elections from 1966 to 1979 saw a change of seat (see Table 3.4). During the years of Thatcherism the further development of these trends was to transform by-elections from the quiescent politics of the late forties and fifties.

4

By-Elections, 1979–1983

FOLLOWING the 1979 general election, after a brief honeymoon period, the first Thatcher administration experienced a steady decline in the national opinion polls. During 1980–1 economic news worsened with the international recession: oil prices doubled in two years; in August 1980 unemployment passed the 2 million mark; inflation was in double digit figures; and in the summer of 1981 there were urban riots in Brixton and Toxteth. Labour moved back into a comfortable lead in the polls throughout 1980 until the sharp upsurge in support for the Alliance in 1981 which reached unprecedented heights around Christmas 1981. In moments of euphoria Alliance politicians began constructing their first Cabinet and party strategists assumed they could achieve a breakthrough with about 60–80 seats in the next general election. This ascendancy was not to remain unchallenged for long, however; the Tory lead was reestablished following Argentina's invasion of the Falklands in April 1982 along with improvements in the economy (see Saunders *et al.* 1987; Norpath 1987). From April 1982 the government remained consistently ahead in the polls until the June 1983 general election. Therefore, if the standard Gallup measures of voting intentions are to be relied upon, at some stage during the three-year period all parties—first Labour, then the Alliance, and lastly the Conservatives—could have attracted over 50% of the poll. This volatility was reflected in by-election results with all except the Nationalists making gains during this period.

THE FOURTH LIBERAL–SOCIAL DEMOCRATIC REVIVAL 1981–1987

The fourth period of resurgence for the Liberals started in 1981, with the creation of the Liberal–SDP Alliance, and continued until the acrimonious aftermath of the 1987 general election. The Social Democrats were founded with the Limehouse Declaration in January 1981, followed by the official launch in late March. During 1980 the Liberals had consistently attracted about 14% of the vote in Gallup polls on their own but support for the Liberal–Social Democra-

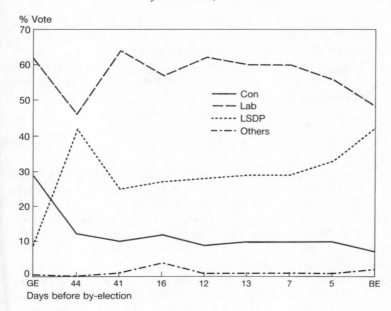

FIG. 4.1. Warrington opinion polls

tic Alliance was double this level by spring 1981. A historic realignment on the centre-left seemed possible as the polls put Labour,
the Conservatives and the Alliance neck-and-neck.

The question remained whether this potential support would
actually materialize in the acid test—at the ballot box. Warrington,
Croydon North-West, Crosby, and Glasgow Hillhead provided a
series of critical by-elections for the Alliance. When founded, given
the difficulties of minor parties breaking through in the British electoral system, there were considerable doubts about the long-term
viability of the Social Democrats. Many commentators felt that their
popularity was a media creation, with ephemeral support which
might evaporate as fast as it had arisen. As Peter Zentner noted,
at the time of the by-election the future of the SDP hung in the
balance: 'With no legal reality to prop it up, with no single leader,
with no agreed policies, and with opinion poll ratings sliding, the
SDP was in a no-man's land between runaway success and possible
eclipse ... it needed to prove itself in the only way that counted
i.e. the polling booths' (Zentner 1982: 156; see also Stephenson

1982). It was felt that any sign of failure might halt the potential SDP bandwagon. By May and June 1981 the leaders were concerned that the initial momentum was slowing down, with a slight slide in the position of the SDP from second to third place in the opinion polls. Warrington, in July 1981, therefore promised to be pivotal for the development of the new party.

WARRINGTON

For their first contest the seat of Warrington, Labour since the war, was not the most promising territory for the SDP. At the start of the campaign commentators reckoned that the new party had little chance: the seat had 'an apparently impregnable Labour majority of rock-hard working class voters in the unpropitious North country' (*Observer*, 19 July 1981). In the 1979 general election Labour enjoyed a 33% majority, while the Liberals trailed in third place with only 9% of the vote. The by-election was caused by the resignation of Thomas Williams, who had held the seat for Labour for twenty years. In his place Labour chose Douglas Hoyle, a left-wing member of Labour's National Executive Committee, an experienced candidate who had represented Nelson and Colne until 1979. The weakness of the grassroots Liberal organization was reflected in the previous local elections when they only contested a single ward.

The constituency was socially mixed: Labour were strongest in the new town, while the Conservatives were based in the northern outlying villages. At the start of the contest the intellectual and patrician Roy Jenkins was not seen as the ideal Alliance candidate for the seat (Shirley Williams had been first choice), but as the contest got underway he proved an adept and popular campaigner. Jenkins brought a wealth of experience of electioneering to the campaign, as a former deputy leader of the Labour Party, notable Home Secretary, Chancellor of the Exchequer and President of the EEC Commission, and a founder member of the Social Democrats.

Jenkins's decision to contest Warrington was courageous. The early polls by NOP and MORI suggested that the Alliance had little chance of winning. At the start Labour were placed ahead with a substantial lead of about 30%, with the Alliance in second place. The series of opinion polls indicated that the position of the parties remained largely unchanged during the campaign (see Fig. 4.1). In their final poll, with fieldwork four days before the election, MORI estimated Labour remained ahead with 56% of the vote, followed by the SDP with 33%, and the Conservatives trailing with 10%. In the final result on 16 July Labour's lead was reduced to 6%, indicating a last-minute swing towards the Alliance. The SDP gained 42% of the vote, thereby threatening one of Labour's safest seats. The Alliance picked up about a quarter of Warrington's former Labour voters, and three-quarters of the Tories. The Conservative, Stan Sorrell, lost his deposit, with his vote cut from 29% to just 7%. Eight minor party candidates, from the Ecology to the Prosperous Britain Party, polled fewer than 600 votes between them.

Although Jenkins did not win the seat, the result was widely interpreted as a triumph for the Social Democrats. In Jenkins's own words: 'My first defeat in thirty years in politics, and it is by far the greatest victory that I have ever participated in.' The by-election served several functions. It established the electoral credibility of the new party, boosted the morale of activists, and demonstrated their ability to attract votes from both major parties. As Ivor Crewe (1981: 31) commented after the result: 'By any objective measure the Warrington by-election was a humiliation for both major parties and a stunning success for the Social Democratic–Liberal Alliance. This was ... worse than a government's normal mid-term unpopularity: it was a collapse of unparalleled proportions.' Warrington cemented the Alliance by demonstrating that well-established Liberals could co-operate effectively with the newer Social Democrats at the grassroots level. Lastly the outcome strengthened Roy Jenkins's hand in the contest for leadership of the Alliance. The by-election at Warrington also represented something of a watershed in terms of the media coverage, attracting intense interest. Before Warrington there had been at most one or two opinion polls published during the campaign; afterwards in key contests there were commonly seven or eight polls published in a three-week period. The media gave these campaigns front-page treatment as dramatic events with significant consequences for party politics.

CROYDON NORTH-WEST

Warrington was followed in October 1981 by Croydon North-West, which proved that the Alliance could expand support with local

Liberal candidates as well as with better-known national political figures. Initially there had been some hesitation about adopting William Pitt as the Alliance candidate. An early MORI poll suggested that Shirley Williams stood a better chance of gaining the seat given her national reputation.[1] In contrast Bill Pitt was largely unknown outside the local area. The candidate's past electoral record was not promising. Pitt had contested Croydon North-West unsuccessfully three times in the past in borough council elections. He lost his deposit in the 1979 general election and gained only 12% of the vote in the May 1981 GLC elections, fought with the same constituency boundaries. Nevertheless the local Liberal party continued to support their local candidate. Pitt had established close ties with the constituency as chairman of the London Liberal party, a housing officer working in the environmental health team in neighbouring Brixton, and active trade unionist in the Lambeth branch of NALGO. The local Liberal organization was weak, with only forty paid-up members. Although the seat was a Conservative marginal in the London suburbs, it did not appear potential Liberal territory, with Labour support concentrated in the inner-city areas where there was a high proportion of black and Asian voters.

Nevertheless at the start of the campaign constituency polls suggested that the by-election could prove a three-horse race, with the Alliance just ahead. The final polls indicated Pitt would win but underestimated the extent of his victory (see Fig. 4.2). The Liberals won by quadrupling their share of the vote from 11% to 40%, a similar swing to that at Warrington. The Alliance gained from the Labour and Conservative parties, although the Gallup poll suggested that much of this support was negative: more than half of those who voted Alliance gave as their main reason their dislike of the other parties.[2]

The outcome was significant for the development of the Liberal–Social Democratic Alliance. The result confirmed the advantages of co-operation for both partners in the Alliance; together they could win seats which had eluded the Liberals on their own. It showed that the Alliance could build up a first-class grassroots organization within the space of a few months, mobilizing over a thousand activists from across the country. The outcome reinforced Alliance

[1] MORI poll published in the *Daily Star*, 18 July 1981 (N. 546)
[2] Gallup poll, *Daily Telegraph*, 20 Oct. 1981 (N. 1010)

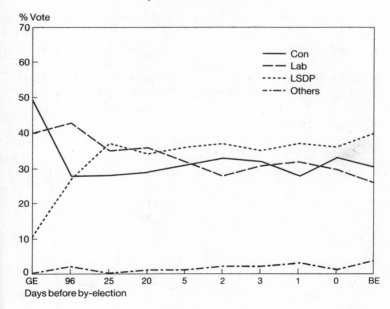

FIG. 4.2. Croydon NW opinion polls

credibility; some concluded that if a local candidate like William Pitt could win, this gave hope to others. It was less easy here than in Warrington to dismiss the outcome as a 'media creation' which could be attributed to the international reputation of a leader like Roy Jenkins. The result was associated with an immediate surge in Alliance popularity: from September to October they moved into the lead in Gallup national polls (from 29% to 40%). The contest demonstrated that the Alliance could fight effectively in Labour *and* Conservative seats. Croydon North-West therefore fuelled speculation that the necessary conditions were ripe for realignment, breaking the two-party dominance in British politics.

CROSBY

In November 1981 this was followed by Crosby, a solid Conservative seat in the North-West. By this stage expectations had shifted—far from being the underdog, most commentators assumed that Shirley

Williams would win for the Alliance, and there was even talk of
the dangers of SDP complacency. Crosby was a prosperous dormi-
tory area for Liverpool commuters, with an older population settled
in the western seaside wards, although the seat included some small
industrial units and a section of the Liverpool docks. Overwhelmingly owner-occupied and middle-class, Crosby had been Conservative since the war, with a Tory majority of almost 20,000 in the
previous general election.

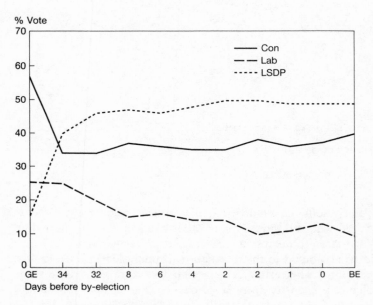

Fɪɢ. 4.3.   Crosby opinion polls

Yet at the start of the contest opinion polls by MORI and NOP
put the Alliance ahead with a 6 to 12 percentage point lead over
the Conservatives (see Fig. 4.3). The local Tory party seemed unable
to meet the challenge of the professional Social Democratic organization which mobilized 1,500 volunteers (Drucker *et al.* 1982*a*). The
series of eight polls suggested that the Labour vote was squeezed
into third place, until on the day Labour were reduced from 25%
to 9.5%. The Alliance won easily with almost half the vote, and
a 10% lead over the Conservatives.

The series of by-election victories, coupled with the popularity of the parties in the national polls, prompted some commentators to suggest that the Alliance was taking off 'like a rocket from Cape Canaveral' (King 1982). After Crosby, at the 1981 Liberal Assembly in Llandudno, David Steel felt sufficiently confident to urge conference delegates to 'Go back to your constituencies and prepare for government.' Yet in retrospect Crosby proved to be the high point for the Alliance. In Gallup national polls the Alliance moved to 50% in December 1981, before experiencing a steady decline in the following months. The sudden and spectacular increase in support proved to be short-lived: what was easily gained was just as easily lost.

GLASGOW HILLHEAD

In the spring of 1982 the outcome in the by-election in Glasgow Hillhead often seemed in doubt. The constituency should have been an easier prospect for the Alliance than Crosby, as a marginal with a Conservative majority of only 7%. The seat was socially divided between the badly housed working class in areas of urban blight along the Clyde, the centre with Victorian terraced flats including many Glasgow University students, and the northern wards with large owner-occupied villas. The constituency had one of the highest proportions of well-educated professional workers in any British seat, which might have been expected to benefit the Alliance.

Yet Jenkins's decision to stand was risky. He needed to return to Parliament if he was to lead the Social Democrats into the next general election. By this stage it was not sufficient to come second; given public expectations, he had to win to stay in the forefront of national politics. If the Alliance was gradually losing popular support in the national polls, it needed another by-election victory to restore its momentum. The 'Scottish' dimension, including the presence of the Nationalists, made prospects difficult to assess. The experienced SNP candidate, George Leslie, might have been expected to draw some of the protest vote from the Alliance. In monthly opinion polls the Alliance, particularly the Social Democrats rather than Liberals, had been performing less well in Scotland than elsewhere. The 'Englishness' (or, more accurately, Welshness) of Jenkins may have produced problems.

The Conservative and Unionist candidate was Gerry Malone, a Catholic Glaswegian lawyer who lived in the constituency. Labour fielded a moderate Londoner, David Wiseman, a community worker and Glasgow district councillor. There were another four fringe candidates, including a 'Roy Harold Jenkins' who added to the confusion by also standing for a Social Democratic Party, although a Woy Jenkins standing for the Student grants Doubled Party (SDP) had earlier been excluded by the returning officer. By all accounts the campaign was serious, with debates about issues rather than personalities, and reports that public meetings were unusually well attended (Drucker *et al.* 1982*b*).

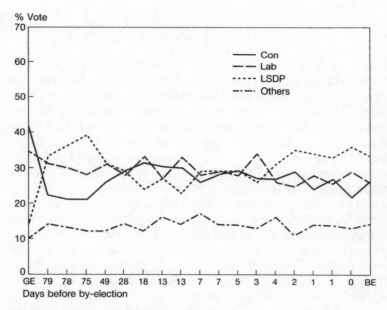

FIG. 4.4.   Glasgow Hillhead opinion polls

The early polls indicated a close and confusing race, with no significant differences between the three major parties (see Fig. 4.4). In early January NOP suggested Labour had a slight edge over the Alliance while ORC put Jenkins marginally ahead. At the start of February Telephone Survey Research Unit (TSRU) placed both parties equal, with the Tories trailing. A fortnight later two polls suggested the Conservatives were just ahead, while another by NOP gave Labour the lead with the Alliance clearly third. The day before the election a Gallup poll gave Labour a 7 percentage point lead, with Jenkins in third place. The position of the Scottish Nationalists in absorbing some of the potential 'protest' vote added a further complicating factor. These indecisive poll results, along with the implications of the contest for the future leadership of the SDP, and the slight decline in their national popularity, fuelled media interest in the contest. During the course of the campaign nineteen polls were published, almost as many as in the February 1974 general election.

On the day Jenkins won the seat with a narrow majority of 2,038 and a lower swing than in the previous Alliance victories, although any precise comparisons with other contests are complicated by the presence of the Scottish Nationalists and the phoney Roy Jenkins. The Labour vote suffered relatively limited damage, leaving them just a few hundred votes behind the Conservatives. The SNP candidate lost his deposit, along with the other four fringe candidates.

As a result of Glasgow Hillhead the Alliance realized they could no longer assume that they could sweep to victory. It had been a hard campaign. On the eve of poll MORI estimated that 6 out of 10 voters in the constituency had been personally canvassed by Alliance campaign workers, while a quarter had actually met Jenkins during the contest (Drucker *et al.* 1982*b*). As Ivor Crewe (1982*b*) summarized the outcome, essentially it suggested that 'the Alliance's bandwagon continued to roll, but more slowly'.

MERTON AND MITCHAM

By the time Roy Jenkins finally succeeded in Glasgow Hillhead the Alliance had won three out of the four by-elections held since it was founded; it seemed to many commentators that it could defeat the established parties anywhere. Government popularity was transformed, however, with the Falklands factor coupled with improved economic trends (Norpath 1987; Saunders *et al.* 1987). As a result, against all the usual by-election trends, the government was able to gain a seat in Merton and Mitcham in June 1982 when Bruce

Douglas-Mann ill-advisedly resigned to fight under his new Social Democratic flag. The seat had been a marginal Labour seat in the 1979 election. With the opposition vote split it required only a minimal shift for the Conservative candidate, Mrs Angela Rumbold, to win.

The Conservatives managed to avoid the usual anti-government swing in other by-elections at the time, including the low-key contests of Beaconsfield and Coatbridge. Then in October 1982 Labour won the highly marginal Birmingham Northfield from the Tories, before losing Bermondsey, which had enjoyed a solid 59% majority, to the Alliance, whilst a month later holding on to the highly marginal seat of Darlington. The swings and roundabouts of by-election politics had never seemed so unpredictable and unstable. All parties won and lost seats in sharp succession.

BIRMINGHAM NORTHFIELD AND GLASGOW QUEEN'S PARK

Birmingham Northfield had traditionally been Labour, with the British Leyland Longbridge car manufacturing plant, a high proportion of skilled manual workers and council tenants. But from 1974 to 1979 in the West Midlands many skilled manual workers switched from Labour to the Conservatives. The by-election was caused by the suicide of Jocelyn Cadbury, who won the seat for the Conservatives in 1979 with a narrow majority of 204. Labour selected a rightwing candidate, John Spellar, an official of the Electricians' Union.

In early polls NOP put Labour and the Conservatives level while the Liberals remained in third place. In the final result Labour recovered the seat largely by default, as the Alliance took slightly more votes from the Tories than Labour. Spellar's fragile hold over the constituency was demonstrated when the government regained the seat in the 1983 general election. With 26% of the votes, the Alliance performance was creditable, but it fell short of expectations, given the swings experienced just a year earlier.

The Birmingham result was widely interpreted as an indicator of Labour's recovery as the main party of opposition, confirmed by their retaining the safe seats of Gower, Peckham, and Glasgow Queens Park. To some observers it seemed as though the spectacular Alliance by-election gains immediately after their launch had proved a short-term media creation, with voters returning to their traditional two-party allegiances in the run-up to the general election. The Alliance seemed to have lost its momentum. Yet Southwark and Bermondsey, in February 1983, was to prove that the outcome of by-elections could not be taken for granted by any party.

BERMONDSEY

Given the social profile of the constituency, commentators might have expected Bermondsey to be a re-run of the routine contest held two months earlier in Glasgow Queens Park. In this inner-city seat in the heart of South London's dockland, with 80% of the electorate in local authority housing and the lowest proportion of owner-occupiers in Britain (2%), Labour should have experienced little difficulty in retaining their solid (39%) majority. At the 1979 general election in Bermondsey Labour had 64% of the vote, the Tories were second with 25%, and the Liberals trailed with 7%. Yet deep internal divisions within the local Labour party were to prove decisive.

The Bermondsey by-election was engendered by the resignation of Bob Mellish, a former Labour Whip, who felt that the radical left were taking over the local party. The adoption of Peter Tatchell led Mellish to support John O'Grady, standing as the 'Real Bermondsey Labour' candidate. As leader Michael Foot first denounced Tatchell in the House of Commons then publicly supported him, thereby highlighting factional strife within the Labour Party. The campaign proved particularly virulent, with the popular press focusing on anti-gay and Militant Tendency smears against the Labour candidate. A series of constituency leaflets added to the personal vilification of Tatchell, who reported threats on his life (Tatchell 1983). The local Labour party claimed that national headquarters failed to provide adequate organizational support, with only a dozen full-time campaigners.

Even with these problems two weeks before the poll Peter Tatchell was confident that he could hold the seat. Labour believed O'Grady's support was slipping (Tatchell 1983). The dynamics of campaign change were registered by the opinion polls. At the beginning of January in an NOP poll Labour were ahead with 47% of the

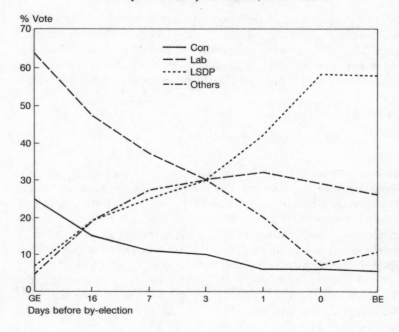

FIG. 4.5.   Bermondsey opinion polls

vote, with the Alliance, Conservatives, and Real Labour party all around 15% to 19%. By 18 February Labour seemed to have dropped 10 percentage points although remaining in the lead. On the eve of poll Thames broadcast an ORC poll suggesting Labour and the Liberals were equal on 30%, with support falling for the Real Labour party and the Conservatives. On the Wednesday evening television news published the results of the Audience Selection poll for the *Sun* indicating that the Liberals would win with a 10 point lead, which proved an underestimate.

   In the final result the Labour vote suffered a spectacular collapse from 64% to 26%. Simon Hughes increased the Liberal share of the vote from 7% to 58%, a post-war record. Within a few weeks Alliance support had been dramatically transformed. The result restored Alliance morale, producing a short-lived six point jump into second place in national Gallup polls. In the run-up to the 1983 general election Bermondsey convinced many Liberals and Social

Democrats that their main strategy should be to replace Labour as the official opposition. Within the Labour Party serious questions were raised about Michael Foot's leadership and the ability of the party to overcome its divisions before the forthcoming general election campaign.

DARLINGTON

The sensational result in Bermondsey led to even greater media attention a month later in Darlington. The scene looked set for another dramatic campaign. Interest was heightened by the pre-general election atmosphere which led political commentators to focus on any available indicators of party popularity. Darlington was highly marginal, with Labour only 2% ahead of the Conservatives in 1979. Darlington could be seen as a weather-vane seat, turning with the political fortunes of the country. The seat had been Labour after the war, reverting to the Conservatives in the fifties, before swinging back to Labour with the first Wilson government. Darlington, relatively prosperous for the North-East, had a large middle-class Conservative vote in the west and south-west of the town. As with Bermondsey, observers thought the selection of candidates important, with the Alliance representative, Tony Cook, proving less effective under public scrutiny than Ossie O'Brien for Labour.

The constituency polls suggested an uncertain outcome (see Fig. 4.6). At the beginning of March MORI indicated that Labour remained ahead although by the middle of the month four polls put the Alliance in the lead. After a widely publicized television campaign debate, where Tony Cook performed badly, the Alliance dropped back into third place. In the final result Labour kept the seat with an increased majority. In a few days, according to the available polls, about 15% of the potential Alliance support slipped back to the old parties. It proved difficult for the tactical anti-Labour voters to know how to cast their vote since neither Conservatives nor Alliance looked like an obvious loser. To some extent the outcome restored Labour confidence, making Bermondsey seem like a temporary aberration and thereby reducing the immediate threat to Michael Foot's leadership. But the result also restored Conservative confidence that in the forthcoming general election they would

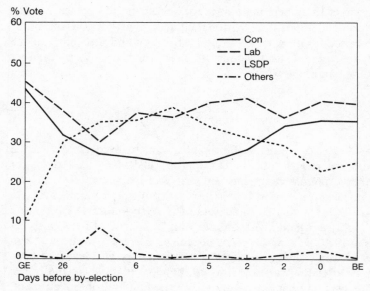

FIG. 4.6.   Darlington opinion polls

face their familiar Labour opposition, rather than the more uncertain threat from the Alliance.

SUMMARY

The evidence from the by-election results during Mrs Thatcher's first administration led the Alliance to hope for a fundamental breakthrough. The initial euphoria caused by Warrington, Croydon North-West, Crosby, and Glasgow Hillhead had subsided but nevertheless the Alliance had good reason to be pleased with their overall performance. During this period the Alliance had increased their share of the by-election vote by almost 20%, capturing support from both major parties (see Table 4.1). In Bermondsey they had achieved their best ever result, gaining over half the vote. In the series of by-elections their mean share of the vote was 29%, putting them in second place behind Labour.

We can conclude that during this period by-elections played a crucial role in establishing the Alliance's credibility as a major force

Table 4.1.   *Changes in by-election results, 1979–1983*

Seat	Date	Turn-out(%)	ChangeCon.	Lab.	LSDP
Manchester C.	27.09.1979	−30	No	−10	0	9
Herts. SW	13.12.1979	−31	No	−9	−12	7
Southend E.	13.03.1980	−8	No	−19	7	12
G'gow C.	26.06.1980	−17	No	−8	−12	—
Warrington	16.07.1981	−4	No	−22	−13	33
Croydon NW	22.10.1981	−10	Yes	−19	−14	30
Crosby	26.11.1981	−6	Yes	−17	−16	35
Glasgow H'head	25.03.1982	1	Yes	−14	−8	19
Beaconsfield	27.04.1982	−22	No	0	−10	10
Merton/Mitcham	03.06.1982	−28	Yes	0	−21	21
Coatbridge	24.06.1982	−19	No	−1	−6	8
Gower	16.09.1982	−15	No	−8	−9	16
S'thwk/Peckham	28.10.1982	−20	No	−16	−10	25
B'ham N'thfld	28.10.1982	−16	Yes	−10	−9	18
G'gow Queen's Pk	02.12.1982	−21	No	−12	−9	9
Bermondsey	24.02.1983	−2	Yes	−19	−38	51
Darlington	24.03.1983	2	No	−8	−6	14
MEAN CHANGE		−14			−12	−11	20
MEAN VOTE	1979–83			26	38	29

in British politics. Without these contests it would have been difficult, if not impossible, for them to advance their bandwagon. Without the continued oxygen of by-election publicity the Social Democrats might have faded from public memory as just another breakaway faction of dissatisfied ex-Labour MPs. The results boosted Alliance morale at a critical juncture. These contests demonstrated that grassroots activists from both parties could work effectively together, putting into practice the Alliance's central theme of co-operation rather than the old politics of confrontation. By-elections allowed the Social Democrats and Liberals to learn appropriate ways of working together, experience which was to prove vital for the following general election campaign. By-elections from Warrington to Darlington proved that the Liberal–Social Democratic Alliance was more than the sum of its parts. Some hoped that on this basis the Alliance could achieve a realignment on the centre left, developing a distinctive social and ideological base which would allow the eventual displacement of the Labour Party.

But the 1983 general election demonstrated, yet again, the difficulties of translating by-election success into Parliamentary seats. With 7.8 million votes the Alliance gained 25.4% of the UK vote, compared with 13.8% for the Liberals alone in 1979. The Alliance were just 700,000 votes behind Labour, representing a larger share of the vote than the Liberal Party had achieved since 1923. In terms of popular support, with 27.6% of the vote, the outcome represented the worst result for Labour since 1918, and the worst result in terms of votes per candidate since the party was founded.

Nevertheless the outcome needs to be seen in context: the Alliance won only 23 seats, thereby experiencing a reduction in their Parliamentary strength from the period immediately prior to the election, since 29 MPs had defected to the SDP. The 1983 result represented only a 3.5% increase in the Liberal vote since their previous post-war peak in February 1974, taking account of the number of seats contested. Further the nature of the Alliance vote seemed remarkably similar to previous Liberal support, rather than achieving a realignment of any key groups in terms of class, region, age, or gender. Unfortunately for the Alliance partisan realignment seemed harder to achieve than many believed in the immediate aftermath of Warrington and Crosby.

5
By-Elections, 1983–1987

In by-elections during Mrs Thatcher's second administration the pattern of greater electoral volatility continued, with about a third of all seats changing hands. Early in the Parliament the elevation of William Whitelaw to the Lords created a by-election in Penrith and the Border. In the immediate aftermath of the general election Penrith proved one of the quieter contests in terms of media attention, attracting minimal press coverage and no published opinion polls. With a comfortable majority of 15,000 in the June general election the Conservatives expected no problems in the by-election just seven weeks later. Penrith should have been natural Tory territory; one of the largest constituencies in Britain, stretching from the Scottish borders to the Pennines and Lakes, heavily dependent on agriculture and tourism. Yet the Alliance felt that there was the potential to squeeze the Labour vote into third place. Part of the Conservative support represented a personal vote for Whitelaw, who had held the seat for twenty-eight years.

The outcome proved dramatic: the Conservative majority was sharply reduced from 15,000 to 552 votes, while Labour lost their deposit. In accordance with Alliance canvass returns, which suggested a strong rise in their support in the last week of the campaign, the Alliance came within 2% of taking their seat (see Fig. 5.1). Commentators attributed the result to the goverment's performance since the June general election, with rows over MPs' pay, the proposed £1,000m. package of spending cuts and the rejection of capital punishment in Parliament. Voters may have resented the timing of the campaign so soon after the general election, as indicated by the sharp decline in turn-out.

CHESTERFIELD

The dramatic swings at Penrith could not be attributed to bandwagons created by opinion polls since there were none. Nor could press coverage be blamed; Penrith attracted little attention until the headline news of the results. In contrast the contest at Chester-

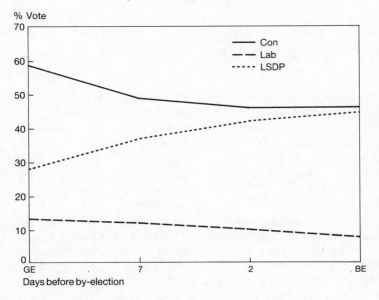

Fig. 5.1.   Penrith opinion polls

field which followed in March 1984 proved a media circus, with fourteen polls published during the campaign, yet the Labour vote remained remarkably steady. The focus of the attention was the candidacy of Tony Benn, who had lost his previous seat at Bristol South-East through boundary changes. The leading spokesperson for the Labour left and former Secretary of State for Industry, Benn had unsuccessfully contested the deputy leadership of the party in 1981. Commentators believed that his defeat in the by-election would have had serious consequences for the future direction of the Labour Party. Chesterfield provided a significant test whether, following their disastrous performance in the 1983 election, Labour could mount a united and effective campaign under the new leadership of Neil Kinnock. Many journalists, drawing parallels with Bermond-sey a year earlier, expected a dramatic contest.

Attracted by the publicity seventeen candidates stood for election, most for fringe causes ranging from the commercial ('Buy your Chesterfields in Thame Party'), to the absurd ('Yoga and Meditation Party'). Yet despite the media hoopla, all polls except Marplan suggested that throughout the campaign Labour enjoyed a comfortable lead of 10 to 27 percentage points.[1] On 23 January early polls by Audience Selection and Gallup gave Labour 46% of the vote, and, on 1 March, that is exactly what Benn achieved (see Fig. 5.2).

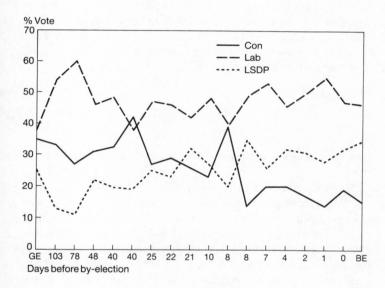

FIG. 5.2. Chesterfield opinion polls

In many ways the outcome was not surprising. Chesterfield was natural Labour territory: near to Sheffield, heavily industrial with many steelworking plants including the large steel and chemical complex at Staveley, although coal mining had declined. Over 40% of the electorate were council tenants, with few in professional and managerial occupations. Throughout the campaign the Labour organization seems to have been effective, with support mobilized from all wings of the Parliamentary party. The main battle was for second place, with the Alliance overtaking the Conservatives

[1] The exceptions were the Marplan polls published in the *Guardian* on 23 Jan. and 23 Feb. 1984.

in the polls in early February. In the end many Conservative voters switched but even so the Alliance failed to mount an effective challenge to Tony Benn. To win, the Alliance needed to gain from both parties and the Labour vote held solid. Any doubts voters may have had about Benn were insufficient to alienate traditional Labour support. In a Harris poll, when asked to evaluate Benn the majority of voters (59%) agreed that he was too left-wing but many felt he was sincere and could represent effectively the interests of Chesterfield.[2] The main impact of the intense media coverage and polling activity was to increase interest in the campaign (turn-out increased by 4%), rather than to mobilize an anti-Benn bandwagon.

CYNON VALLEY, STAFFORD, AND SURREY SOUTH-WEST

There followed a series of three low-profile by-elections caused by the death of the Labour MP for Cynon Valley and the Tory representatives for Stafford and Surrey South-West. The contests were held on 3 April 1984, at the same time as the local government elections, so that the Alliance could not invest the usual level of organizational resources into each contest. Given solid majorities from 26% to 35% at the last election, the outcome seemed predictable, arousing minimal interest in the press. Cynon Valley was in the heart of Labour territory in the coal-mining valleys of Mid-Glamorgan, between Merthyr Tydfil and the Rhondda. The seat had been Labour since the war. Surrey South-West was a classic Tory seat, in the outer commuter belt with stockbroker towns such as Godalming and Farnham. Stafford was more mixed, with some Labour wards in the town, but the agricultural areas were strongly Conservative; electors had returned Sir Hugh Fraser as Tory MP since 1945. In these by-elections Labour slightly improved their support for Ann Clwyd in Cynon Valley, while in Stafford and Surrey South-West there was a 10% swing from the Conservatives to the Alliance. The media paid greater attention to the local elections, held at the same time, considered a more reliable guide to trends across the country.

[2] Harris poll in the *Observer* 27 Feb. 1984.

PORTSMOUTH SOUTH

Most commentators assumed that Portsmouth South in June 1984, with a 25% Tory majority, would prove a similar low-key event. Commentators noted that the campaign seemed to generate little local interest. The elections to the European Parliament, held on the same day, attracted all the media coverage.

The Alliance candidate, Mike Hancock, was well known in the area as a local councillor. Labour probably suffered from a candidate, Sally Thomas, who actively supported CND in a constituency dependent upon the naval dockyard. The Conservative was perceived as an outsider, more popular with Conservative Central Office than the local party. The routine campaign attracted minimal national press coverage. The only poll, by NOP published in the *Daily Mail* two days before the election, showed the Conservatives in the lead with 43%, followed by Labour on 31% and the Alliance last with 25%.

As a consequence the result came as a shock; few expected the Social Democrats to win, with 38% of the vote compared with 34% for the Tories. In looking for explanations the Conservative candidate blamed the low turn-out. In a mid-term contest many may have stayed at home but compared with other recent by-elections the decline in participation (by 19%) was far from exceptional. The Conservative Party internal report suggested that the party had been complacent, failing to put sufficient organizational resources into the campaign. When NOP returned to their original sample, in their post-mortem to see why their poll differed from the result, they found local factors and tactical considerations led to a swing in the last few days. Based on the recalled vote NOP suggest that their original sample was accurate but subsequently many voters had changed their minds.

Yet although the result surprised observers, it was consistent with longer-term by-election trends. The increase in the Alliance vote (by 12%) was average for the Parliament; indeed they achieved better results at Penrith and at Chesterfield without taking the seats. The decline in the government's share of the vote (by 16%) was also far from unusual: there were worse results for the government in a third of all by-elections during this Parliament. Therefore Portsmouth South was significant for the loss of the seat, rather than the size of the swing.

ENFIELD SOUTHGATE

It was another six months before the next by-election, at Enfield Southgate in December 1984, brought about by the death of the Conservative member in the Brighton bombing. In the circumstances the opposition hesitated about contesting the by-election but eventually Labour chose Peter Hamid, a West Indian local councillor, while the Alliance selected Tim Slack, from outside the constituency. The Tory candidate was a young adviser from their Research Department, Michael Portillo. Suburban Southgate was mainly middle-class owner-occupiers who commuted to the City, although the Labour candidate hoped to appeal to the substantial ethnic minority population. In the general election the Conservatives had a 35% majority, and the Alliance had second place with 25% of the vote.

Again this was to prove a campaign generating little national interest with only one poll published in the *Observer* five days before the result. The Harris poll found Conservative support slightly down on the general election, with the Alliance and Labour neck-and-neck on 22% to 23%. But Harris also asked about tactical preferences: whom voters would choose if the Liberals stood a chance of winning and Labour did not. This presented a different picture which proved closer to the final outcome. On the day Michael Portillo was returned with 49% of the vote, while Labour dropped to 12% in third place. It seems that the tactical squeeze benefited the Alliance but was insufficient to threaten the Tory majority. The Conservatives probably benefited from a competent candidate, an efficient organization led by a full-time agent, sympathy generated by the circumstances of the by-election, and lessons about the dangers of complacency learnt at Portsmouth South.

BRECON AND RADNOR

Enfield provided a strong contrast to the following contest, Brecon and Radnor, in July 1986. The largest seat in mid-Wales, Brecon and Radnor had been Labour until 1979 but the seat boundaries had been altered by re-districting to exclude some of their strongest areas in the mining villages. In 1983 the Conservatives held 48% of the vote, with Labour and the Alliance neck-and-neck on 25% and 24% respectively. The Alliance chose a quiet but competent candidate, Richard Livsey, a lecturer in agriculture with farming roots in the neighbouring constituency. There were three fringe candidates as well as those for the Conservatives (Christopher Butler), Labour (Richard Willey), and Plaid Cymru (Mrs Janet Davies).

Observers expected that government support would suffer in the mid-term of their administration, but at an early stage it seemed a three-way contest. The first poll in early June, by MORI for the *Daily Mirror*, suggested Labour were ahead with 39%, followed by the Conservatives (31%), and the Alliance (28%) (see Fig. 5.3).

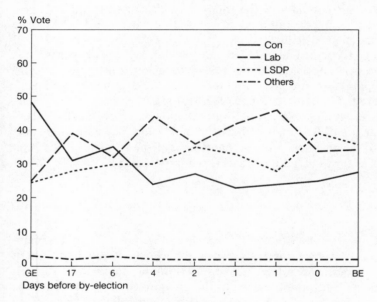

FIG. 5.3.   Brecon and Radnor opinion polls

Another two MORI polls reinforced perceptions that Labour were pulling ahead; the final MORI poll gave them a decisive 18 percentage point lead. But this was in marked contrast with the results of a survey by Beaufort Research for HTV which placed the Alliance only 1% behind Labour. In the end the only survey to come close was the exit poll by BBC 'Newsnight', which correctly identified the Alliance as the winner, with the Conservatives driven into third place, their worst performance during the Parliament. Labour improved its vote but the Alliance just edged ahead with a wafer-thin (1.5%) lead.

The subsequent post-mortem into the performance of the polls suggested that large agricultural constituencies such as Brecon pose considerable sampling problems; traditional Liberal support is often located in scattered rural farms and isolated villages rather than small towns. These may prove difficult to contact for fieldworkers imported into the constituency, given commercial constraints of time and travel. Probably there was also a last-minute swing: Gallup's post-election survey found that of those who made up their minds in the last few days of the campaign half shifted to the Alliance. MORI's recall of their original sample found that a third of Alliance voters claimed to have decided how to vote after their final poll was conducted. Only an exit poll on the day would register this movement. As David Butler (1986) commented after the election, the polls face problems where the electorate is highly turbulent: 'More than at any time since 1923 Britain faces a three-party race. An increasingly volatile electorate can move in many ways and falsify predictions.' The main effect of the polls and media attention was to stimulate interest in the contest, as demonstrated by the high level of turn-out, and to intensify party campaign activity.

TYNE BRIDGE

In contrast Tyne Bridge, in December 1985, proved a routine campaign. In a solid inner-city seat in the heart of Labour's northern strongholds, with all the indicators of multiple deprivation, the outcome seemed pre-ordained. In the previous general election Tyne Bridge was the safest Labour seat in the North-East. The constituency had one of the highest rates of unemployment in the country, owing to the decline in docking, shipbuilding and the heavy armaments industry. Almost half the population were council tenants while two-thirds were working class.

Labour selected a moderate candidate, Dave Clelland, the leader of Gateshead council. Journalists concluded that the real battle was between the Alliance and Conservatives for second place. The Tories chose a candidate from outside the constituency, Jacqui Lait, a member of the Reform Group who stressed middle-of-the-road Toryism. The SDP faced three main problems: they were unable to exploit the 'extremist' labels with either of their opponents, their base in local politics was weak, and they started in third place with only 18% of the vote in the previous general election.

The contest proved largely uneventful, with little media attention and only one campaign poll, carried out by BBC *Newsnight* on 24–25 November, which suggested that Labour support was steady while the Alliance had moved into second place. The main local issues were the ones where Labour enjoyed a strong lead: unemployment, crime and vandalism, housing and the health service.[3] The most dramatic change was in levels of participation; for a mid-term election in a safe seat during bitter winter weather only four out of ten electors turned out to vote. As expected the results were close to the average for this Parliament, with a 12% swing from the Conservatives to the Alliance. The Labour candidate was returned with a largely unchanged share of the vote and a comfortable majority over the Alliance in second place. The Conservative vote was squeezed from 25% to 11%, consistent with by-elections in similar safe Labour seats.

FULHAM

In April 1986, just when it seemed safe to generalize about by-elections, Fulham seemed to go against the established trends. The Alliance might have expected to do well in this contest given three factors: their by-election record, the opinion polls, and the nature of the constituency. The Alliance had come first or second in every by-election this Parliament. In April their support was high in the national polls. According to Gallup surveys, in the wake of deep Cabinet splits over the Westland affair and controversy about British Leyland, the Conservatives had slumped into third place nationally (see Fig. 5.4). In Gallup polls taken in the first few months of 1986, during their mid-term slump, the Tories were as low as 29%, one of their worst ratings under Mrs Thatcher, while Labour and the Alliance were equal, around 34%. In Fulham the Alliance should have been the natural home for disaffected Tories.

The Alliance might also have expected to perform well in Fulham given the character of the seat. The constituency was a marginal seat; Martin Stevens, the previous Conservative MP, had a majority

[3] BBC 'Newsnight' poll, 25 Nov. 1985 (N.1,007)

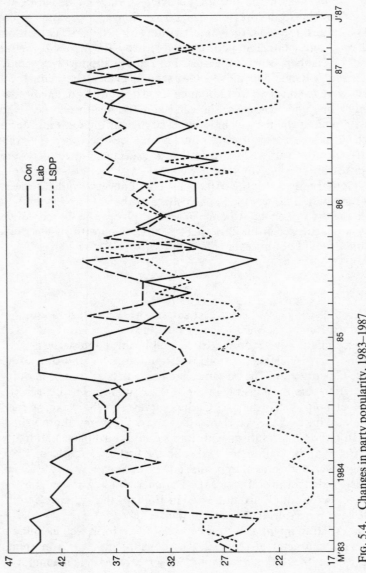

FIG. 5.4. Changes in party popularity, 1983–1987

of under 5,000. Before 1979 the seat had been held by Michael Stewart, the Labour Foreign Secretary. It was originally an inner-city area, but over the years extensive gentrification had transformed many parts of the constituency. Fulham was socially mixed. In the affluent wards there were owner-occupied Edwardian terraced homes, with a high proportion of professional and managerial occupations. Many of the younger professionals who could not afford nearby Chelsea lived in mansion flats around the Fulham Broadway. In contrast the large Clem Attlee estate was solidly working-class, and in Margravine ward one in five were registered unemployed.

Yet from the start of the campaign the Alliance faced several disadvantages. Based on their 1983 performance the SDP began a long way behind the other parties. Roger Liddle, the SDP candidate, was the leader of the Alliance group on Lambeth council. He was opposed by a moderate Labour candidate, Nick Raynsford, well-known locally for his campaigns on housing rights. The constituency Labour party was middle-of-the-road, active, and well-organized. The Alliance could not use the extremist label against their opponents, as they had in Bermondsey or Chesterfield. Such tactics were undermined by the actions of the Labour party's National Executive, with the introduction of disciplinary proceedings against the Liverpool militants at the time of the by-election.

Lastly the Alliance could not attack the local council in Hammersmith and Fulham as it was controlled by a Conservative–Liberal administration, while Labour were able to highlight local housing problems and cuts in services. Since 1978 the Liberals had held the political balance on Hammersmith and Fulham council, siding only once with Labour out of more than 300 council meeting votes. During this period there had been sharp increases in council rents and a radical programme of privatization for the council's direct labour organization, housing services, and transport fleet. This record undermined the Alliance's claim to provide an alternative to Conservative policies on social services.

The series of ten polls during the Fulham contest present a remarkably stable picture (see Fig. 5.5) despite all the media hype, the extensive campaigning by local activists, and numerous visits from party leaders. From the start all polls put Labour ahead, with about 40% to 45% of the vote, and at the end Labour won 44%. The decisive shift giving Labour the seat came before, not during, the official campaign. In the series of polls the Alliance were consistently

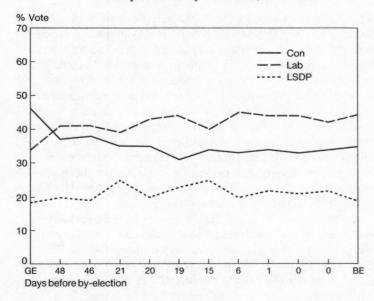

FIG. 5.5. Fulham opinion polls

ranked third with a largely unchanged share of the vote. This was
confirmed in the final result—the second worst Alliance performance
this Parliament. Despite the high-profile campaign, with extensive
media publicity and frequent polls, the Alliance failed to mobilize
a bandwagon in their favour. In Fulham the polls served to reinforce
their position in third place, emphasizing for anti-government voters
that Alliance support was a wasted vote. The outcome boosted
Labour's morale, since it proved that they could do well in by-
elections, although this was the first time that they had gained a
seat in four years. The Tories dismissed the loss as a predictable
case of the mid-term blues, confident that the seat would be restored
in the next general election.

RYEDALE

After Fulham attention turned to by-elections at Ryedale and West
Derbyshire, both held on 8 May 1986. The government was recover-
ing from the political fall-out of the Westland affair but these were

expected to be quiet contests in safe Tory seats. Ryedale, the largest rural seat in England, stretches fifty miles from Scarborough on the east coast through the North Yorkshire moors to the outskirts of the city of York. The constituency looked like natural Conservative territory, with a scattered population engaged in agriculture and tourism, professionals in York, and many in country retirement. Ryedale had been solidly Tory since the war although the Liberals had been successful in recent local government elections, holding a majority of council seats. During the seventies Labour had become progressively weaker in Ryedale, down to 10% in 1983. Alliance campaign strategists realized they had the potential to squeeze Labour and to pick up dissatisfied Tories, although they had to improve on their average by-election performance this Parliament, and do much better than their position in the national polls, to pose a serious threat to the Conservatives.

The campaign focused on local problems—the rural bus services, the Filey coastguard, and agricultural subsidies—but nationally the dominant issue was the American bombing of Tripoli in mid-April. Constituency polls registered two decisive shifts in public opinion. The first, marked by a substantial drop in Conservative support, occurred before the start of the official campaign. The earliest BBC

Table 5.1. *Opinion polls in Ryedale by-election, 1986*

	GE 1983	BBC I March	BBC II April	Gallup May	Result 8 May
Con.	59	47	44	40	41
Lab.	10	17	19	14	8
LSDP	31	35	37	47	50
Con. Lead	29	12	7	−7	−9

Note:	BBC I	BBC 'Newsnight' poll, fieldwork 19–22 Mar. 1986, N.634.
	BBC II	BBC 'Newsnight' poll, fieldwork 24–5 Apr. 1986.
	Gallup	Fieldwork 29 Apr.–4 May 1986, N.997.

'Newsnight' survey, in April, found the Conservative lead over the Liberals was cut from 29% to 12% (see Table 5.1). There was evidence of further potential change: when asked whether they would consider voting tactically, to keep out the party they most disliked if their own could not win, over half of the Labour voters said they might switch to the Alliance.

The second decisive movement in public opinion occurred in the last week of the campaign, with the main transfer of votes between Labour and the Alliance. This suggests that Ryedale can be explained by a long-term erosion of government support coupled with a short-term tactical switch in the last few days. The Alliance won with just over half the vote in the constituency. As in Portsmouth South, the campaign had attracted little press attention and few polls, yet the result proved dramatic. Most commentators and even the Alliance candidate, Elizabeth Shields, seemed surprised by taking the seat, which to most observers had appeared one of the safest Conservative seats in the country (see Fig. 5.6).

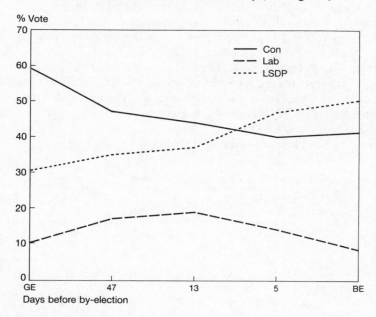

FIG. 5.6.   Ryedale

WEST DERBYSHIRE

Commentators expected that the West Derbyshire by-election, held at the same time, might be more dramatic. The Alliance had hopes of a strong performance in this by-election, called following the resignation of Matthew Parris, who left to become a television presenter. In 1983 the Conservatives gained over half of the vote (56%) but it appeared the Alliance might be well positioned to squeeze the Labour vote in third place. West Derbyshire, dominated by agriculture, tourism and light industry, included much of the Peak District National Park. Labour had always performed well in the Belper wards, part of George Brown's old constituency on the outskirts of Derby, but the Alliance were stronger in the rural areas in local elections.

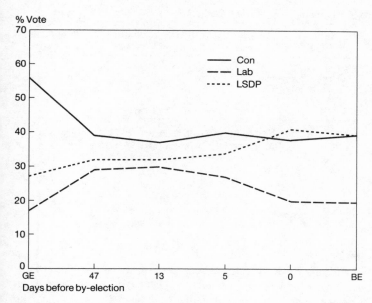

FIG. 5.7. West Derbyshire opinion polls

The earliest constituency poll, by BBC 'Newsnight' in March, suggested that the Conservative lead had declined sharply from 29% to just 7%, (see Fig. 5.7) and West Derbyshire promised to be a three-way contest. The April BBC survey registered almost no change in party support, although there was evidence for further potential shifts, as four out of ten Labour voters said they would consider voting tactically to keep out the party they most disliked, if their own could not win. Given the close position of the parties, the problem for the Alliance was in clearly establishing that they, rather than Labour, were the main challengers to the Conservatives. The position of the parties seemed to remain largely unchanged until the last few days, although there was some slippage in the Labour vote, as shown by the Gallup poll four days before the election (see Table 5.2). The final result saw limited tactical transfers to the Alliance but these were insufficient to win, and after numerous recounts they ended within one hundred votes of challenging the Tories.

Table 5.2. *Opinion polls in West Derbyshire by-election, 1986*

	GE 1983	BBC I March	BBC II April	Gallup May	Result 8 May
Con.	56	39	37	40	40
Lab.	17	29	30	27	20
LSDP	27	32	32	34	39
Con. Lead	29	7	5	6	1

Note:	BBC I	BBC 'Newsnight' poll, fieldwork 19–22 Mar. 1986, N.634.
	BBC II	BBC 'Newsnight' poll, fieldwork 24–5 Apr. 1986.
	Gallup	Fieldwork 29 Apr.–4 May 1986, N.997.

NEWCASTLE UNDER LYME

In June 1986 the resignation of the MP John Golding, due to a conflict with his work as General Secretary of the National Communication Union, led to the contest in Newcastle under Lyme. In the Potteries region, the constituency had been Labour since the war although by 1983 the seat was highly marginal, with only a 5.5% majority. Socially the constituency was diverse, combining traditional mining communities with suburban areas. The campaign was dominated by local and personal issues, especially the candidacy of Mrs Llin Golding, the wife of the previous MP, which raised accusations of a Golding 'dynasty'. It was a relatively quiet campaign in early June, which coincided with the traditional Potteries' holiday week, so that many voters were away and the election was characterized by low turn-out. In line with by-elections during the previous year there was a swing of 17% from the Conservatives to the Alliance, allowing them to come within 800 votes of taking the seat from Labour. Commentators attributed the results to a weak Labour organization, and a Liberal–SDP campaign characterized by 'dirty tricks', but the Labour result was consistent with their average performance during the Parliament.

TRURO

Towards the end of Mrs Thatcher's second term there were two by-elections which we will compare in detail in the following chapters: Knowsley North, a routine campaign in a solid Labour seat, and the classic SDP victory at Greenwich. The last by-elec-

Table 5.3. *Changes in by-elections, 1983–1987*

Seat	Date	Turn-out	Seat change	Con.	Lab.	LSDP
Penrith	28.06.83	−17	No	−13	−6	17
Chesterfield	01.03.84	4	No	−17	−2	15
Cynon Valley	03.04.84	−8	No	−7	3	−1
Surrey SW	03.04.84	−13	No	−10	−2	11
Stafford	03.04.84	−11	No	−11	4	7
Portsmouth S	14.06.84	−13	Yes	−16	4	12
Enfield S'gate	13.12.84	−19	No	−9	−6	12
Brecon	04.07.85	−1	Yes	−21	9	11
Tyne Bridge	05.12.85	−23	No	−14	1	11
Fulham	10.04.86	−5	Yes	−11	10	1
Ryedale	08.05.86	−5	Yes	−18	−2	20
W. Derbyshire	08.05.86	−3	No	−16	3	12
Ncl. u. Lyme	17.06.86	−15	No	−17	−1	17
Knowsley N	13.11.86	−13	No	−14	−8	20
Greenwich	26.02.87	1	Yes	−23	−4	28
Truro	13.03.87	−9	No	−7	3	3
AVERAGE CHANGE		−10		−14	0	12

Note: All figures represent percentage change from the previous general election to the by-election.

tion of the Parliament was Truro in the South-West, caused by the tragic death of David Penhaligon. In the previous general election the Labour vote was minimal (4.5%); it could hardly be squeezed

Table 5.4. *Summary of by-elections, 1979–1989*

Govt.	Con.		Lab.		LSDP[a]	
	%Vote	Change	%Vote	Change	%Vote	Change
Con. 1979–83	26	−12	38	−11	29	+20
Con. 1983–87	29	−14	31	0	38	+12
Con. 1987–89						

Note: a. This represents the mean share of the vote for the Liberals and Social Democrats where they contested by-elections irrespective of whether they fought the seat in the previous general election.

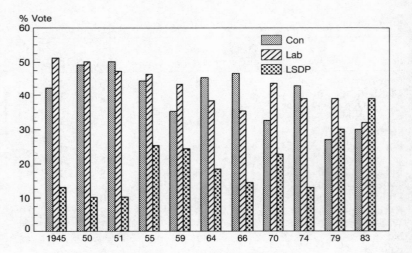

FIG. 5.8.   Party support in by-elections, 1945–1987

any lower. The Conservatives in second place fought a decent campaign but they could do little against a solid (19%) Liberal majority. In the event Matthew Taylor managed to improve the Liberal majority slightly, with 60% of the vote, which served to reinforce Alliance confidence in the run-up to the general election, although the change in the vote was fairly minimal.

Table 5.5. *Changes of seat in by-elections, 1979–1989*

Govt.	BE No.	Changes in seats No.	%
Con. 1979–83	17	6	35
Con. 1983–87	16	5	31
Con. 1987–89	8		

Note: This excludes exceptional cases including uncontested by-elections in university seats and the Bristol SE by-elections awarded on petition.

SUMMARY

During the second Conservative administration Labour showed some signs of recovery in their by-election performance, by increasing support in Brecon and Radnor, and winning Fulham. But the Liberals and Social Democrats made the most impressive by-election gains, in Portsmouth South, Brecon and Radnor, Ryedale, and Greenwich. The Alliance also made the most consistent gains in votes in every by-election except Cynon Valley (see Tables 5.3 and 5.4). Although not achieving the same public impact as their successive victories in 1981–82, the Alliance gained a higher share of the vote than the other parties (38%) in all the by-elections since 1983. In Mrs Thatcher's second term, as in her first, one in three by-election seats changed hands (see Table 5.5).

The extent of change should not be exaggerated, however; even in recent years many contests like Tyne Bridge in 1985, Cynon Valley in 1984, or Knowsley North in 1986 fail to generate dramatic results. Therefore we need to go on to explore why some contests prove volatile, and what this implies about the dynamics of by-election campaigns, by considering detailed case-studies where survey evidence is available in the Greenwich and Knowsley North contests.

6

The Routine Fare: Knowsley North

ON the basis of the campaigns outlined so far we have identified two basic categories of by-elections. On the one hand there are the dramatic contests with unexpected winners and losers, the famous by-elections typified most clearly by Glasgow Hillhead, Hamilton, Lincoln, Bermondsey, and Orpington. These are the classic by-elections remembered long after the event, which can have a significant impact on the national political scene. On the other hand there are the more routine by-elections exemplified by Tyne Bridge, Glasgow Queens Park, and by Southwark and Peckham during Mrs Thatcher's second term, generating minimal attention and predictable results. The solid Labour seat of Knowsley North in November 1986 exemplifies these low-key campaigns while a few months later Greenwich clearly falls into the volatile category. We will therefore compare these campaigns as detailed case-studies, using the available survey evidence to analyse the conditions producing these different outcomes.

THE CONSTITUENCY

Located on the outskirts of Liverpool, Knowsley North is the classic sort of inner-city seat which in a general election should have been solidly Labour. One of Britain's poorest seats, it has more semi-skilled and unskilled workers than any other constituency, high crime, and extensive vandalism. Solidly working-class, with the third highest unemployment rate in Britain, in the 1983 general election it proved, not surprisingly, to be the eighth safest Labour seat, with a majority of over 17,000 for the Labour MP, Robert Kilroy-Silk.

The constituency included thousands of families decanted from slum areas of Liverpool to Kirkby during the fifties, with over 90% of Kirkby housing municipally owned. By the time of the by-election almost two-thirds of the electorate were living in council accommodation, compared with about a quarter in Britain as a whole. The seat was socially homogeneous, with urban deprivation across the whole constituency, although there were some differences between

Table 6.1. *Demographic indicators by ward in Knowsley North (%)*

Ward	Manual SEG[a]	Council tenants[b]	Unempl. pop.[c]	Pensioner pop.[d]	Labour vote[e]
Cantril	68	75	36	17	Unopp.
Tower Hill	70	84	21	7	81
Northwood	66	85	18	10	74
Kirkby C.	68	80	18	10	73
Knowsley Pk	68	76	17	15	70
Prescott E.	74	72	11	14	65
Cherryfield	76	82	18	12	65
Whitefield	59	65	17	12	56
Prescott W.	49	39	6	23	45
Park	66	51	14	10	25
ALL	65	61	17	13	59

Notes: See Appendix for details.

a. Manual Socio-Economic Groups (7, 8, 9, 10, 11, 12, 14, 15): 1981 Census 10% Small Area Statistics.

b. Percentage of resident population in local authority accommodation: 1981 Census 100% SAS updated by Director of Housing, Knowsley Borough Council April 1986.

c. Percentage of adult population registered unemployed, Manpower Services Commission, Registered Unemployment Claimants, Knowsley North, August 1986.

d. Percentage of population over 60, Census 100% SAS.

e. Vote by ward in the 1986 borough elections.

the relatively better-off Park and Prescott West wards and the more deprived areas of Cantril and Tower Hill to the north (see Table 6.1). As Hugo Young described the blight:

Some of the Kirkby estates are as bleak as anything built in Britain ... Except in the one shopping centre, there is little activity. Across large acres there are no shops or pubs. There is no cinema or hospital in the constituency. Nor, now, is there a proper bus service, deregulation having wiped out several routes as 'uncommercial'. Yet Knowsley North has fewer car owners than almost anywhere else. The two commonest signs of life are unemployed men walking their dogs and black taxis plying for trade. (Young 1986)

THE CANDIDATES

The media focused almost exclusively on two themes: the personalities of the candidates and splits in the local Labour party. Headlines tended to focus on the divisions between the Militant left and the more moderate Labour candidate imposed by Labour's National Executive Committee. The by-election was occasioned in late September by the resignation of Robert Kilroy-Silk, who left in a mood of bitterness and anger, driven out by conflict with the hard left and Militant Tendency sympathizers in his local party. The leading contender to take over the seat was Les Huckfield, the Labour Member of the European Parliament for Merseyside East, who was closely associated with the hard left although not a member of the Militant-Tendency faction. In the candidate selection process by the end of September Les Huckfield led the field with twenty-seven local nominations, compared with eleven for George Howarth.

Yet Les Huckfield's nomination would have been deeply embarrassing for the National Executive. At the time Kinnock was in the process of taking action against members of Militant Tendency on Liverpool council, expelling Tony Mulhearn and Derek Hatton from the party in the September Blackpool conference. The executive was reluctant to interfere in the selection process. Conventionally this has been seen as an area where the local party has considerable autonomy, subject only to formal NEC approval. Previous attempts to force a candidate on an unwilling local party, such as the adoption of Patrick Gordon Walker by Leyton in 1965, have sometimes backfired. Nevertheless the executive felt that this was a necessary step as the adoption of a hard-left candidate might produce another Bermondsey. The publicity would undermine Kinnock's public stance against the Militant Tendency at the Blackpool conference and the popular press would use the incident to cast doubts on Kinnock's ability to control the 'loony left'. Although Les Huckfield had gathered the highest number of nominations the National Executive decided to suspend the Knowsley North selection process in late September, appointing a three-person committee to investigate the process. By mid-October the NEC decided by a close vote of 13: 9 that Les Huckfield was disqualified.

Accordingly the Executive recommended that the constituency should pick George Howarth, a moderate Kinnock-supporter who had been Deputy Leader of the borough since 1982/3. In separate legal actions both Les Huckfield and the local party tried to obtain injunctions against the NEC to prevent Howarth's adoption but these legal moves were rejected in the High Court. The local party boycotted the campaign, which created headlines about divisions in the Labour camp. Labour Party headquarters in Walworth Road drafted in outside volunteers to take their place and there is no evidence that this significantly damaged their campaign. For the final weekend Labour said they mobilized 500 recruits for canvassing, of which only 62 were locals. Nor did the absence of the candidate seem to do any real harm. Nine days before polling George Howarth was confined to a hospital bed, without any apparent impact on the campaign. As one commentator noted, from the start George Howarth mattered for what he is not, rather than what he is. 'That he was not Leslie Huckfield or a member of Militant Tendency, was all that concerned the Labour leadership when it ruthlessly imposed him. If the candidate is merely a negative, it hardly matters if he is not there' (H. Young 1986).

By the close of nominations there were six candidates. The main challenge to George Howarth was provided by Rosemary Collins for the Liberal and Social Democratic Alliance, an outspoken local councillor who waged an aggressive grassroots campaign. Rosemary Collins focused her campaign on local grievances, particularly housing, and attacking the Militant Tendency. The problem was that the issues of leaky roofs and unsafe concrete pavements were insufficient to generate an enthusiastic bandwagon in the absence of a strongly left-wing candidate to attack. The Liberal campaign was managed by the seasoned veteran Andy Ellis, with visits by most of the prominent Alliance politicians. During the last weekend's canvass the Alliance claimed to bring about 1,200 activists into the constituency. For the Liberals it was seen as an opportunity to restore their momentum following the disastrous defence rows in the Eastbourne conference in the previous autumn. Since their conference the Alliance had been sinking steadily in the national polls. With a general election on the horizon the Alliance badly wanted a by-election victory to increase their national popularity. The Conservatives selected Roger Brown, although from the start it seemed to many a lost cause.

THE CAMPAIGN

Most of the campaign debate concentrated on splits within the Labour Party and disenchantment with the Labour council. Discussion at press conferences focused on the local issues of housing repairs, unemployment, high rates, and bus services. The Alliance and the Conservatives tried to make political capital from the problems facing the Labour Party in Liverpool, and there is some evidence in the BBC survey that voters shared their concerns. When asked about the policies pursued by Liverpool City Council more than half (57%) the Knowsley voters said they thought the effect had been bad for Merseyside; only 20% approved. When asked how they would describe the Merseyside Labour party over half the sample saw it as extreme, including two-thirds of Conservatives and three-quarters of those who intended to vote Alliance (see Table

Table 6.2.   *Extremist images of the Labour Party, Knowsley North (% of respondents by party identification)*

	All	Lab.	LSDP	Con.
Local party	53	44	78	65
National party	25	15	48	45

Note: Q. In the local area in Merseyside how would you describe the major parties? Is the Labour party extreme or moderate? And at the national level in Britain ...

Source: BBC 'Newsnight' Survey, Knowsley North, 1–2 Nov. 1986, N.736.

6.2). Voters were clearly aware of the divisions in the local party. The problem Rosemary Collins faced in trying to campaign on the issue of the 'loony left' was that voters distinguished between the local Labour party and George Howarth, the choice of the National Executive under the leadership of Neil Kinnock. At the time of the by-election the NEC moves to expel Derek Hatton, Tony Mulhearn, and other Militants from the Liverpool Labour party were being carried out at Walworth Road headquarters in the full glare of Fleet Street publicity. This may have influenced perceptions of Neil Kinnock's leadership; when asked how they saw the national Labour Party almost two-thirds of the Knowsley electorate saw it as moderate. Without a hard-left candidate the Alliance were unable to benefit from disaffected Labour voters.

The selection of Labour candidate therefore made it difficult for the Alliance to mobilize a tactical shift, which depends in large part on protest voting. The Alliance faced another problem here: credibility. There was evidence in BBC surveys of considerable tactical potential. During the campaign almost half the electorate (47%) said they would seriously consider switching to another party to keep out the party they most disliked, including 53% of Conservatives and 46% of Labour voters. The Alliance was the second choice of about 85% of those Labour and Conservatives who would consider switching. If mobilized this could have had a dramatic effect on Alliance support. The problem was that given the size of the Labour majority over successive general elections, reinforced by polls within the campaign which placed Labour comfortably ahead, less than 10% believed that the Alliance could win. Among those who intended to vote Alliance, only a quarter thought their party could beat Labour. Even spokesmen for the Alliance were cautious about their prospects, acknowledging in the last week that there was still a long way to go to catch up with Labour.

The Alliance also performed weakly in terms of support on the major campaign issues. When asked in BBC 'Newsnight' surveys which issues were important to them in deciding how to vote, respondents from all parties nominated a trilogy of issues where the Labour Party has traditionally established a long-standing lead: unemployment, the health service, and education. These were also the issues where voters proved the most critical of the government's performance, even Conservatives. In the light of the severe unemployment problems blighting the constituency over 90% of the electorate disapproved of government policy, while about 80% were critical of the way the government had handled the National Health Service and education (see Table 6.3). In contrast issues where the Conservatives performed more strongly, such as inflation, defence and nuclear energy, were of lower salience. On the key defence issue of unilateral versus multilateral disarmament two thirds of all voters, and more than half of Labour voters, disapproved of official Labour policy. The problem for the Conservatives and the Alliance was that less than half of all Knowsley voters considered the defence issue very important. The policy agenda therefore forced the contenders to fight on Labour territory.

The strengths and weaknesses of the government on the major issues were reflected in their broader image (see Table 6.4). As pre-

Table 6.3.   *Salient Issues and Government Approval, Knowsley North (%)*

	Importance[a]	Approval of Government[b]			
		All	Lab.	LSDP	Con.
Unemployment	83	5	3	3	24
Health	81	11	6	10	41
Education	78	13	7	18	38
Inflation	50	22	10	37	60
Defence	46	21	13	25	60
Nuc. energy	35	30	21	34	69
T. unions	38	31	24	37	75

Notes: a. Percentage nominating issue as 'very important'.
b. Q. Do you approve or disapprove of the way the government has handled—?
(percentage approve).
Source: BBC 'Newsnight' Survey, Knowsley North, 1–2 Nov. 1986, N.736.

Table 6.4.   *Images of the government (by party identification–Knowsley North (%))*

	Positive responses	Lab.	LSDP	Con.
Determined	82	78	90	95
Patriotic	64	61	72	80
Efficient	40	32	47	80
Honest	18	12	13	61
Truthful	12	6	11	42
Caring	10	12	39	

Note: Q. Here are some qualities that people sometimes think that governments should have. Could you tell me whether or not the present government is—?
Source: BBC 'Newsnight' Survey, Knowsley North, 1–2 Nov. 1986, N. 736.

vious studies have found, the government was widely perceived as determined and patriotic, a possible legacy of the Falklands factor and Mrs Thatcher's long-standing image as the 'Iron Lady'. On the other hand with memories of the Westland crisis still fresh, few saw the government as honest and truthful, while only one in ten thought them caring.

THE RESULT

In the previous general election the Conservatives were in second place. The earliest poll, by BBC 'Newsnight' on 1–2 November 1986, suggested that the usual anti-government movement was evident (see Table 6.5). From the start of the campaign the Conservatives

Table 6.5. *Opinion Polls in Knowsley North, 1986*

	Lab.	Con.	LSDP
General election, 1983	65	20	15
BBC poll, 1–2 Nov. 1986[a]	67	10	22
BBC poll, 12 Nov.[b]	57/59	8	32/34
BBC poll, 13 Nov.[c]	60	6	33
By-election, 13 Nov.	56	6	35

Note: a. Quota survey N.736
   b. Telephone recall survey
   c. Exit poll.

were forced into third place, with the Alliance the main beneficiaries while Labour support remained stable. As the campaign progressed there was relatively little movement. The polls registered a slight decline in the Labour and Tory vote, with the Alliance increasing their share of support to about 33%, although they remained too far behind to pose a serious challenge to Labour.

On polling day George Howarth achieved a solid victory, gaining over half (56%) of the vote, though the Labour vote fell from their 1983 result. Labour performed particularly well in their traditional areas of strength, notably among the unemployed, council tenants, manual workers, as well as with Catholics and younger voters (see Table 6.6). The Conservatives were reduced from 20% to 6%, one of their lowest shares of the vote in any post-war by-election. Fewer than 2,000 voters supported the Tories although given the constituency this result was not seen as unexpected. The swing was close to the mean loss of support for the Conservatives in Mrs Thatcher's second administration.

The Alliance share of the vote increased by 20%, similar to the swing at Ryedale, and higher than at Portsmouth South, where Alliance candidates triumphed. The problem was the scale of the Labour majority challengers had to climb. The Tory vote was squeezed to its hard-core supporters. The only way the Alliance could make further gains was to convert disenchanted Labour supporters or to mobilize probable abstainers. As Hugo Young (1986) noted during the campaign, in Knowsley 'it will be hard to get

Table 6.6.   *Vote by Social Group in Knowsley North, 1986*

% Pop.		Lab.	LSDP	Con.	%
100	ALL	67	22	10	100
	Socio-Economic Group				
6	Professional/Managerial	64	16	20	100
30	Other Non-Manual	58	30	12	100
65	Manual	76	16	8	100
	Employment Status				
49	Employed	68	21	11	100
17	Unemployed	80	12	8	100
	Housing Tenure				
37	Owner-Occupier	61	24	14	100
61	Council Tenant	77	17	6	100

Source: BBC 'Newsnight' Survey, Knowsley North, 1–2 Nov. 1986, N. 736.

anything moving among people divided between tribal Labour, ada-
mant non-voting, or inextinguishable pessimism about the capacity
of any politician anywhere to do anything sensible.' An exciting
campaign which promised a close result, with extensive media coverage, might have managed to increase participation but in the event
turn-out declined from 70% to 57%. Without a hard-left candidate
insufficient Labour voters were persuaded to switch to the Alliance
for negative reasons. Almost half of the voters decided to sit it
out at home and, as we might expect from previous studies, abstention was particularly strong among the under-thirties, manual
workers, the less educated, and council tenants.

By comparing voting intentions at the beginning (1–2 November)
and end of the campaign (12 November) with a sub-sample of voters
who were re-interviewed by telephone we can estimate how many
remained stable (see Table 6.7). An analysis of gross change suggests
that the Alliance vote was fairly soft—they gained from those who
were initially undecided, but they also lost some support to Labour
during the campaign. Overall they held on to 72% of their original
supporters. There was therefore flux, but no consistent flow of the
vote towards the Alliance. Labour were more successful in retaining
85% of their supporters from the first poll. As we would expect
given net change the Conservatives proved weakest, losing half of
their original supporters. Overall we can estimate on the basis of
BBC 'Newsnight' surveys that about one-third changed their voting

Table 6.7.   *Change during the Knowsley North campaign*

	POLL II				
	Lab.	LSDP	Con.	Oth./DK/ Ref./Ab.	%
POLL I					
Lab.	85	8	1	6	100
Alliance	15	73	3	9	100
Con.	—	25	50	25	100
Oth./DK/Ref./Ab.	25	43	7	25	100

Sources: Poll I BBC 'Newsnight' Quota Survey, 1–2 Nov. 1986, N. 736; Poll II BBC 'Newsnight' Telephone recall, 12 Nov., N. 240.

intentions during the last two weeks of the campaign while two-thirds (64.5%) were stable.

SUMMARY

The key question remains: why was Knowsley North relatively stable while other by-elections have proved more changeable? Why did the Alliance fail to mobilize the sort of bandwagon which occurred in some other inner-city seats such as Bermondsey and Warrington? What does Knowsley tell us about contests in similar safe Labour seats, such as Tyne Bridge, Glasgow Queens Park or Cynon Valley?

The particular circumstances of this campaign provide a partial explanation. The basis of the constituency, with its high level of social deprivation, unemployment and council housing, situated in the urban sprawl of Merseyside, made it prime Labour territory. Unlike some other inner-city seats the constituency was fairly homogeneous socially and politically; it was difficult for the Alliance to build an effective grassroots campaign at ward level. The divisions between the local Labour party and the NEC may have opened the way for a more explosive contest, but in the end the successful imposition by the leadership of a moderate candidate prevented the opposition from dividing the Labour vote.

Without a negative charge the Alliance could only increase their support at the expense of the party in government, but they were unable to challenge the solid Labour majority established over successive general elections. During the campaign the Alliance did not appear to be a serious threat to Labour; few thought the Alliance

Table 6.8.   *Safe Labour by-elections, 1979–1985*

	Maj.	Con.		Lab.		LSDP	
	GE	% Vote	Change	% Vote	Change	% Vote	Change
Manchester C.	49	12	−10	71	0	14	+9
Glasgow C.	56	9	−8	61	−12	—	—
Warrington	33	7	−22	48	−13	42	+33
Coatbridge	33	26	−1	55	−6	8	+8
S'th'wk/Peckham	32	12	−16	50	−10	32	+25
G'gow Queens Pk	40	12	−12	56	−8	9	+9
Bermondsey	39	6	−19	26	−38	58	+51
Cynon Valley	35	7	−7	59	+3	20	−1
Tyne Bridge	31	11	−14	58	+1	30	+11
AVERAGE ABOVE	39	11	−12	65	−9	27	+18
Knowsley North	44	8	−12	56	−8	35	+20

Note: Safe Labour seats are defined as those with a majority of over 30% in the previous general election.

could win. Even the Liberal leadership publicly acknowledged that they were facing an uphill struggle. In this context it was difficult to create an effective middle of the road bandwagon to mobilize disaffected Conservative and Labour voters. It was easier for such groups to protest by staying at home. Focused at the level of pavement politics, the campaign never generated the excitement which might have won over the Labour vote. Based on the available survey evidence we can therefore conclude that the main change in support came at an early stage, before the official campaign opened. In a mid-term contest disaffected Conservatives switched to the Alliance. But after this initial movement the Alliance failed to promote a subsequent shift sufficient to displace Labour, based on campaign-specific factors, such as particular candidates, campaign events, the tactical situation, and grassroots organization. To explain this further we need to examine the contrasts with volatile by-elections, exemplified by Greenwich, before looking more systematically at the conditions leading to electoral change.

7

The Political Earthquakes: Greenwich

IF Knowsley North can be seen as typical of the routine contests, Greenwich can be taken as a case-study for the volatile by-elections such as Bermondsey, Ryedale or Orpington. From the announcement of the by-election, following the death on 24 December 1986 of the Labour MP Guy Barnett, Greenwich had all the hallmarks of a high-profile contest. First the timing of the by-election guaranteed maximum publicity. From the autumn of 1986 intense speculation about when the Prime Minister would go to the country heightened interest in any indicators of party strength.

Secondly, throughout 1986 the national opinion polls suggested an uncertain political prospect. It was not clear who might win a general election. Early in 1986, following the Westland affair, most national polls showed Labour clearly ahead of the government. In Gallup polls of voting intentions across the country the Tories were placed third from January to March 1986. In spring the Labour lead strengthened following the American bombing of Libya; in the Gallup poll in May 1986 27% of the electorate supported the Conservatives, their second worst performance that Parliament. But during autumn 1986 the Conservatives recovered some lost ground, owing to the divisions within the Alliance on defence policy, evident at the Eastbourne Liberal conference. From October to December most polls suggested the major parties were neck-and-neck, with the Alliance trailing in the low twenties. Towards the end of January 1987 uncertainty was heightened by conflicting results in the national polls. Within a few days of each other Gallup published a poll in the *Daily Telegraph* showing Labour 5% ahead, while Harris in the *Observer* gave the Tories an 8% lead, and Marplan in *Today* suggested that the parties were level-pegging. At the same time a MORI poll of marginal seats in *The Times* seemed to produce different projections to the national polls.[1] In this heightened political atmosphere any by-elections which promised an indication of the mood of the electorate would have been the subject of intense media

[1] MORI poll in *The Times*, Jan. 1987.

speculation. The results of Greenwich in February 1987 were widely expected to affect the timing of the general election, with a good result for the Tories influencing Mrs Thatcher to go to the country early. To some extent Greenwich can be seen as analogous to Darlington, held in the intense glare of media publicity just three months before the 1983 general election, or Liverpool Edge Hill in March 1979.

PARTY PROSPECTS

The third factor generating publicity was that Greenwich could be seen as a genuine three-way marginal. At the start of the campaign, based on the polls and past voting results in the constituency, all parties had some grounds for hope. Of all the by-elections since 1983, Greenwich was the most marginal, with a Labour majority of only 3.4%. In the previous general election the Conservatives were firmly established in second place, well placed to overturn the Labour majority. In the week before the by-election Conservative support seemed to be rising in the country as a whole: in five national polls the Conservatives had moved back into the lead.

On the other hand, based on early indicators Labour might also have hoped for a good result at Greenwich. A year earlier Labour demonstrated a strong performance in the similar inner-London seat of Fulham, winning the by-election with an 11% swing. The first poll in Greenwich by Harris for the *Observer*, published on 11 January before the selection of their candidate, gave Labour 60% of the vote, implying an almost unbeatable 35 percentage point lead over the Conservatives. The seat had been solidly Labour since 1935, an inner-city constituency in the East End with a high proportion of council tenants. The previous MP, Guy Barnett, had held the seat for fifteen years. Barnett had first entered through a by-election caused by the resignation of Richard Marsh, Minister of Transport in the Wilson government, who left in 1971 to take over the chairmanship of British Rail. In the 1971 by-election Labour increased their solid majority, taking two-thirds of the vote. The Liberals did not even contest the by-election.

Although Greenwich may have appeared marginal, the 1983 result could be attributed to the exceptional circumstances of the disastrous Labour campaign under Michael Foot. In the four general elections preceding 1983 the Labour vote had never fallen below

Table 7.1. *Greenwich election results, 1970–1987 (% vote)*

	Lab.	LSDP	Con.	Other	Maj.	
1970	57	6	36	0	21	Lab.
1971 (BE)	67	0	28	5	39	Lab.
1974 (Feb.)	51	20	29	0	23	Lab.
1974 (Oct.)	56	17	27	1	29	Lab.
1979	52	11	33	4	19	Lab.
1983	38	25	35	2	3	Lab.
1987 (BE)	34	53	12	2	19	SDP
1987 (June)	35	41	23	1	6	SDP

Source: Craig, (1980).

50% (see Table 7.1). Based on their support in general elections over the preceding decade we can calculate the 'normal' Labour vote as about 49%. In the preceding May 1986 local elections Labour won the Greenwich ILEA seat, with identical boundaries to the constituency, with 50% of the vote, compared with 27% who voted Tory and 21% Alliance. The question was whether Labour could recover their 'normal' share of the vote in a by-election, or whether long-term demographic change had transformed the nature of the constituency.

Yet the Alliance also had good reason to expect to win Greenwich given their overall performance in previous by-elections. A projection based on the results of the London by-elections since 1981, from Croydon North-West to Fulham, would have given the Alliance 48% of the vote, far ahead of Labour (see Table 7.2). To

Table 7.2. *Greater London by-elections 1981–1987*

			Change in the vote[a]		
Seat	Date	Maj.	Con.	Lab.	LSDP
Croydon NW	22 Oct. 1981	9	−19	−14	30
Merton/Mitcham	3 June 1982	1	0	−21	21
Peckham	28 Oct. 1982	32	−16	−10	25
Bermondsey	24 Feb. 1983	39	−19	−38	51
Enfield S'Gate	13 Dec. 1984	35	−8	−6	12
Fulham	10 Mar. 1986	12	−11	10	1
MEAN		21	−12	−13	23

Note: a. See Appendix.

take Greenwich the Alliance just needed to repeat their performance in the preceding contests in Newcastle under Lyme and Knowsley North. Although they started third, the Alliance were only 13% behind Labour in the previous general election. With a quarter of the vote in 1983 the Alliance had a strong base upon which to build.

THE CONSTITUENCY

The location of Greenwich in a politically mixed area of London, on the south bank of the Thames, opposite the Isle of Dogs in the heart of London's docklands, reflected the nature of the three-way contest. Greenwich was close to the only Alliance seats in London; Woolwich (John Cartwright) to the west, Bermondsey and Southwark (Simon Hughes), along with the Tower Hamlets local authority. To the south were the Conservative constituencies of Lewisham East and Eltham, while to the north were the traditional East End Labour strongholds of Bow and Poplar and Newham South (see Fig. 7.1).

The constituency was socially as well as politically mixed (see Table 7.3). The seat remained predominantly working-class, and despite the decline of the docks almost half of the population were employed in manual occupations. Further almost half of the population were council tenants located in tower blocks and traditional estates, compared with about a quarter in Britain as a whole. In certain areas, such as Ferrier and West wards, over 97% of the electorate were in local authority accommodation (see Table 7.3). At the time of the by-election about 14% of the adult male population were registered unemployed while 8% were from ethnic minorities. Yet there were also strong contrasts in the seat, with gentrified wards and some fine Georgian terraces close to the famous Greenwich Royal Observatory, the National Maritime Museum, and the Royal Naval College. Like nearby areas bordering the Thames, the decline of docking and heavy industry had led to a growth in employment in services. Fashionable yuppies from the City had moved in to renovate property following the rapid increases in London house prices.

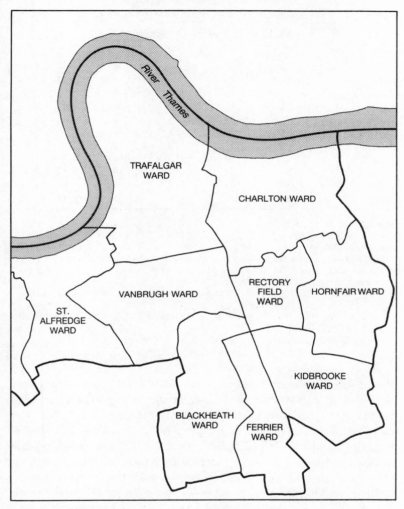

FIG. 7.1. Greenwich constituency

THE CANDIDATES

The timing, the party prospects, and the proximity of the seat to Westminster and Fleet Street suggested it would be a highly public event. The selection of the Labour candidate guaranteed it. Deirdre

Table 7.3. *Demographic indicators by ward in Greenwich (%)*

Ward	Manual SEG[a]	Council tenants[b]	Unempl. pop.[c]	NCWP pop.[d]	Labour vote[e]
Vanbrugh	34	35	6	6	29
Blackheath	16	18	4	4	30
Trafalgar	55	36	8	7	36
Hornfair	58	71	9	4	41
Kidbrooke	48	54	6	4	46
St Alfege	41	42	12	8	50
Rectory Field	49	57	10	9	51
Charlton	56	34	12	18	54
West	53	63	14	14	55
Ferrier	43	81	14	7	66
ALL	45	47	9	8	44

Notes: See Appendix for details.

a. Manual Socio-Economic Groups (7, 8, 9, 10, 11, 12, 14, 15): 1981 Census 10% Small Area Statistics.

b. Percentage of resident population in local authority accommodation: 1981 Census 100% SAS updated by *Greenwich Housing Facts*, Jan. 6 1987, Annual Report of Greenwich Council Housing Services, 1985/6.

c. Percentage of adult population registered unemployed, *Employment Gazette*, Sept. 1986, Dept. of Employment.

d. Percentage in households with head of household born in New Commonwealth or Pakistan, 1981 Census 100% SAS.

e. BBC 'Newsnight' Survey, Greenwich III, 21 Feb. 1987.

Wood was widely perceived in the popular press as an extreme-left candidate at a time when Neil Kinnock was trying to pull the party towards the soft left. Some commentators suggested that the extremist label was exaggerated although Deirdre Wood had consistently voted with the left on ILEA and the GLC. On such fashionable ideological litmus tests as support for invitations to Sinn Fein delegates to visit London, for black sections within the party, and for councils defying the law over rate-capping, Deirdre Wood was to the left of the Labour leadership. Much of the campaign focused on personal criticisms of the Labour candidate, although there was general condemnation following the *News of the World*'s articles about Mrs Wood's father. Some attacks in the popular press may have caused a sympathetic backlash by going too far. Deirdre Wood was assisted by Frank Dobson, chairman of the London Labour party, Labour campaign co-ordinator and candidate 'minder'. The Conservatives selected John Antcliffe, a young (25-year-old), self-confident Rothschild's merchant banker. While running an energetic campaign, the Conservative candidate was generally considered not the most effective choice for this type of seat. The Alliance sought to portray him as yet another chinless 'Hooray Henry', a public school/Oxbridge product doing 'something in the City', a type apparently favoured for by-elections by Tory Central Office. Although Antcliffe was a local resident and member of the borough council, on the basis of his age there were questions about his experience. Association with the City was not considered advantageous given financial scandals concerning insider trading and the Guinness affair. There were also suggestions that Conservative Central Office failed to throw sufficient resources into the contest, leaving a small group from the local party to drum up support. In the early stages much of the Tory campaign was focused on fierce personal attacks on the Labour candidate and the 'loony left', although this may have served to benefit the SDP rather than the Tory candidate. Colin Moynihan, MP for Lewisham East, was the main Conservative spokesman, helped during the campaign by brief visits from many members of the government front bench.

Lastly in Rosie Barnes the SDP clearly had a popular candidate who grew in stature and confidence as the campaign progressed. Presenting an image as an ordinary middle-aged business woman and down-to-earth mother of three, married to a Greenwich SDP councillor, the Alliance candidate proved an effective choice. With a working-class background, Rosie Barnes progressed through the classic ladder of grammar school and redbrick university to become a market-research specialist, married to a professional in venture capitalism. A former Labour voter, Rosie Barnes joined the SDP as a founder member in 1981. In early press conferences the SDP candidate seemed hesitant and unsure of herself yet by the end of the campaign, despite the presence of the party leaders, she managed to dominate the final Alliance rally. The campaign was masterminded by Alec McGivan, veteran of many by-elections, with John Cartwright, MP for neighbouring Woolwich, as party spokesman.

THE CAMPAIGN

During the campaign press coverage increased as, according to the opinion polls, the Alliance appeared to be making significant gains.

Thirteen polls were published during or after the contest, including six carried out by BBC 'Newsnight' (see Table 7.4). The first poll by Harris in early January placed Labour at 60%, which may well

Table 7.4.   *BBC Newsnight polls in Greenwich*

Survey	I	II	III	IV	V	VI
Fieldwork	31 Jan.–1 Feb.	8 Feb.	21 Feb.	25 Feb.	26 Feb.	28 Feb.
Pub.	3 Feb	10 Feb.	23 Feb.	—	26 Feb	1 Mar
Sample	Quota	Panel recall	Quota	Panel recall	Random	Panel recall
In'view	Face to face	Phone	Face to face	Phone	Exit poll	Phone
N.	671	270	914	321	2286	507
Samp. pts.	38		40		10	
Voting intentions						
Lab.	48	43	43	36	37	
LSDP	24	31	39	52	51	
Con.	26	25	16	11	10	
Other	2	1	2	1	2	

Source: See Appendix.

have overestimated their support; indeed Labour Party organizers placed little weight on the results. The main significance of the poll was that it created certain unrealistic expectations about party strength. As a result subsequent polls gave the impression that as front-runner the Labour Party was consistently losing ground. By setting exaggerated expectations of Labour support the poll generated the impression of greater change in the early stages of the campaign than probably existed.

According to the polls, as shown in Fig. 7.2, we can identify three decisive shifts in the contest. Before the start of the official campaign a poll by BBC 'Newsnight' (Greenwich I), with fieldwork completed on 1 February, suggested that Labour enjoyed a solid lead with 48% of the vote. There was no statistically significant difference between the Conservatives on 26% and the Alliance on 24%, although most commentators drew a distinction between the parties in second and third place. Therefore it should be stressed that the first major shift came even before the campaign started. According to early polls, the Conservatives experienced the sharpest drop in support, down 11% since the general election. At this stage Labour were the beneficiaries, with support for the Alliance largely unchanged since the previous general election.

The second shift came with the selection of the Labour candidate, which seemed to produce an immediate decrease in Labour support. 'Newsnight' returned to some of the voters who had been interviewed on 1 February to check their voting intentions a week later. Among those who were recalled by telephone on 8 February the poll (Greenwich II) suggested that there had been a shift of about 5% from Labour towards the Alliance, pushing the SDP into second place. Given the panel design such a shift was significant, although the use of the telephone for the recall interviews, along with the small sample size (N. 271), caused considerable controversy (Kellner 1987). There was some confusion about the difference between a telephone poll, basing its sample on the proportion of the electorate with access to telephones, and a telephone recall poll, basing its re-interviews on a sample with known demographic characteristics. The results were disputed by the Conservatives, although this probably only added further publicity to the poll. Most press coverage during the following week included speculation based on this poll that an Alliance bandwagon was about to roll which would squeeze the Tory vote into third place. Despite intense interest in the state of play no more polls were published by the major companies until the last week of campaign. It is impossible to establish whether Newsnight were the earliest to monitor a shift in public support, or whether the publication of the poll helped to generate, or reinforce, the shift. Nevertheless subsequent surveys confirmed the 'Newsnight' results, notably the Harris polls published on 16 and 19 February (see Fig. 7.2).

The third significant shift seems to have occurred in the final days of the campaign. On the final Saturday (21 February) 'Newsnight' carried out the third in its series of surveys, (Greenwich III) interviewing a fresh sample of 914 electors. The results suggested that the Alliance vote had increased to 39% largely at the expense of the Conservatives, with Labour support staying steady in the lead. Responses to questions on tactical voting suggested that there was still room for change during the last few days of the campaign. When asked 42% of Conservatives said they would consider switch-

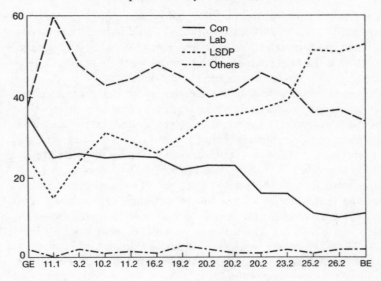

F<small>IG</small>. 7.2.   Greenwich by-election polls

ing their vote if their own party could not win, and over 90% of
these nominated the Alliance as their second choice. By the last
weekend some voters had not made up their minds, about 9% saying
they remained undecided.

The decisive shift which gave Rosie Barnes the seat seems to have
occurred between the 'Newsnight' poll at the weekend (Greenwich
III) and on the eve of the election (Greenwich IV). When a sub-
sample (N. 321) were re-interviewed by telephone on Wednesday
25 (Greenwich IV) the SDP had moved into the lead, with 52%
of the poll. Labour support had fallen to 36%, with the Conservatives
trailing on 11%. This was very close to the final result the following
day. In the final result the Alliance triumphed with 53% of the vote,
while Labour declined to 34%, and the Conservatives to 12%.

THE RESULTS

The Social Democrats attracted votes fairly evenly across the social
spectrum, irrespective of age group and housing tenure, although

their support was weakest amongst the manual working class in wards such as Ferrier and West (see Table 7.5). During the campaign the Alliance increased their support particularly strongly amongst

Table 7.5.　*Demographic profile of the Greenwich vote*

	Lab.	LSDP	Con.	%	Coeff. of assoc.[a]
ALL	44	40	16	100	
Socio-economic group					
Professional/manag.	24	51	25	100	
Other non-manual	40	41	19	100	
Manual	55	34	11	100	.08
Gender					
Men	46	37	17	100	
Women	43	41	16	100	.01
Housing tenure					
Owner-occupier	34	43	24	100	
Private tenant	44	44	12	100	
Council tenant	53	35	12	100	.05
Age group					
Young (18–25)	51	36	13	100	
Early middle (26–45)	44	38	18	100	
Late middle (46–64)	38	43	19	100	
Elderly (65+)	45	41	15	100	.01

Note: a. Gamma coefficients of association, measuring association between social group and voting choice for the major parties.
Source: BBC 'Newsnight' Survey, Greenwich III, (21 Feb. 1987), N. 914.

women and the professional/managerial socio-economic groups, their areas of greatest strength. The Alliance took support from both major parties. They gained a third of those who recalled voting Labour in the previous general election, along with two-thirds of those who had voted Conservative.

The result gave the SDP their first victory for three years. The Alliance increased their share of the vote by 28%, their best performance since Bermondsey. The national polls indicated an immediate jump in Alliance popularity. The three major polls with fieldwork preceding Greenwich estimated Alliance support at about 22%, which increased to 30% in the two polls with interviews after the

Greenwich result.[2] Following the January re-launch, Greenwich restored some of the damage to Alliance Party morale which had been caused by the defence row at the Liberals' Eastbourne Assembly.

For Labour, although their share of the vote declined by only 4% (less than at Knowsley North), the loss of the seat provoked bitter internal recriminations which continued to reverberate in the press and party for the next few weeks. The significance of Greenwich was that the outcome revived speculation that in the forthcoming general election the Alliance would gain sufficient momentum to move into second place. It raised tactical voting as the joker in the pack which might undermine conventional assumptions about the relationship between votes and seats. In an article in the *Sunday Times* Michael Cocks, the former Labour Chief Whip, blamed the extremism of the party in London, with its emphasis on minority interests which were unpopular with traditional Labour voters (Cocks 1987). In a letter leaked to the press Neil Kinnock's press secretary, Patricia Hewitt, added to the row within the party by criticizing the London 'loony left' for losing traditional votes by emphasizing issues like gay and lesbian rights. Others blamed the result on the series of personal attacks against Deirdre Wood in the press, although there were suggestions that many of the media smears originated from senior members of the Labour Party who sought to prevent her selection as candidate. Yet others suggested the problem lay in the opinion polls which were accused of creating, or at least encouraging, tactical voting.

The Conservatives were more discreet in their inquest although equally disturbed by the result. In Greenwich the Tories experienced their worst loss of votes in any by-election since the Isle of Ely in 1973, down 23%. As one observer noted, privately this caused Tory nightmares that Greenwich would start an Alliance bandwagon which would roll on into the general election. The volatile electorate, coupled with the possibility of tactical voting, created worries in Tory Central Office that national polls might prove unreliable as indicators of party prospects in the forthcoming general election

---

[2] The national polls before the Greenwich result were by Harris for the *Observer* (fieldwork 17–19 Feb.), by Marplan for *Today* (fieldwork 20–24 Feb.), and by MORI for the *Sunday Times* (fieldwork 20–25 Feb.). The post-election polls were by Harris for TV-AM (fieldwork 27 Feb.–1 Mar.) and by Gallup for the *Daily Telegraph* (fieldwork 27 Feb.–3 Mar.).

(Tyler 1987; Wilson 1987). In calculating whether to call an election in late spring or the autumn, the polls suggested that the Alliance were in third position in the country as a whole, but Greenwich created an element of uncertainty. If the SDP could make dramatic gains during the campaign in Greenwich, then, some back-benchers worried, why not in many of the seats where they provided the main opposition to the Tories?

EXPLANATIONS OF GREENWICH

The results of Greenwich are clear; their meaning is not. The Social Democrats may have been returned owing to an effective campaign, with a well-oiled by-election machine, a popular candidate, and an efficient organization. If so, Greenwich implies that the Alliance are particularly good at by-elections, where they can invest maximum organizational resources, but they have difficulties in translating this success into general election campaigns. Or Greenwich might represent a positive endorsement of Social Democratic policy, on the issues from the social market economy to community politics. Or perhaps many, disliking the alternative 'Hooray Henry' and 'Loony London left' party images, may have cast a tactical vote for Rosie Barnes. No single explanation is adequate but using the BBC 'Newsnight' series of six pre-election and post-election surveys in Greenwich we can start to disentangle the relative significance of these factors, including the role of party organizations, campaign issues, and tactical bandwagons.

CAMPAIGN ORGANIZATION

The press suggested that part of the explanation lay in the Social Democrats' campaign organization which made intensive use of direct mailing to target voters. The campaign was directed by Alec McGivan, the national SDP organizer who had worked on by-elections since Warrington, with advice from the Washington DC firm of Matt Reese Associates. Following American campaign techniques the Social Democrats aimed to contact individuals, especially opinion leaders within the community such as doctors, teachers, and publicans, with personally addressed letters carefully tailored to their likely concerns. In a fairly sophisticated operation the strategy was to target communications, for example teachers were told about Alliance policy on nursery schools while letters to council tenants included information about SDP policy on the right to buy. To produce the literature and mailing lists intensive use was made of computers, with canvass returns fed daily into a network from local terminals in seven wards. The Alliance were able to draw on a small army of activists in the area from their local strongholds in Woolwich, Bermondsey, and Tower Hamlets. Usually the Alliance had 100 to 150 workers helping each day. It has been estimated that by the last weekend the Alliance were able to draft in over 1,000 party workers for their final leafleting campaign. From the start the Alliance focused on a few central themes: the attractiveness of their candidate and the theme that the Alliance combined practical judgement with social care ('head and heart'). Lastly they stressed the tactical situation, that given the polls the Conservatives could not win so only a vote for the Alliance could prevent the election of an extreme left-wing candidate.

Compared with this professional presentation observers noted that the Conservative campaign was under-resourced, with a moribund local party and minimal assistance from Central Office (Tyler 1987). Labour used the campaign techniques which had proved effective a year earlier at Fulham, including direct mail. They brought in a range of well-known speakers for press conferences from front-bench spokesmen to the actress Glenda Jackson. Neil Kinnock lent his personal weight to the campaign, touring the constituency in the last few days.

It is difficult to assess the impact of campaign organizations on the outcome. The conventional view is that in general elections party activists have only a minimal impact on constituency results, although their role might be more significant in by-elections (Butler and Kavanagh 1985; Kavanagh 1970; Drucker *et al.* 1982*a*; Swaddle 1988). Campaigns serve three primary functions for political parties: reinforcement, recruitment, and conversion. In terms of reinforcement parties aim to build on their areas of greatest strength, confirming waverers and mobilizing traditional supporters. In terms of recruitment parties want to win over the undecideds and abstainers, targeting those with no established partisan attachment such as first-time voters. Lastly the most difficult task for parties is conversion, switching voters who started the campaign with another preference.

From the start of the Greenwich campaign to polling day the Social Democrats managed to maintain 96% of their original vote. During the campaign their increase in support came from over half (55%)

Table 7.6. *Vote switchers during the Greenwich campaign (%)*

Voting intentions 31 Jan.	Actual by-election vote 26 Feb.				
	Lab.	LSDP	Con.	Other D/K Ref.	Total
Labour	87	10	0	2	100
Alliance	2	96	1	1	100
Conservatives	11	48	41	0	100
Undecided	24	55	5	16	100

Source: BBC 'Newsnight' Post-Election Panel Survey, Greenwich VI, 27–8 Feb. 1987, N. 507

of those who were initially undecided, 10% of Labour voters, and almost half (48%) of those who were initially Conservative (see Table 7.6). In Greenwich is there evidence that it was the work of SDP grassroots party activists which proved particularly effective in mobilizing their potential supporters, convincing the undecided and converting the opposition?

The BBC 'Newsnight' surveys suggest that the Conservatives were less successful in their campaign: one week before polling day only half of the electorate knew the name of the Conservative candidate, compared with three-quarters who were able to identify Deirdre Woods and Rosie Barnes (see Table 7.7). At the grassroots level in terms of party workers, 13% of Labour and Alliance voters reported being canvassed by their own parties, compared with only

Table 7.7. *Recognition of candidate's name by party supporters*

% Correct recognition	All	Lab.	LSDP	Con.
Deirdre Wood. (Lab.)	75	78	79	68
Rosie Barnes (LSDP)	72	66	86	69
John Antcliffe (Con.)	52	44	58	65

Note: Q. Some people have heard of the candidates in the by-election and some have not. How about you? Can you tell me the name of the—[Conservative/Labour/Liberal/SDP] candidate?
Source: BBC 'Newsnight' Survey, Greenwich III 21 Feb. 1987, N. 914.

6% of Conservatives. The days of large-scale rallies are gone, and most voters had not seen any of the candidates at a political meeting; but again Social Democrats were slightly more likely to have attended such a meeting. There is therefore some survey evidence to support the view that the Social Democrats ran an effective grass-roots campaign, although it is difficult to evaluate the impact of this activity on Alliance support.

CAMPAIGN ISSUES

Nor is there evidence that voters were converted by the positive content of the Alliance message. Over three-quarters of Greenwich voters suggested that three issues were most important in the campaign: the health service, unemployment, education. On these questions of social policy the Labour Party enjoyed a decisive lead (see Table 7.8). There was quite a strong association between these issues

Table 7.8.   *Party best on the salient issues, Greenwich*

Issue	Lab.	LSDP	Con.	Coeff. of assoc.[a]
Health service	53	19	16	.54
Unemployment	48	18	19	.52
Trade unions	45	13	26	.49
Education	44	18	23	.64
Nuclear energy	30	16	31	.56
Defence	32	17	36	.58
Inflation	28	14	42	.58

Notes: Q. Which party do you think would be most likely to take the right decisions on the following issues?
a. Gamma Coefficients of association.
Source: BBC 'Newsnight' Survey, Greenwich (31 Jan.–1 Feb. 1987), N. 671.

and voting intentions. The Conservatives were ahead on the less salient issues of inflation, defence, and nuclear energy, with the Alliance third. Overall Social Democrats proved less positive towards their own party than Labour or Conservative voters on six out of seven issues in the 'Newsnight' survey. This suggests support for the Alliance was largely negative: if the by-election had been decided on the most important prospective issues alone Labour should have won.

TACTICAL SHIFTS

The most convincing evidence that the late shift towards the Alliance was tactical comes from the BBC 'Newsnight' post-election Greenwich survey (Greenwich VI). After the event it is clear that many switched to the Alliance primarily for negative reasons. When asked the main reason for their vote, almost half of the Alliance voters nominated dislike of the other candidates or other parties (see Table

Table 7.9. *Negative versus positive support by party supporters (%)*

	All	Lab.	LSDP	Con.
Dislike other candidate	16	2	27	9
Dislike other parties	18	12	23	7
Like own candidate	12	7	17	0
Like own party	54	78	34	84
TOTAL	100	100	100	100

Note: Q. Which one of the following comes closest to the main reason for your vote: I dislike the other candidates, I dislike the other parties, I like the—candidate, I like the—party.
Source: BBC 'Newsnight' Post-Election Panel Survey, Greenwich VI, 27–28 Feb. 1987, N. 507.

7.9). Few Alliance supporters gave a positive reason for their vote. Although the SDP candidate may have proved more attractive than the others, only 17% of Alliance voters nominated Rosie Barnes as the main reason for their support. A third said they voted Social Democrat because they liked the party, compared with 78% of Labour and 84% of Conservative supporters. This confirms the view that the Alliance is the party of protest *par excellence*, the natural camp for those temporarily alienated by their traditional party (Himmelweit *et al.* 1985). The problem for the Liberals and Social Democrats was to convert fluctuating protest votes into more permanent partisan loyalties. In the 1987 general election Rosie Barnes was returned again for Greenwich, although with a reduced majority.

As outlined the potential for tactical shifts had been evident early in the campaign. In the BBC surveys of 31 January and 21 February about 41% of Conservatives said they would consider switching to keep out the party they most disliked, and their overwhelming second choice was the Alliance. The Greenwich campaign fulfilled all the conditions which are necessary to mobilize the tactical shift.

That is, voters were given considerable *information* about party prospects, the information suggested that by the end of the campaign
the parties were in a distinct *rank order*, and many were highly
negative towards the Labour front-runner. By the last week, given
the polls, canvass returns, media commentators, and even Tory party
activists, most Conservatives recognized that the Alliance stood a
better chance against Deirdre Wood than their own candidate. Few
Tories (16%) thought that their own party could hope to win, or
even come second (18%). As a result many Tory tacticals seem to
have decided to switch in the last few days of the campaign. The
tactical nature of Alliance support was confirmed when after the

Table 7.10.   *Preferred winning party by vote (%)*

	All	Lab. voters	LSDP voters	Con. voters
Con.	21	1	24	89
Lab.	35	89	5	2
LSDP	39	5	68	0
Other	3	3	1	7
Don't know	2	2	2	2

Note: Q. Which party would you most like to have won the by-election?
Source: BBC 'Newsnight' Post-Election Panel Survey, Greenwich VI, 27–8 Feb. 1987,
N. 507.

election voters were asked in the BBC survey who they would most
like to have won (see Table 7.10). Among those who finally voted
for the SDP a quarter would actually have preferred the Conservatives to have taken the seat, and the same proportion of Alliance
voters (24%) said that if there were a general election tomorrow
they would support the Conservatives.

Therefore the available evidence suggests that the decisive shift
in Greenwich was due in large part to last-minute tactical voting,
encouraged but not created by the Alliance campaign. As David
Butler (1987) noted after the event, the impact was caused by the
extent of the shift: 'There is nothing new about tactical voting. But
Greenwich, to a new degree, provided a spectacular education about
its possibilities.' The spectre of tactical voting caused concern in
both major parties. If it manifested itself in the subsequent general
election it could upset all the neat calculations about the relationship
between votes and seats which are based on the assumption of a

uniform swing. Yet with hindsight we know that Greenwich proved a deceptive guide to the results of the general election. We need to go on to explore on a more systematic basis the conditions leading to tactical voting, to understand why the potential shifts were mobilized in volatile by-elections like Greenwich and Ryedale while failing to appear to the same extent in the subsequent general election, or even in other by-elections.

PART II

Trends in By-Election Results

8

Electoral Volatility and Partisan Dealignment

In the second part of the book we need to move beyond particular constituency results to develop theories which can account for systematic trends. In this chapter we will start by considering explanations of electoral volatility based on theories of partisan alignment, dealignment, and realignment, to understand why by-elections have been transformed from the quiescent two-party politics of the fifties to the more unpredictable multi-party contests of the eighties.

EXPLANATIONS OF ELECTORAL CHANGE: DEMOGRAPHIC TRENDS

In the classic account of voting provided by Butler and Stokes three major sources of electoral change were identified: long-term trends involving the physical replacement of the electorate, partisan realignment where voters transfer their traditional party loyalties and lastly the short-term response of the electorate to the immediate issues and events of politics (Butler and Stokes 1974: 6). Between a general election and a by-election there will always be some changes in the physical composition of the electorate, as some voters transfer into and out of a constituency, older generations die and younger voters register for the first time. It has been estimated that the scale of these demographic changes is sufficient to provide a 10% turnover of the electorate within a five-year Parliament (Butler and Stokes 1974: 5). Of the total change in the electorate between the 1979 and 1983 elections, one-third related to physical changes concerned with death and coming of age (Rose and McAllister 1986: 151). Some of this change may cancel out (for example as younger Tories replace older Tories), but it may have a differential effect on party support (for example if younger Greens replace older Labour supporters).

The demographic balance of a constituency may change in a relatively short time: the development of new housing in the docklands, the closure of a major industry like the tin mines in Cornwall, patterns of immigration in the West Midlands, or local government policies towards council house sales. In the mid-eighties the process of gentrification diluted Labour's working-class base in Fulham and Greenwich. In contrast in Tyne Bridge inner-city decay and unemployment reduced the population; elderly voters remained while the younger generation with marketable skills departed for better work prospects. In constituencies with many resident students, such as Newcastle Central or Bath, the composition of the electorate may change substantially if an election is held within or outside of the academic year. Demographic trends may alter the composition of a seat but changes in the composition of the electorate are insufficient by themselves to explain the extent of by-election swings, and swing-backs, experienced by parties within the space of six months or a year.

CHANGES IN PARTISAN ALIGNMENT

The second kind of change suggested by Butler and Stokes was a long-term change in the electorate's party identification through the process of partisan dealignment and realignment. The classic theory of partisan identification suggests that during periods of stable alignment voters are anchored to the Labour and Conservative parties for long periods of time, with an abiding loyalty which guides voting choice over successive elections (Butler and Stokes 1974: 211–28). Butler and Stokes found that during the 1960s many electors in Britain displayed minimal interest in political concerns, party policies, or issues in Parliament, although most continued to cast their ballot. Electors therefore sought short-cuts in information to guide their voting choice. The electorate tended to vote along the lines of others around them, taking cues from their family, friends, and colleagues, developing a long-run habitual identification to guide their future voting choice. The primary factor influencing most voters was their social situation, particularly family and occupational class, which led to their habitual party loyalties. For Butler and Stokes party identification was highly stable; it appeared to develop early in life prior to policy preferences and it appeared to strengthen with time. This suggested party identification was an affective orientation, similar to a religious affiliation.

The concept of party identification has two essential features: it refers to a durable or habitual loyalty which persists across successive elections and it relates to a voter's self-definition, how individuals usually think of themselves (see Converse and Pierce 1985; Budge, Crewe, and Farlie 1976; Campbell *et al.* 1960). In terms of by-elections, if the conditions of partisan alignment persist, we would expect considerable electoral stability. Voters may occasionally 'defect' from habitual voting in a by-election although it could be predicted that there would be a 'homing tendency', for voters to return to their 'normal' party once the immediate pressures towards defection had disappeared.

The conditions which generate partisan alignment, dealignment and realignment has been the subject of considerable controversy, providing one of the classic themes in electoral studies and generating an extensive literature in Britain and the United States (see, for example, Alt 1984; Crewe, Alt, and Sarlvik 1977*a*; Crewe 1985, 1984, 1982*b*; Burnham 1970; Heath, Jowell, and Curtice 1985; Franklin 1985; Flanagan, Dalton, and Beck 1985; Crewe and Denver 1985). For the purposes of this argument we can adopt the dynamic model provided by Paul Beck (1984) which interprets the process of partisan change as essentially cyclical (see Fig. 8.1). During

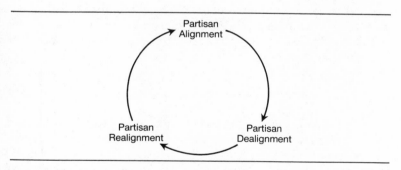

FIG. 8.1. Cycles of partisan loyalties

periods of stable partisan alignment most of the electorate can be expected to display long-term party loyalties, which are strongly associated with politically salient social cleavages, notably divisions of social class, housing tenure, and region. During these periods British elections will be predictable contests between Labour and the Conservatives decided by the switch of relatively few votes.

THE THEORY OF PARTISAN DEALIGNMENT

Nevertheless over time generational, social and ideological change could be expected gradually to weaken these party loyalties, leading to a decline in the number of Labour and Conservative party identifiers. During periods of partisan dealignment, without the anchor of party loyalties, we would expect elections to display the following characteristics:

1. greater volatility within and between elections;
2. a consistent decline in support for the two major parties;
3. short-lived swings, and swing-backs, in third party support;
4. increased protest and tactical voting;
5. fluctuating or lower levels of turn-out;
6. a weaker association between social class and voting choice; and, lastly,
7. a fall in party identification.

The linkages between social cleavages and partisan identification could be expected to weaken, with class dealignment, leading to a greater role for 'issue' voting. Despite electoral dealignment there may continue to be minimal change at the level of the Parliamentary parties, at least initially, as the first-past-the-post electoral system makes it difficult for third parties to gain seats unless their support is spatially concentrated.

THE THEORY OF PARTISAN REALIGNMENT

Yet in the cyclical model the process cannot be expected to remain static. Periods of partisan dealignment will eventually be superseded, via critical elections, by the developments of new party loyalties. Partisan realignment is seen as a complex, long-term process in which new social cleavages and issues lead to a fundamental change in the enduring loyalties of groups of the electorate. Realignment involves 'short, sharp re-organizations of the mass coalition bases of the major parties which occur at periodic intervals' (Burnham 1970: 20). The conditions leading to partisan realignment have been subject to considerable controversy. The essential points have been put most succinctly in Walter Burnham's classic account, which suggests that in critical elections three factors act as catalysts which re-define the established political map: generational change, social developments, and new political issues. In prototypical realigning elections, such as Roosevelt's in 1932 or Attlee's in 1945, one party fundamentally changes the political agenda, thereby attracting the enduring loyalties of new coalitions of groups. In Burnham's model realignments are the equivalent of electoral earthquakes, periodically re-defining the established political landscape.

It is relatively straightforward to recognize critical elections with hindsight, given their far-reaching impact on the party system, but identification of these events, let alone prediction, is far more difficult for contemporary observers. Nevertheless commentators have suggested that just such a critical election might have occurred in 1979, with Thatcher's victory representing a watershed which led to a fundamental realignment in the British party system. There is a large measure of agreement among observers that the traditional pattern of two-party politics characteristic of the fifties and sixties was disturbed from 1974 to 1979, but there is far less consensus concerning the subsequent direction of change. Two alternative interpretations of realignment are possible.

On the one hand the creation of the Liberal–Social Democratic Alliance in 1981 increased speculation that the conditions might be ripe for a realignment on the centre left. During the early eighties it was hoped by some, and feared by others, that the Alliance could carve out a distinctive ideological identity and social base, leading to the long-term and terminal decline of the Labour Party. Subsequent events, notably the deep splits within the Alliance following the 1987 general election, the divisions between the Democrats and SDP, and their subsequent performance in the polls, dampened any expectations of an immediate realignment on the centre-left.

Following three successive Conservative victories, other observers have suggested that Britain has experienced a fundamental realignment on the right. The process of realignment need not necessarily lead to the development of new parties, if existing parties can adapt successfully to social and ideological change. Hence in Roosevelt's classic 1932 realignment the Democratic Party was able to rejuvenate its support by building a successful coalition of the urban poor, Southern blacks, ethnic minorities, and Northern liberals around a distinctive public policy programme. The essential features of realignment are that it leads to an enduring shift in the balance of power, in which one party seizes control of national government, re-orients its policies, and remains in command for a generation.

Some have suggested that under Mrs Thatcher's leadership the Conservative Party have been able to expand the natural basis of their support by capitalizing on social and ideological change associated with the development of an enterprise society during the eighties, notably the expansion of the middle-class service economy and the growth of home-ownership and share-ownership, coupled with the decline in trade union membership (for a discussion of the electoral impact of these trends see Norris 1990). Observers suggest the realignment has taken place by expanding the appeal of Conservatism to new groups of voters, the skilled working class in the private sector, the first-time home owner in the Midlands, younger service-sector professionals in the South-East, while retaining the old basis of Tory support.

If there has been partisan realignment on the centre-left or right we would expect by-elections in the eighties to show evidence of the following characteristics:

1. consistent Alliance or Conservative gains which are retained in subsequent elections;
2. more stable campaigns;
3. increased levels of electoral participation;
4. changes in the social group basis of party support;
5. stronger party identification;
6. decreased protest or tactical voting.

In the light of these theories of partisan dealignment and realignment we need to examine the evidence to see which account provides the most satisfactory explanation for trends in British by-elections.

EVIDENCE OF PARTISAN DEALIGNMENT

The main indicator used as evidence of partisan change is the concept of electoral volatility, referring to the ease of transition of voters from one party to another. We can compare four indicators of net volatility, each of which has certain advantages and disadvantages, to summarize change from the general election to the by-election:

1. changes of seat;
2. the conventional ('Butler') swing of the vote
3. the Pederson Index;
4. and the percentage difference in support for all parties.

CHANGES OF SEAT

We can start by comparing trends in seats changing hands from the general election to the by-election, which many commentators and politicians take as the main indicator of electoral change. This measure has certain advantages for journalists: it is straightforward, dramatic and focuses on the consequences of by-elections with significant implications for party politics. As documented in earlier chapters, the evidence from this indicator shows a consistent trend towards increased volatility over the years: from 1945 to 1955, excluding exceptional cases, out of more than a hundred contests only one seat (Sunderland South) switched from Labour to the Tories (see Table 8.1).[1] Labour managed more consistent gains in the mid-fifties, with one in seven by-elections changing hands, but the decisive turning-point occurred in the mid-sixties. From 1966 to 1979 the incumbent party was defeated in one in three by-elections (see Fig. 8.2). Defeats remained at this level from 1979 to 1989; commentators often assume that seat volatility increased with the creation of the Liberal—Social Democratic Alliance in 1981, with well-publicized victories such as Glasgow Hillhead, Crosby, and Greenwich, but this overlooks the dozen Tory gains from 1967 to 1969, or the half-dozen Labour victories from 1962 to 1964 (see Table 8.2). There have been similar trends in general elections: the 1950 and 1951 elections were highly stable; out of 1,250 contested seats only 46 (4%) were won or lost (see Table 8.3). In contrast from the 1966 to the 1987 general elections 276 seats switched hands, or one in every ten contests.

Many constituencies which changed hands in by-elections would conventionally be regarded as safe seats; the average majority in the previous general election was 18%. Some seats which switched had substantial majorities, such as Bermondsey in 1983 (39%), Ripon

[1] 'Seat changes' excludes exceptional cases including uncontested by-elections in 1946 in university seats, the Bristol SE by-elections awarded on petition and all contests in Northern Ireland. The analysis includes 3 seats where the elected MP resigned the party whip, standing as an independent candidate to test public opinion in the by-election. It should be noted that Glasgow Camlachie also switched hands in Jan. 1948 but this is excluded as a special case since it was not contested by the Labour Party in 1945. The MP elected in 1945 represented the Independent Labour Party although he subsequently took the Labour whip. The defeat in the 1948 by-election was due to a split in the vote between Labour and the Independent Labour Party. The Conservative share of the vote remained largely unchanged.

Table 8.1.   *Changes of seat in by-elections, 1945–1990*

		BE No.	Changes in Seats[a] No.	%	%
Lab.	1945–50	47	0	0	⎫
Lab.	1950–51	14	0	0	⎬ 1
Con.	1951–55	44	1	2	⎭
Con.	1955–59	49	7	14	⎫
Con.	1959–64	61	8	13	⎬ 14
Lab.	1964–66	13	2	15	⎭
Lab.	1966–70	37	15	41	⎫
Con.	1970–74	30	10	33	⎬ 33
Lab.	1974–79	31	7	23	⎭
Con.	1979–83	17	6	35	⎫
Con.	1983–87	16	5	31	⎬ 33
Con.	1987–90[b]	9	3	33	⎭
TOTAL		368	64		

Notes: a. This excludes exceptional cases including uncontested by-elections in university seats and the Bristol SE by-elections awarded on petition.
   b. June 1987 to March 1990.

in 1973 (35%), Birmingham Ladywood in 1969 (35%), and Walthamstow West in 1967 (36%). The SNP's victory at Glasgow Govan in 1988 broke post-war records, overturning a Labour majority of 53%. In contrast, as we have already noted, against expectations certain marginals did not change, for example Darlington in 1983 (2%) and Newcastle under Lyme in 1986 (6%). By itself the majority of a seat proved a poor predictor of seat change: the simple Pearson correlation between the majority of a seat in the previous general election and whether it eventually changed hands in a by-election was statistically significant but fairly weak ($r = .21$ $p > .001$).

   In terms of regional trends the greatest seat volatility has been in the Midlands and Greater London; the Conservatives have performed strongly in these areas, winning constituencies such as Ashfield, Walsall North, and Leicester South-West, with almost half of their seat gains in these regions (see Table 8.4). In line with national trends, the sharpest decline in the Tory vote has been registered in Scotland. Labour have performed relatively poorly in the Midlands seats, while gaining seats in their heartland areas of Scotland and Wales.

   Nevertheless whether seats are won or lost is an insensitive mea-

Table 8.2. *Labour and Conservative by-election gains, 1945–1990*

Con. Gains	Date	From	Lab. Gains	Date	From
1. Sunderland S.	1953	Lab.	1. Lewisham N.	1957	Con.
2. Liverpool Garston	1957	ENP	2. Carmarthen	1957	Lib.
3. Ealing S.	1958	ENP	3. Rochdale	1958	Con.
4. Brighouse/Spen.	1960	Lab.	4. G'gow Kelvingr.	1958	Con.
5. Leyton	1965	Lab.	5. Middlesborough W.	1962	Con.
6. Glasgow Pollok	1967	Lab.	6. Dorset South	1962	Con.
7. Cambridge	1967	Lab.	7. G'gow Woodside	1962	Con.
8. Walthamstow W.	1967	Lab.	8. Bristol SE	1963	Con
9. Leicester SW	1967	Lab.	9. Luton	1963	NL/C
10. Acton	1968	Lab.	10. Rutherglen	1964	Con.
11. Dudley	1968	Lab.	11. Bromsgrove	1970	Con.
12. Warwicks. Meriden	1968	Lab.	12. Merthyr Tydfil	1972	Ind.
13. Oldham W.	1968	Lab.	13. Southwark	1972	ENP
14. Nelson/Colne	1968	Lab.	14. B'ham N'thfield	1982	Con.
15. Walthamstow E	1969	Lab.	15. Fulham	1986	Con.
16. Swindon	1969	Lab.	16. Vale of Glam.	1989	Con.
17. Wellingborough	1969	Lab.	17. Mid Staffordshire	1990	Con.
18. Woolwich W.	1975	Lab.			
19. Walsall N.	1976	ENP			
20. Workington	1976	Lab.			
21. B'ham Stechford	1977	Lab.			
22. Ashfield	1977	Lab.			
23. Redbridge/Ilford N.	1978	Lab.			
24. Merton/Mitcham	1982	SDP			

Note: 'Gains from' indicates the name of the incumbent party at the time of the by-election. ENP = English National Party. NL&C = National Liberal and Conservative.

Table 8.3. *General and by-election changes of seat, 1945–1987 (GB)*

	By-Elections			General Elections		
	Change	Total	% Chge.	Change	Total	% Chge.
1945–55	1	105	1	46	1,250	4
1955–66	17	123	14	120	1,890	6
1966–87	43	131	33	276	3,165	9
ALL	61	359	17	442	6,305	7

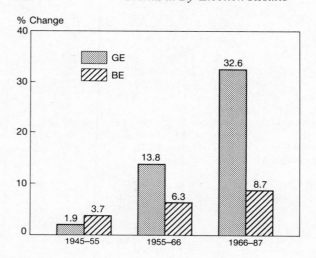

Fig 8.2.   By-election changes in seat, 1945–1987

Table 8.4.   *Regional trends in by-election volatility*

Region	BE No.	BE Chge.	% Chge.	Seat gains			Change in vote %		
				Con.	Lab.	LSDP	Con.	Lab.	LSDP
Scotland	53	9	17	1	3	3	−8	−4	6
Wales	21	4	19	0	2	1	−6	−5	6
North	24	4	17	2	1	1	−4	−4	7
North-West	40	6	15	4	0	2	−6	−3	8
Yorks.& Hum.	27	3	11	0	1	2	0	−2	−1
E. Midlands	20	4	20	2	0	2	−6	−8	10
W. Midlands	28	7	25	4	2	1	−1	−7	5
E. Anglia	11	2	18	1	0	1	−5	−4	9
Gr. London	68	15	22	8	3	4	−1	−4	4
South	63	7	11	3	2	1	−2	−3	4
ALL	359	62	17	24	14	19	−3	−4	5

sure of volatility, as constituencies can change hands with a minimal
shift in votes, depending upon their marginality in the previous
general election. At the end of Mrs Thatcher's first term of office
Labour gained Birmingham Northfield while the Alliance took Ber-

mondsey, but one had a majority of 0.3% while the other had a majority of 39%. This measure is also limited to the change in seats from the general election to the by-election (or vice versa) rather than multiple electoral flux within the campaign. Therefore this needs to be supplemented by other measures.

VOTING SWING

The second measure of volatility, commonly employed in previous studies, is the concept of 'voting swing'. The conventional ('Butler') swing in a constituency measures the average increase in the Conservative share of the vote minus the decrease in the Labour share of the vote.[2] Most research on by-elections has focused on the anti-government swing, between the government and the main opposition party. By-election votes have usually been compared with the previous general election results (the swing) or the following general election result (the swing-back), or an average of the two (see Stray and Silver 1983, 1979; Mughan 1986a, 1988).

Evidence from trends in the conventional voting swing suggests that there has not been a consistent increase in Conservative–Labour volatility in by-elections and general elections (see Table 8.5). The swing to the Conservatives reached its first peak under the 1966–70 Wilson administration, with a second peak under the 1974 Wilson/ Callaghan government. The swing towards Labour is apparent during the Conservative administrations of 1955–64, 1970–4 and 1983–7. In short, rather than dealignment, this suggests a picture of trendless fluctuations.

Nevertheless there are serious problems about using this measure. The concept of anti-government voting swing was a simple and useful way of analysing electoral change in general elections during the fifties, when Labour and the Conservatives took most of the seats, but it has become increasingly out of date as conventional voting swing fails to take account of shifts in multi-party support. The concept can be seen as particularly inappropriate for by-elections, where almost a third of all seats which switched have been

---

[2] An alternative is the two-party ('Steed') swing which is the change in the Conservative share of the sum of the Conservative and Labour vote. All votes not given to Conservative and Labour are in effect treated as abstentions.

Trends in By-Election Results

Table 8.5. *Conventional ('Butler') swing of the vote, 1945–1987*

	BE	GE
1945–50	4.6	2.9
1950–51	4.4	1.7
1951–55	0.2	1.3
1955–59	−4.9	1.1
1959–64	−5.8	−3.1
1964–66	1.6	−2.8
1966–70	12.0	4.9
1970–74 (Feb.)	−5.5	−0.8
1974–74 (Oct.)	—	−2.2
1974–79	9.4	5.4
1979–83	−1.1	4.1
1983–87	−7.8	−1.7

Note: This represents the change in each party's share of the vote from the previous general election to the by-election. The by-election swing from February to October 1974 is excluded as there was only one contest during this period (Newham South).

gained by the Liberals, Social Democrats and Nationalists.[3] Secondly, while swing may have been useful in the past, as a predictive measure, it is not a 'behavioural measure' unless very restrictive assumptions are made (W. L. Miller and Mackie 1973). Thirdly, the concept only measures net volatility, the change in constituency results from one election to the next, rather than the multiple flux of the vote. Lastly, movement between the parties and abstention are included in the final figure purporting to measure change between the parties (Taylor and Payne 1973). As a result of these problems the Nuffield 1987 General Election study abandoned the use of swing in analysing the regional distribution of party support (Curtice and Steed 1988).

THE PEDERSON INDEX

The third method of summarizing electoral change is the Pederson Index, (the Index of Dissimilarity), which was developed within the context of multi-party politics in Europe to try to overcome the problems associated with the conventional concept of voting swing (Pederson 1980). The Pederson Index is measured by summing the

---

[3] The value of the use of swing in analysing general election results has been questioned in recent years. See Curtice and Steed (1988).

percentage point change in each party's share of the vote in a constituency compared with the previous election, and dividing by two. Unlike the voting swing, the Pederson Index takes no account of the direction of change. The Pederson Index tends to confirm that there has been a trend towards more volatile by-elections since the mid-sixties, reaching a peak in the first Thatcher administration, although the pattern is not clear-cut, and there was an earlier peak from 1959 to 1964, following the Liberal and Labour revivals (see Table 8.6).

Table 8.6.   *Pederson Index, 1945–1987*

	BE	GE
1945–50	11.0	3.9
1950–51	7.2	6.8
1951–55	3.9	1.7
1955–59	9.8	3.2
1959–64	16.0	5.9
1964–66	6.2	4.4
1966–70	12.5	6.0
1970–74 (Feb.)	14.0	13.3
1974–74 (Oct.)	—	3.1
1974–79	12.3	8.2
1979–83	19.0	11.8
1983–87	14.6	3.2

Note: This represents the change in each party's share of the vote from the previous general election to the by-election. The by-election swing from February to October 1974 is excluded as there was only one contest during this period (Newham South).

SHARE OF THE VOTE

The Pederson Index is more appropriate than voting swing in a situation of multi-party politics common to by-elections; nevertheless it suffers from the disadvantage that each party is given equal weight regardless of its size (Crewe 1985). For example gains for the National Front or the Raving Monster Loony Party are treated as equivalent to a shift in Liberal or Labour support. It therefore seems preferable to supplement this with the most straightforward measure which is available, the percentage difference in each party's

Table 8.7.   *Change in mean share of the vote, 1945–1987 (%)*

	Con.		Lab.		LSDP	
1945–50	+4	(−1)	−3	(−4)	0	(−40)
1950–51	+7		−2		−1	(−13)
1951–55	−1		−1		0	(−36)
1955–59	−9	(−1)	+1		+1	(−42)
1959–64	−14	(−1)	−2		+7	(−42)
1964–66	+2		−2		+2	(−2)
1966–70	+7		−17		−2	(−22)
1970–74	−11	(−1)	−4		+5	(−19)
1974–79	+10		−9		−5	(−1)
1979–83	−12		−11		+20	(−3)
1983–87	−15		0		+12	
MEAN	−4		−4		+3	

Note: This represents the change in each party's mean share of the vote in constituencies where parties contested both the previous general election and the by-election.

The figures in parentheses indicate the number of seats excluded as the party did not contest the previous general election, the by-election, or either contest.

share of the vote from a general election to a by-election (Table 8.7), which confirms the evidence of increased electoral change noted since the mid-sixties.

These data can be summarized by classifying volatile seats as those with a significant change (more than 15%) in the share of the vote for *any* of the parties, from the general election to the by-election. The results (see Table 8.8 and Fig. 8.3) suggest that in the post-war decade nine out of ten by-elections showed high stability; in the sixties this declined to seven out of ten, but in the eighties this proportion fell to four out of ten, which is consistent with the thesis of partisan dealignment.

Lastly it should be noted that the evidence considered so far provides a conservative estimate of electoral change, as it is limited to *net* volatility, the flow of the vote between elections, as measured by changes in the total share of the vote obtained by each party in Parliamentary constituencies. This does not take account of *gross* volatility, the total amount of switching by individual voters, that is the flux of the vote, between any two points of time. Net volatility can be seen as analogous to a river flowing downstream while gross volatility is more like the movement of waves back and forth under the sea. The latter produces multiple complex turbulence

Table 8.8.   *Classification of by-election seats, 1945–1987 (%)*

	Stable		Volatile	
1945–50	87 ⎫		13 ⎫	
1950–51	93 ⎬	92	7 ⎬	8
1951–55	98 ⎭		2 ⎭	
1955–59	82 ⎫		18 ⎫	
1959–64	57 ⎬	71	43 ⎬	29
1964–66	92 ⎭		8 ⎭	
1966–70	78 ⎫		22 ⎫	
1970–74	73 ⎬	75	27 ⎬	26
1974–79	71 ⎭		29 ⎭	
1979–83	41 ⎫	42	59 ⎫	58
1983–87	44 ⎭		56 ⎭	
MEAN	77		23	

Note: See text for definitions.

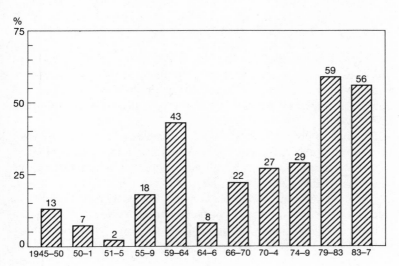

FIG 8.3   Volatile by-elections, 1945–1987

where individuals waver or switch their voting intentions, from the general election to the by-election, or from the start of the campaign to polling day, or from one moment to the next.

For most by-elections we do not have the information to estimate gross volatility, as we need to know how individuals change their voting intentions over time, requiring panel surveys which return to the same respondents at intervals, or cross-sectional surveys with recall data about previous voting choice. With a few exceptions (the by-elections in Greenwich and Knowsley North), such survey information is not available. The data concerning constituency results therefore provide only a conservative estimate, as the change in each party's share of the vote in a constituency is the product of a much larger amount of individual vote-switching. If vote-switching is multi-directional ('churning') then the flux does not necessarily lead to any substantial changes in each party's share of the vote: all parties may gain and lose at the same time. It should be emphasized that a highly volatile electorate may therefore produce a stable outcome:

In a period of dealignment the pool of relatively unattached electors swells: more voters are 'up for grabs'. But this does not necessarily undermine the established two-party system, let alone realign it in a predictable direction. The two parties may take voters from each other. If they do it simultaneously, turbulence in the electorate can still produce a stable outcome (stable dealignment). (Crewe 1984: 52)

With partisan dealignment the old party loyalties are loosened but this does not necessarily lead to realignment, or the long-term re-establishment of party loyalties in a new mould. Only if the electors flow in a consistent direction will the conditions for realignment take place.

The information which is available concerning trends in by-election volatility therefore tends to confirm the studies of voting behaviour in general elections which have suggested that during the seventies Britain experienced the process of partisan dealignment, a marked loosening of the electorate's ties with Labour and the Conservatives. In support of this thesis studies have noted a substantial fall in official party membership, a decrease in the two-party share of the electorate, increased negative voting, greater switching towards third parties, and the growth of electoral volatility between, and within, election campaigns (see, for example, Alt 1984; Sarlvik and Crewe 1983; Crewe 1984; see also Crewe, Sarlvik and Alt 1977*a*; W. L. Miller *et al.* 1990; Rose and McAllister 1986; Whitley 1983; Franklin 1985; Heath, Jowell, and Curtice 1987; Heath 1988).

Party loyalties continue to structure the electorate; in the 1987 general election almost nine out of ten voters acknowledged a party identification (see Table 8.9). Yet there has been a marked fall in

Table 8.9.　*Trends in voters' party identification, 1964-1987 (%)*

	All with party identification	Very strong party identification
1964	93	44
1966	92	44
1970	91	42
1974 (Feb.)	90	30
1974 (Oct.)	90	27
1979	87	22
1983	87	21
1987	86	19

Source: British General Election Studies (Heath, Jowell, and Curtice 1988).

the proportion of strong identifiers; in 1964 44% of the electorate were committed partisans, ('very' strong Conservative, Labour or Alliance identifiers), which dropped to 19% by 1987. This tends to suggest dealignment rather than realignment, as the change has affected Labour and Conservative support equally, irrespective of social class, gender, and age (Crewe 1985).

EVIDENCE FOR PARTISAN REALIGNMENT

Nevertheless proponents of realignment suggest that we need to consider whether the party system has been experiencing fundamental change in recent years. In particular we need to examine the evidence from by-elections to see whether 1979 was a critical election, leading to a significant and enduring shift in the party balance on the centre-left or right. The Liberals, Social Democrats and Nationalists certainly hoped that the by-election breakthroughs they experienced promised a more fundamental break-down of the established two-party system, with the displacement of Labour on the centre-left.

Table 8.10.   *By-election seat gains and losses, 1945–1989 (seat nos.)*

	Con.	Lab.	Lib.	SDP	Other	Total
From Con.	—	12	10	3	4	29
From Lab.	20	—	4	1	1	26
From Lib.	1	1	—	—	0	2
From other	3	3	0	0	—	6
TOTAL	24	16	16		5	63
Net Gain/Loss	−5	−10	+12	+4	−1	

Certainly the Liberals have been the major beneficiaries of by-election change, winning sixteen by-elections from 1945 to 1987, while the Labour Party net performance proved the weakest (see Table 8.10). Some Liberal and SDP MPs have managed to translate a by-election victory into long-standing support; they include David Steel (Roxburgh, 1965) Cyril Smith (Rochdale, 1972), Alan Beith (Berwick, 1973), Simon Hughes (Bermondsey, 1983), and Rosie Barnes (Greenwich, 1987). In the Parliament following the 1987 general election, despite the loss of Roy Jenkins (Glasgow Hillhead, 1982), Mike Hancock (Portsmouth South, 1984), Elizabeth Shields (Ryedale, 1986), and Clement Freud (Isle of Ely, 1973), a third of the Social and Liberal Democratic MPs had originally entered their current seat via the by-election route.

An analysis of the seats which the Liberals won demonstrates that they made gains across the country, from inner-city Liverpool Edge Hill, and suburban Sutton and Cheam, to rural Ryedale. There is no particular pattern by region, marginality or type of seat (see Tables 8.11 and 8.12). The Liberals performed most strongly under Conservative administrations, winning two-thirds of their gains from the Tories, with notable successes under the Heath administration.

Even where the Liberals failed to win seats they often performed strongly, increasing their share of support from the previous general election in almost nine out of ten by-elections which they contested, with the most substantial gains during the Conservative administrations of Macmillan, Heath, and Thatcher (see Figs. 8.4 and 8.5). During Mrs Thatcher's second administration, the Liberal–Social Democratic Alliance improved their share of the vote in all but one contest (Cynon Valley), receiving on average 38% of the vote, higher than Labour or the Conservatives (see Table 8.13). The main

Table 8.11.   *Liberal by-election wins, 1945–1989*

Constituency	Date	MP	Gained from
1. Devon, Torrington	27.03.1958	Mark Bonham Carter	Con.
2. Kent, Orpington	14.03.1962	Eric Lubbock	Con.
3. Montgomeryshire	15.05.1962	Emyln Hooson	(Lib. hold)
4. Roxburghshire	24.03.1965	David Steel	Con.
5. B'ham Ladywood	26.06.1969	Wallace Lawler	Lab.
6. Rochdale	26.10.1972	Cyril Smith	Lab.
7. Sutton/Cheam	07.12.1972	Grahame Tope	Con.
8. Isle of Ely	26.07.1973	Clement Freud	Con.
9. Yorkshire, Ripon	26.07.1973	David Austick	Con.
10. Berwick upon Tweed	08.11.1973	Alan Beith	Con.
11. Liverpool Edge Hill	29.03.1979	David Alton	Lab.
12. Croydon NW	22.10.1981	William Pitt	Con.
13. S'wk/Bermondsey	24.02.1983	Simon Hughes	Lab.
14. Brecon/Radnor	04.07.1985	Richard Livsey	Con.
15. Ryedale	08.05.1986	Elizabeth Shields	Con.
16. Truro	26.02.1987	Matthew Taylor	(Lib. hold)

Table 8.12.   *Social Democratic by-election wins, 1981–1989*

Constituency	Date	MP	Gained from
Crosby	26.11.1981	Shirley Williams	Con.
Glasgow Hillhead	25.03.1982	Roy Jenkins	Con.
Portsmouth South	14.06.1984	Mike Hancock	Con.
Greenwich	26.02.1987	Rosie Barnes	Lab.

exceptions to this tendency came in the early fifties, when the Liberals were at their lowest level of support in the national polls following the disaster of the 1950 general election, and again in the mid-seventies during the period of the Lib.–Lab. pact when David Steel entered into a Parliamentary alliance with the Callaghan Labour government. In the early nineties it remains to be seen whether the Liberal Democrats can stage an effective recovery, with the centre party vote fragmented, and the emergence of the Greens following the 1989 Euro-election. In national opinion polls support for the Liberal Democrats fell to single figures following the merger in spring 1988, and slid further during the following years. Most commentators were pessimistic about their prospects. Nevertheless on the basis

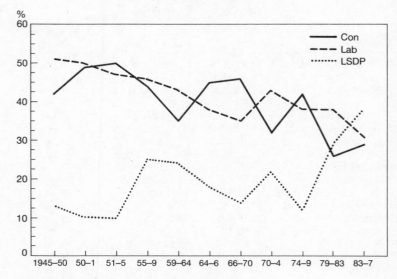

FIG. 8.4.   By-election share of vote, 1945–1987

of their past by-election performance, and changes in the nature of the electorate, we would expect that in the long term third parties (the SNP, the Greens, and the Democrats) would be capable of staging a rally in certain favourable by-elections.

In analysing party performance we need to distinguish between the increased share of the vote due to third party interventions and the increase due to public support. In this analysis it should be noted that we need to control for party intervention. In the fifties it was common for the Liberals and Nationalists to contest a by-election seat where they had not stood in the previous general election (and vice versa). In these cases the resulting change in the third party share of the vote can be attributed to the organizational strength of the constituency party as much as to shifts in public support. In measuring changes in votes for third parties (including the Liberals, Social Democrats, Scottish Nationalists and Plaid Cymru, and all other minor candidates) we therefore need to distinguish four categories of by-elections:

1. ALL: the mean change in the vote in all contests.
2. WITHDRAWALS: the mean change in the vote where a third party contests the previous general election and not the by-election.

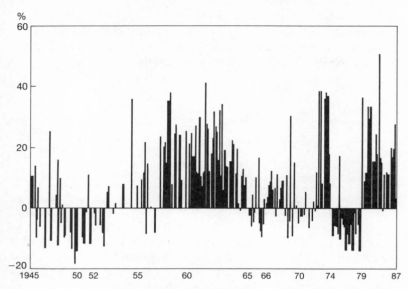

Fɪɢ. 8.5. Liberal vote change, 1945–1987

Table 8.13. *Mean share of the vote in by-elections 1945–1987 (%)*

Govt.		Turn-out	Con.	Lab.	LSDP[a]
Lab.	1945–50	62	42	51	13
Lab.	1950–51	69	49	50	10
Con.	1951–55	59	50	47	10
Con.	1955–59	64	44	46	25
Con.	1959–64	64	35	43	24
Lab.	1964–66	64	45	38	18
Lab.	1966–70	62	46	35	14
Con.	1970–74	56	32	43	22
Lab.	1974–79	57	42	38	12
Con.	1979–83	56	26	38	29
Con.	1983–87	64	29	31	38
Mᴇᴀɴ	1945–87	62	41	43	21

Note: a. This represents the mean share of the vote for the Liberals (Social Democrats) where they contested by-elections irrespective of whether they fought the seat in the previous general election.

3. INTERVENTIONS: the mean change in the vote where a third party contests the by-election and not the previous general election.
4. BOTH: the mean change in the vote where a third party contests both the previous general election and the by-election.

Table 8.14.   *Change in Liberal (Alliance) vote 1945–1987*

		No.	Lib. GE	Lib. BE	Lib. change
Withdrawals	(GE only)	24	9.8	—	−9.8
Consistents	(GE & BE)	135	17.4	22.5	+5.1
Interventions	(BE only)	75	—	17.9	+17.9

Note: For a definition of these categories see text. Liberal vote until 1981; then combined Alliance vote.

We can classify by-elections where there are Liberal withdrawals (where they contested only the previous general election); Liberal interventions (seats where they contested only the by-election) and Liberal consistents (where they contested both the by-election and the general election). The results show (see Table 8.14) that the Liberal share of the vote increased in contests where they intervened (+17.9%) and, at a lower level, where they fought both contests (+5.1%).

If the Liberals and Social Democrats made a consistent series of by-election gains which were retained in subsequent general elections this would suggest that, at least in these contests, the Liberal Democrats were capable of mounting an effective challenge to the two-party system. Realignment requires the establishment of a long-term base of core identifiers who support the Liberal Democrats over successive elections. On the other hand if support for the Liberal Democrats proved ephemeral, swinging back in general elections, this would suggest partisan dealignment.

An analysis of the swing-back from the previous by-election to the following general election suggests that support mobilized in by-elections proves largely, although not wholly, ephemeral. In the 1987 general election the Alliance managed to retain some of their by-election gains made during the previous Parliament; Rosie Barnes was returned for Greenwich and Richard Livsey (just) for Brecon and Radnor; but others lost, including Elizabeth Shields in Ryedale and Mike Hancock in Portsmouth South. As shown in Table 8.15

Table 8.15. *Swingbacks from by-election to 1987 general election*

	Con. change	Lab. change	LSDP change
Penrith	+14.3	+3.6	−15.9
Chesterfield	+9.9	−0.9	−5.0
Cynon Valley	+4.8	+10.2	−7.6
Surrey SW	+10.2	−1.1	−8.9
Stafford	+11.0	−6.1	−4.2
Portsmouth S	+9.1	−13.5	+5.4
Enfield Southgate	+9.2	+6.9	−14.7
Brecon/Radnor	+7.0	−5.1	−1.0
Tyne Bridge	+7.8	+5.9	−14.9
Fulham	+16.9	−7.7	−8.4
Ryedale	+12.0	−0.3	−11.7
W. Derbyshire	+13.6	−8.1	−4.2
Ncl. u. Lyme	+8.8	−0.2	−7.9
Knowsley N.	+4.5	+13.6	−18.3
Greenwich	+11.7	+1.1	−12.4
Truro	+9.3	+3.1	−11.4
MEAN CHANGE			
GE '83 to BE	−15.3	+0.4	+12.3
BE to GE '87	+10.0	+0.1	−8.8
NET CHANGE	−5.3	+0.3	+3.5

Note: The figures represent the change in the percentage share of the vote from the previous by-election to the 1987 general election.

the Conservatives recovered about two-thirds of the support which they had previously lost to the Alliance in by-elections, while Labour regained support in their own seats such as Knowsley North. Yet there was some residual positive effect for the Alliance. In the by-election seats the Alliance increased their share of support from the 1983 to the last general election by 3.5%, whereas across the country their support declined by 2.3%. Therefore there has been dealignment: some voters who switched to the Alliance in a by-election were retained for the subsequent general election but for most the change represented only a temporary defection.

The alternative argument for realignment is that the 1979 election represented a watershed for the Conservatives, with the country experiencing a fundamental realignment on the right. Is this the case from the evidence of by-election results? During the first Thatcher administration the Conservative share of the vote in by-elections reached its lowest post-war record, dropping from 50% in 1951–5 to 26% in 1979–83 (see Table 8.13). From 1979 to 1987 the Conservatives lost support in every by-election except Beaconsfield. Some of the record anti-government swings could be attributed to the phenomenon of the Alliance, but these swings continued in contests like Richmond, Yorkshire in 1989, even after the break-up of the old Alliance. Much of this support was restored in subsequent general elections, but this serves to confirm that the electoral system has been experiencing dealignment not realignment: there has been no repeat of the series of Conservative gains managed from 1967 to 1969.

CONCLUSIONS: EXPLANATIONS OF BY-ELECTION VOLATILITY

On the basis of this analysis we can develop a classification of by-elections into four categories, outlined in Fig. 8.6. Where *partisan alignments* dominate we would expect most of the electorate to be relatively stable in their voting choice over successive elections. By-elections would reflect this quiescence, with minimal shifts in support

		Gross volatility	
		Low	High
NET VOLATILITY	LOW	Stable partisan alignment	Stable partisan dealignment
	HIGH	Partisan realignment	Unstable partisan dealignment

FIG 8.6. Typology of volatility

from the general election to the by-election. National trends in party popularity could be expected to predominate over local concerns, issues, and events. The evidence suggests this pattern was characteristic of the by-elections during the post-war decade which produced highly predictable results for the major parties.

In contrast under *stable dealignment* we would expect the electorate in by-elections to be characterized by multi-directional and turbulent change. In this situation all parties will find it easier to attract transient support than to build any enduring ties. Short-term campaign-specific factors will become more influential as more voters decide at a later stage. Negative 'protest' voting will increase. There will be widespread temporary defections from one candidate to another, and from voting to abstention, depending on campaign-specific events such as the nature of the candidates, local issues, party organizations, tactical considerations, and media coverage, but no party will manage to build the momentum of a bandwagon whereby support consistently flows their way. The multiple change will cancel itself out in terms of the final results, as each party gains and loses equally. As in a battle there will be heavy casualties on all sides but none will emerge ultimately victorious.

This situation is closely related to *unstable dealignment*, where a party may experience short-lived by-election gains but the swings will eventually be cancelled by the swing-backs. In this situation there may be dramatic by-election victories but this does not signify long-term shifts in party loyalties. With the fickle electorate what is gained too easily may be just as quickly lost. The pattern of unstable dealignment seems characteristic of by-elections from the mid-sixties onwards, with transient gains by all parties which frequently revert back in subsequent general elections.

Lastly in a period of *partisan realignment* we would expect support to shift fairly consistently across a series of by-elections towards the one party, with swings sustained over successive elections. By-election support would be based on positive rather than negative considerations, and on national rather than campaign-specific factors, with voters developing a long-term attachment to the party. The evidence we have considered suggests that the most consistent by-election winners are the Liberals, but these gains were based on dealignment rather than realignment. The Liberals experienced strong resurgences during certain periods (1956–8, 1962–3, 1972–4, 1981–7) but they have not managed to establish deep-rooted and lasting changes in party loyalties which persist across a series of elections.

Under conditions of partisan dealignment, if party loyalties no longer structure the vote, we have to consider what other factors explain by-election results. Butler and Stokes (1974: 422) concluded that the short-time fluctuations in support shown in by-elections, local elections, and opinion polls are due to specific issues and particular events, ephemeral influences which alter the party balance depending on how deeply basic party loyalties cut through the electorate: 'A hard budget, an unpopular prime minister, a severe winter, a sense that the Government has grown tired in power—influences such as these are overlaid on the more enduring bases of party support and produce the fluctuations which are displayed in many indicators of the state of the parties.'

Crewe also argues that in the absence of traditional party loyalties a range of campaign-specific factors come to the fore: 'the outgoing government's record, the major issues of the day, the party leaders' personal qualities, specific and perhaps quite trivial incidents—took on a greater significance.' (Crewe 1984). Yet if we accept campaign-specific factors have become more significant, what sort of 'issues' count? Local or national? Retrospective or prospective? Economic or social? We will go on to explore the implications of these developments in the context of the theory of retrospective voting, which can be seen as particularly appropriate to explain consistent trends in by-election results.

9

Retrospective Theory and Government Performance

PARTISAN dealignment helps to explain why volatility has increased in by-elections but so far we have not sought to explain the *direction* of change; in particular why the party in government consistently tends to lose support in these contests. This trend can be explored in the light of the theory of retrospective voting, a perspective which has attracted growing interest in recent years. The aim of this chapter is to develop a modified version of this theory, as a broad analytical framework which can be used to account for the particular characteristics of by-elections, before going on to examine its empirical basis.

At its simplest the retrospective model assumes that the primary basis for voters' choice is their evaluation of the government's past record, although this vague notion is open to a wide range of interpretations. In the literature there is extensive controversy about a series of questions concerning retrospective voting (for a review see Frey and Schneider 1981; Monroe 1979, 1983, 1984; Paldam 1981). What is the exact time-frame for voter's evaluations (Lewis-Beck 1988; A. H. Miller and Wattenberg 1984)? What is the role of affective feelings and cognitive judgements (Conover, Feldman, and Knight 1986)? What is the relative influence of economic, social, and foreign policy factors on evaluations of the government's performance (Clarke, Stewart and Zuk 1986; Gopoian and Yantek 1988)? What is the impact of personal economic circumstances (simple pocket-book voting) versus evaluations of the state of the national economy (Kiewiet 1983; Kinder and Kiewiet 1979; Whiteley 1984; Kinder and Mebane 1983)? What is the relationship between actual economic conditions (the rate of unemployment, economic growth, inflation, or levels of personal income) and voters' perceptions of the government's economic performance (see for example Hibbs and Fassbender 1981; Conover, Feldman, and Knight 1986; Eulau and Lewis-Beck 1985; Goodhart and Bhansali 1970)? What is the relationship between approval of the government's record and government popularity? (Hudson 1984, 1985) Is there a well-established cyclical pattern in government popularity which is associated with economic conditions? (Hudson 1985; Stray and Beaumont 1987; W. L. Miller and Mackie 1973).

The idea that a government's fate depends upon performance in the eyes of the electorate, particularly success in handling 'bread-and-butter' economic conditions, has a long tradition but it raises complex issues. The classic basis of the general model was developed in the late fifties by Anthony Downs and V. O. Key, before being extended more recently by Morris Fiorina (Downs 1959; Key 1966; Fiorina 1981). The value of the retrospective model has been examined in an extensive range of studies in the United States and Britain although there is little consensus about the results, in part because none have employed exactly the same set of assumptions or statistical controls (for a review see Kiewiet 1983; Kiewiet and Rivers 1984; Eulau and Lewis-Beck 1985). Without entering into the wider controversies the question this chapter will address is whether the retrospective account of voting behaviour can be seen as an appropriate model to explain British by-elections. Do these contests provide an indication of government popularity or a referendum on government performance?

THEORIES OF RESTROSPECTIVE VOTING

In the classic account provided by Anthony Downs, rational citizens aim to maximize their utility by selecting parties for government which will be most beneficial to themselves. In making their choice the most important factor will not be party promises but the current record of the incumbent since this allows instrumental voters, with a minimum of information costs, to make their decisions on established facts rather than vague conjectures. The theory suggests that voters will evaluate party platforms in the light of what the government achieved in office, and what they believe the other parties would have done. Accordingly citizens judge future policies by past performance.

A more extensive version of this theory has been developed in the United States by Morris Fiorina (1981), who suggests that citizens rationally discount much information about campaign platforms, given the record of politicians in fulfilling their promises and the uncertainty surrounding the most appropriate means to achieve desired policy goals. Although voters are unclear about prospective policies they have a certain amount of reliable information upon which to base their choice, namely citizens know what life has been like under the last government. Voters will therefore rely more heavily upon retrospective evaluations of past performance, than upon vague plans, proposals, and promises about what politicians will do in the future.

Retrospective theory assumes that citizens are more concerned with the outcome of government actions than the policies used to achieve them. Voters do not need to pay attention to detailed and technical policy debates; about the money supply, the balance of payments deficits, or the strength of sterling. Voters can sit back, let the politicians and experts argue, and see what works. Through direct experience voters have reliable information to guide their choice: they know whether their wages have kept pace with prices, what public service has been like in local hospitals, whether they have been paying high rates, whether the buses run on time. On this basis, in conjunction with indirect information from the media, the electorate can use their vote in by-elections to express their evaluations of the government's past performance, responding to the direct and indirect ·questions: Are you better off today than you were at the time of the last general election? And is your community, your region, and the country better off as a result of the government's actions?

There are certain generally agreed conditions which have to be met for retrospective or prospective issues to have an impact on electoral behaviour. First, voters must feel that the issue is important; government spending on overseas aid may be considered inadequate by many but this will not affect their vote if, as usual, the issue is low on their list of priorities. Voters must also perceive a party difference on the issue; if all politicians are perceived to agree on the need for economic growth and protection of the countryside, then these issues will not shift votes (Campbell *et al.* 1960). But to have an impact prospective issues have to meet a third condition: voters have to believe that the proposal is credible. The public might think it important to get rid of all nuclear weapons in Britain, the parties might take opposing stands on the issues, but if people do not think that the proposals represent practical 'do-able' suggestions then when it comes to instrumental voting the issues will not cut much ice. By definition retrospective issues, about what the government has done, do not have to meet this last condition, and may therefore have more impact on voting.

SIMPLE AND MEDIATED EVALUATIONS

In seeing whether this model fits by-elections we need to bear in mind Fiorina's distinction between simple evaluations, which are the result of judgements about the respondent's personal situation, and mediated evaluations which are formed from assessments of the government's general performance (Fiorina 1981). The theory is not suggesting that simple pocket-book voting dominates, that electors are motivated purely by their personal circumstances and narrow self-interest, that if pensions rise under Labour or mortgage rates go down under the Tories, as a direct result those who benefit will vote them back into office. Rather the theory suggests that voters give more weight to their experiences of what the government *has* done for themselves, their family, their community, and the country than what the government or opposition say they are *going* to do. It has been suggested that simple and mediated evaluations are related, for example that an individual's perception of the government's economic performance reflects their personal experience of unemployment, although the relative impact of simple and mediated evaluations on voting choice in Britain remains an open question (Conover, Feldman, and Knight, 1986; Weatherford 1983).

Studies of United States politics have concluded that voter evaluations of national economic conditions have had a greater impact on electoral outcomes than have perceptions of personal economic situations (Kinder and Kiewiet 1979, 1981; Kinder and Mebane 1983). Kinder and Kiewiet have called this tendency socio-tropic politics: 'In reaching political preferences, the prototypic socio-tropic voter is influenced most of all by the *nation's* economic condition. Purely socio-tropic citizens vote according to the country's pocket-book, not their own' (1981: 132). In the retrospective account voters are primarily concerned with results, rather than the policies which produce the results. For the present it can be left as an open question how voters arrive at their evaluations of the government's performance. If this theory can be supported it suggests that by-elections can be seen as an evaluation of past performance, signalling where society has been rather than where society should go, with voters discounting much of what politicians say and deciding how to vote on the simpler question: 'has government delivered?'

INSTRUMENTAL PARTY LOYALTIES

Yet if voters are deciding on the basis of government performance, how does the theory account for the influence of party loyalties? What of Labour and Conservative loyalists who hardly ever change their vote no matter what the government does? As we have seen in the traditional Butler and Stokes model, based on surveys carried out in the sixties, party loyalty was seen as an affective orientation, developed in early socialization within the family and workplace, and reinforced through successive elections (Butler and Stokes 1974). Compared with party identification, voters' attitudes towards issues were thought to be of secondary importance in voting choice since these attitudes were considered largely derivative, transient, and inconsistent.

As shown in the previous chapter there is considerable evidence that strong partisanship has declined over the years although many voters continue to express adherence to one of the major parties. Party loyalists do not necessarily desert the government even if it is going through a period of unpopularity; otherwise election swings would be much stronger. How does the theory of retrospective voting account for this? According to Fiorina it is not to be expected that the electorate decides *de novo* at each election since voters experience the results of successive administrations in coping with economic, social, and foreign policy problems. Over the years in a reasonably stable democracy the electorate can see the relative effectiveness of Conservative and Labour politicians in dealing with major issues such as inflation, pensions, or taxation.

As a result partisan loyalty can be interpreted as an instrumental evaluation summarizing the Labour and Conservative track record over time. If voters can be seen as analogous to consumers in the political market-place, the theory suggests that they will buy the goods which they have found meet their needs most effectively. But over the years through repeated evaluations they will develop a brand loyalty so that if one purchase fails they will not immediately switch goods, but will assume it was a faulty product. If successive purchases fail, however, then consumers could be expected to change brand. In recent by-elections, therefore, the electorate could be expected to be influenced primarily by an evaluation of the present government's record, judged in the light of experience of the previous Callaghan, Heath, and Wilson administrations. Retrospective theory acknowledges that for many voters party loyalty remains important but interprets the concept as instrumental rather than affective.

THE RESTROSPECTIVE THEORY OF BY-ELECTIONS

The retrospective theory may be seen as particularly appropriate for by-elections since in these contests voters face a distinctive 'logic of choice': unlike at general elections, voters know that their actions will not determine who rules in Westminster. Only in exceptional circumstances will the outcome of a single by-election bring down a government, although it has been suggested that in the early twenties Newport helped to hasten the departure of Lloyd George, whilst Westminster St George saved Baldwin as leader of the opposition in 1931, and in the mid-seventies Callaghan was forced into the Lib.–Lab. pact after losing his overall Parliamentary majority (Butler 1973; Butler and Kavanagh 1985). In most cases, however, the immediate impact of by-election results is upon public opinion and party morale. As a result the electorate may feel freer to treat their by-election vote as an evaluation of the current administration, 'sending a message to No. 10', whilst returning to the traditional party fold in general elections when the impact of their vote will have different consequences. If this theory can be substantiated it would explain why third parties can experience dramatic shifts in their favour in by-elections, particularly in constituencies held by the government, whilst it is more difficult for them to sustain this support during general elections. Therefore retrospective theory suggests that changes in government popularity would have the most immediate and direct effect on voting choice in by-elections. In turn, as shown in Fig. 9.1, we would expect government popularity to be a function of evaluations of *present* government performance and partisan identification, interpreted instrumentally as a summary measure of *past* government performance.

In this sense local by-elections can be seen, with some legitimacy,

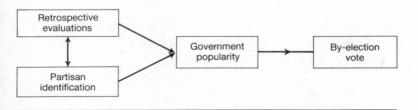

Fig. 9.1 The simple retrospective model of by-elections

as representing a referendum on government performance. Yet there are problems about applying traditional retrospective theory, without qualification, to the particular characteristics of by-elections. First, long-term trends in government popularity can rarely explain the sudden shifts in support which can occur during a three-week by-election campaign. According to the opinion polls, in certain circumstances government popularity may be affected by short-term events, such as the Falklands crisis, the Westland affair, or industrial unrest during the 'winter of discontent', but in most cases evaluations of the government change only gradually. Secondly retrospective theory can help to account for changes in support for the government and opposition during the post-war decade, but it has more difficulty explaining trends in by-elections during periods of multi-party politics, such as the shifts from Labour to the Alliance in Bermondsey, Greenwich, and Ryedale. Thirdly the model outlined does not take account of factors occuring within the campaign, which many commentators regarded as critical to the outcome of certain contests, such as the selection of particular candidates or media coverage.

Accordingly the traditional theory of retrospective voting needs to be modified to fit the particular characteristics of by-elections. In the amended retrospective model of by-elections, outlined schematically in Fig. 9.2, there are two stages in which support can change. The first stage is the one we have already described, that is, the long-term decline in the government's share of the vote in by-elections, which is closely related to changes in government popularity. This development occurs from the previous general election to the start of the campaign, as indicated by the early polls taken before the contest gets under way.

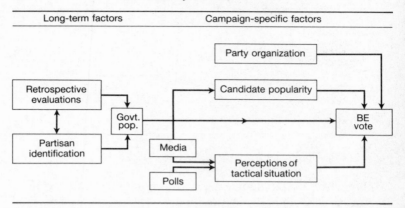

Fig. 9.2   The two-stage retrospective model of by-elections

The second stage is the change in party support during the by-election, caused by campaign-specific factors: the popularity of particular candidates, perceptions of the tactical situation, and the effectiveness of local party organizations. We would expect the media coverage and the published polls to have an *indirect* effect on the campaign, influencing voters' opinions about the candidates and their expectations about the tactical position of the parties in the race. Given their nature, campaign-specific factors are more unpredictable. If third parties can mobilize support with a popular candidate and effective organization, recruiting voters who are temporarily dissatisfied with the government or opposition, they may be able to generate the necessary momentum for electoral success. We would expect campaign-specific factors to have their greatest impact in the more volatile contests but to prove insignificant in stable by-elections.

To test the empirical basis of the simple retrospective model, we need to examine three questions:

1. Is there a systematic pattern of government losses in by-election results?
2. If confirmed, is there an association between a range of constituency results and government popularity, as measured by national opinion polls?
3. If so, can we go further to establish a causal relationship at the

individual level between evaluations of the government's performance and voting choice?

TRENDS IN GOVERNMENT LOSSES

An examination of by-election results quickly reveals the loss of government support to be remarkably consistent; indeed this can be nominated as one of the few predictable 'laws' of by-elections. Since 1955 the government share of the vote has declined in 95% of British by-elections, that is in all except 14 out of 253 contests. During Mrs Thatcher's first two administrations the Conservatives' share of the vote fell in every by-election except Beaconsfield.[1] The only significant exceptions to this pattern, when the government maintained support, were the early years of Attlee's post-war government, and the 1951–5 Conservative administration, when the Liberals were exceptionally weak. Conservative governments have tended to lose about 10% of their share of the vote in post-war

Table 9.1. *Change in the by-election vote by party in government, 1945–1987*

Govt.	Change in percentage vote			No. of By-elections
	Con.	Lab.	LSDP	
Conservative	−9.7	−1.7	+14.4	217
Labour	+5.8	−7.8	+3.3	142
ALL	−3.6	−4.1	+9.6	359

by-elections, although this tends to be almost balanced by Tory gains when in opposition (see Table 9.1). Labour governments have lost a similar level of support in office but failed to stage an equivalent recovery when in opposition. Further, as will be shown in Chapter 13, the loss of government support is a cross-cultural trend evident in Canadian and Australian by-elections.

The striking consistency of the mid-term government losses suggest that it may be possible to draw parallels with mid-term congressional elections in the United States where, since the establishment of the two-party system in 1860, the political party of the

[1] Although even post-Falklands the Tory vote only increased in Beaconsfield by a marginal 0.1%.

incumbent President has lost seats in all but one mid-term contest. The exception was 1934, following the critical realignment under Roosevelt two years earlier (Tufte 1975, 1978; Abramowitz 1985; Abramowitz, Cover, and Norpath 1986; Kernell 1977; Hinckley 1981). While these trends in mid-term losses for the party in government are well established, the reasons explaining this phenomenon are not well understood.

CYCLICAL LOSS OF SUPPORT

The loss of government support from the previous general election to the by-election tends to follow fairly predictable cyclical patterns over time (see Table 9.2). From the first to second year of each administration after an initial 'honeymoon' period most governments experience a progressive fall in support (see Fig. 9.3). By

Table 9.2. *Government loss of by-election votes, 1945–1987 (%)*

Govt.		Year of office				
		1st	2nd	3rd	4th	5th
Lab.	1945	−2.2	−6.2	−6.5	−3.7	
Lab.	1950	−1.7	−2.0			
Con.	1951	−1.1	.5	−0.8	1.9	
Con.	1955	−4.3	−6.3	−10.4	−11.9	−5.4
Con.	1959	−7.6	−15.5	−18.4	−15.5	−9.2
Lab.	1964	−2.7	−8.9			
Lab.	1966	−13.1	−18.0	−19.2	−12.5	−9.7
Con.	1970	0.4	−5.0	−10.5	−17.4	
Lab.	1974	−5.0	−13.6	−11.5	−3.2	−12.6
Con.	1979	−9.5	−13.5	−19.2	−7.8	−14.0
Con.	1983	−11.6	−12.2	−16.0	−18.2	
MEAN 1945–87		−5.3	−9.2	−12.5	−9.8	−10.2

Note: Change in the mean share of the vote by the party in government from the previous by-election to the general election.

the third year most administrations have reached the 'mid-term blues' after which the electoral fortunes of governments follow a divergent pattern. Some tend to recover in their fourth or fifth years of office (for example Macmillan's government in 1959), while others tend to fall further in the run up to the general election (for example the Heath administration in 1973–4). Therefore it cannot be assumed that the swing of the electoral pendulum will produce an automatic recovery from the mid-term blues; it depends on the political factors which shape these short-term fluctuations in electoral support.

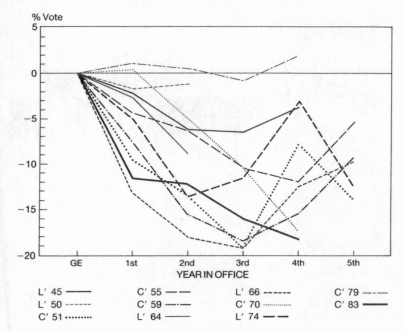

% Vote

YEAR IN OFFICE

L' 45 ———	C' 55 — —	L' 66 ------	C' 79 —·—
L' 50 ------	C' 59 —·—	C' 70 ············	C' 83 ———
C' 51 ··········	L' 64 ———	L' 74 — —	

Fig. 9.3   Government loss of support in by-elections, 1945–1987

This process can be graphically illustrated by the trends in support for the parties from the general election to the by-election. As shown in Fig. 9.3, the change in the Conservative share of the vote is broadly cyclical, particularly since the mid-sixties, with increases when in opposition and losses in government. Sharp declines in Tory support are registered before the Labour victory in 1964, with recoveries in the late sixties, before sudden falls again under Heath and Thatcher. Labour shows a weaker version of the cyclical pattern, with a marked loss of support when in government but with only a limited improvement in their share of the by-election vote in opposition, notably in the period under Sir Alec Douglas-Home and again in 1972–73. As Fig. 9.4 shows, Labour's performance in by-elections tends to be fairly weak at the best of times.

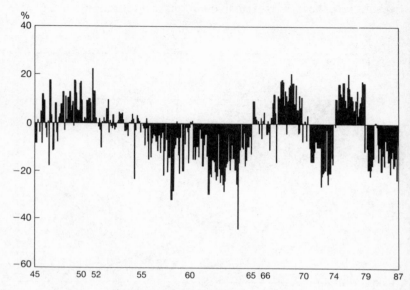

Fig. 9.4   Change in Conservative by-election vote, 1945–1987

THE LOSS OF GOVERNMENT SEATS

These electoral trends have had a clear impact on the loss of by-election seats experienced by the party in government, with Labour administrations faring slightly worse than the Tories. Since the war 61 seats have changed hands in by-elections, of which over three-

Table 9.3.   *Seats lost by party in government, 1945–1987*

	MP in previous election			
	Con.	%	Lab.	%
Conservative	26	93	10	32
Labour	2	7	22	69
All	28	100	32	100

quarters were lost by the party in government (see Table 9.3). In the process the Tories lost 30 seats, although this has to be balanced against their 24 gains, notably their whole string of victories against Labour during the Wilson years from 1967 to 1969, and again during the economic crisis from 1976 to 1977 (see Table 9.4). Labour's victories have been more sporadic, although there were indications of their increasing popularity in a series of by-election gains in the years preceding the return of the Wilson government in 1964. On balance the Labour Party has suffered the greatest loss from the process, gaining 15 seats but losing 27.

CONSTITUENCY RESULTS AND GOVERNMENT POPULARITY

On this basis we have established that there are systematic trends in the loss of support for the party in government, with third parties the main beneficiaries. The question which remains to be considered is whether, as retrospective theory suggests, the loss of government support in by-elections is strongly associated with other measures of government popularity. The first indicator is *time-series* data which can be employed to analyse the relationship between changes in aggregate by-election results and government popularity in national opinion polls. In Britain the most reliable source of continuous data since the war is provided in Gallup monthly surveys of voting intentions.[2]

These measures of national party popularity mirror the pattern of by-election cycles already noted. The swings recorded by the opinion polls are less extreme but, compared with their vote in the previous general election, most governments experience a mid-term slump in party popularity which is often, but not always, followed by some recovery (see Tables 9.4, Fig. 9.5). The opinion polls confirm the cyclical pattern of 'mid-term blues'; most governments experience a steady decline in support around their third year in office, which can be followed by a sharp recovery (such as Callaghan managed in 1978 or the Conservatives experienced following the Falklands in 1982–3) or continued lows.

There is a strong and significant association between the change

[2] It should be noted that regular monthly polls by Gallup are not available until 1947. This excludes any comparison for twenty-four by-elections before Jarrow in June 1947.

Table 9.4. *Cycles of government popularity in national polls*

Year of office	1st	2nd	3rd	4th	5th
Lab. 1945	−1.0	−6.3	−6.3	−6.9	−5.0
Lab. 1950	−2.0	−6.3			
Con. 1951	−5.5	−2.5	−2.3		
Con. 1955	−4.1	−7.1	−10.9	−3.8	−1.7
Con. 1959	−2.5	−5.2	−11.8	−14.9	−3.7
Lab. 1964	−1.9	−5.6			
Lab. 1966	−1.1	−10.2	−15.9	−2.0	
Con. 1970	−3.7	−6.4	−7.6	−11.2	
Lab. 1974 (Feb.)	5.1				
Lab. 1974 (Oct.)	3.9	2.6	−3.9	8.4	2.4
Con. 1979	−4.5	−15.0	−14.8	−0.7	
Con. 1983	−0.8	−5.4	−14.1		
AVERAGE	−1.5	−6.1	−9.7	−4.4	−2.0

Note: Popularity is measured as the average difference over each 12-month period between expressed voting intentions in Gallup national surveys and the actual vote in the previous general election.

Source: Calculated from D. Butler and G. Butler, *British Political Facts 1900–1985* (Macmillan, London, 1986).

in support for the government in national opinion polls and in local by-election results (simple Pearson correlation $r = .53$ Sig. $p = .01$); when the government becomes unpopular in the country as a whole this tends to be reflected in their share of support in local by-elections (see Tables 9.5 and 9.6). The association between changes in support in opinion polls and by-elections is strongest for the Conservative Party (Pearson $r = .88$); as shown in Fig. 9.6, where they do well in one indicator they tend to do well in the other, although by-elections tend to display more exaggerated swings in support. In an analysis using ordinary least squared multiple regression the change in Conservative national popularity accounted for 59% of variance in their by-election results.

There are parallel trends for Labour (see Fig. 9.7) although the association is slightly weaker (Pearson $r = .72$), since from the mid-sixties onwards the party has often performed better in the national polls than in by-elections, which suggests that Labour have problems mobilizing their potential support in these contests. In a regression analysis Labour's popularity in the opinion polls accounted for 32% of variance in their by-election results. In the post-war decade the

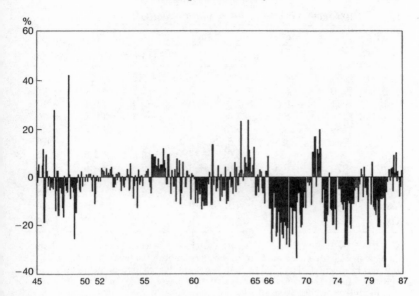

Fig. 9.5   Change in Labour by-election vote, 1945–1987

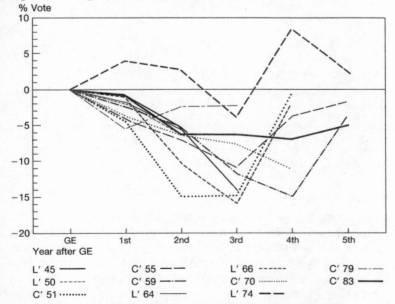

Fig. 9.6   Government loss of support in opinion polls, 1945–1983

Table 9.5.   *Changes in by-election results and Gallup polls*

Govt.		Con.		Lab.		Lib.[a]	
		BE	Gallup	BE	Gallup	BE	Gallup
Lab.	1945	+4.8	+6.1	−2.3	−6.6	−0.3	+2.1
Lab.	1950	+6.8	+2.2	−2.0	−2.7	−1.4	+0.3
Con.	1951	−0.6	−2.9	−0.8	−2.4	+0.1	+5.0
Con.	1955	−8.9	−7.4	+1.0	+0.1	+0.9	+7.6
Con.	1959	−14.3	−9.5	−1.5	+0.8	+6.8	+8.8
Lab.	1964	−1.5	−1.5	−2.0	−1.5	−1.8	+1.5
Lab.	1966	+6.7	+6.0	−17.3	−10.8	+1.8	+2.6
Con.	1970	−10.5	−8.0	−3.8	+3.3	+4.8	+5.1
Lab.	1974	+9.6	+11.1	−9.1	−0.1	−4.9	−8.4
Con.	1979	−11.6	−5.4	−10.5	−3.1	+19.5	+11.5
Con.	1983	−15.3	−6.1	+0.4	+7.7	+12.3	+0.6
MEAN		−3.6	−2.2	−4.1	−1.5	+2.7	+4.3

Note: For by-elections this represents the change in each party's mean share of the vote in constituencies where parties contested both the previous general election and the by-election. The Gallup data represent the change in each party's share of the vote from the previous general election to the month of the by-election.

a. Liberal until 1981, then Alliance.

Table 9.6.   *Correlations between changes in by-election results and Gallup polls*

Govt.	L'45	L'50	C'51	C'55	C'59	L'64	L'66	C'70	L'74	C'79	C'83	ALL
Corr.	.14	.64*	.03	.50*	.43*	.09	.32	.27	.66*	.66*	.43*	.53*
N. BE	22	14	44	49	60	13	37	30	31	17	16	333

Note: Pearson correlations. *Sig. $p = .001$.

Liberals tended to do slightly worse in by-elections than in the opinion polls, but this pattern was reversed around the time of their third revival in 1972–4, with a much stronger by-election performance following the creation of the Alliance. The correlation between their position in the opinion polls and in by-elections was relatively strong ($r = .75$) and the regression analysis explained 26% of variance in Liberal support (see Fig. 9.8).

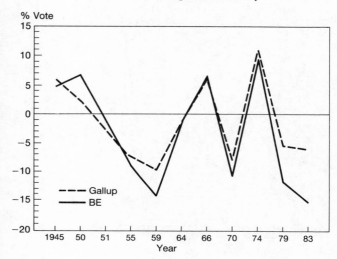

Fig. 9.7   Change in Conservative support

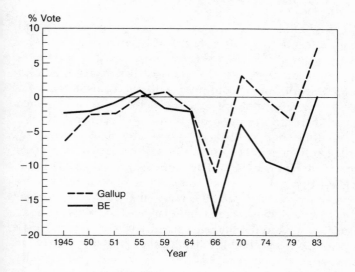

Fig. 9.8   Change in Labour support

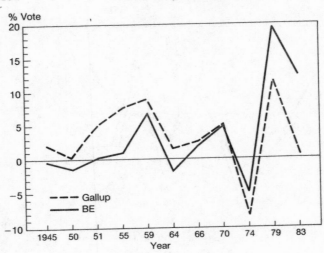

Fig. 9.9   Change in Liberal support

INDIVIDUAL EVALUATIONS OF GOVERNMENT PERFORMANCE

On this basis we can conclude that aggregate constituency data tend to substantiate the retrospective theory of by-elections; there is a significant relationship between party support in national opinion polls and in by-election results. Nevertheless it remains to be seen whether this theory can be confirmed with survey evidence from individual voters. Constituency data are useful to monitor change over time but there are serious problems with the 'ecological fallacy': by-election results and government popularity may be strongly associated but this does not necessarily establish a causal connection (Robinson 1950; Kramer 1983). This is the major weakness of previous studies. Particular by-election results may be influenced by a rise in national party popularity, but conversely, a by-election result like Greenwich may increase national levels of party support. The difficulty is how to disentangle causality where the effect may be reciprocal. Do by-election results influence party popularity, or does party popularity influence by-election results? Further the association may prove spurious, the result of a third factor, which boosts both local and national party popularity, such as the extensive media coverage of the Alliance when they were first founded. For all these reasons aggregate data are widely seen as an inferior substitute for individual-level data. Empirical results based solely on aggregate analysis, however elaborate, are normally regarded with due caution until confirmed by individual-level studies.

Therefore to increase confidence in the retrospective model the results need to be confirmed using cross-sectional or panel surveys of *individual* voters. Using the BBC by-election surveys we can examine the relative impact on voting choice of retrospective evaluations, prospective issues, social structure, and partisan loyalties. To simplify the analysis the detailed results will be presented for the Ryedale, West Derbyshire, and Fulham surveys, carried out at the same time, to control for changing perceptions of the government's performance, before replicating the analysis where consistent items are available in other surveys in the series.

MEASURES OF RESTROSPECTIVE EVALUATIONS

There are problems about designing survey items to measure mediated evaluations of government performance. The most appropriate avoid reference to specific policies or politicians, to minimize the problems of rationalization and circularity. The BBC surveys asked people to indicate the saliency of a series of fourteen issues in the election, then to indicate approval of the government's performance on these issues. For retrospective evaluations to influence by-elections they need to fulfil the necessary conditions of issue-voting outlined earlier; that is, voters have to see the issue as salient and one where there is a difference between the parties. Voters may disapprove of the Tory record on unemployment, it may be seen as the most important issue, but if they believe that unemployment was as high under the the previous Labour government this may not have a significant impact on voting. Retrospective theory suggests where these conditions are met the electorate will give greater weight to evaluations of the government's past performance than other factors in the contest.

The results of this analysis suggest that the mediated government performance measures proved to be strong and significant discriminators of by-election voting choice (see Table 9.7). In the Fulham, West Derbyshire, and Ryedale by-elections three issues were seen

Table 9.7.   *Evaluation of government performance by voting choice (by party)*

Issue		Con. voters	LSDP voters	Lab. voters	Coeff. of assoc.
Unemployment	Approve	33	5	2	
	Disapprove	46	89	97	.79*
Education	Approve	40	7	7	
	Disapprove	41	80	86	.71**
NHS	Approve	42	12	6	
	Disapprove	45	82	91	.60**
Taxation	Approve	71	30	13	
	Disapprove	17	54	74	.56**
Privatization	Approve	71	29	10	
	Disapprove	14	54	78	.58**
Trade unions	Approve	76	47	11	
	Disapprove	9	32	76	.41**
Inflation	Approve	84	55	22	
	Disapprove	10	33	56	.41**

Note: Q. Do you approve or disapprove of the way the government has handled—
a. Gamma Coefficient of Association. **Sig. p .01, *Sig. p .05.

Source: BBC 'Newsnight' Surveys, Fulham, Ryedale, and W. Derbyshire, Mar. 1986, N. 1,574

as most important: unemployment, education, and the National Health Service. On unemployment and the health service nine out of ten Labour voters were critical of the government's record, compared with four out of ten Conservatives (see Fig. 9.9). Since these surveys were carried out in the aftermath of the 1986 Budget it is not surprising that taxation proved to be strongly related to voting choice; almost three-quarters of the Labour voters were critical of the government's handling of this issue, while in contrast almost three-quarters of Conservatives approved. There was a similarly high level of voter polarization on the issues of the government's performance with trade unions and privatization. Voters who supported the Liberal–Social Democratic Alliance were consistently more central, although on unemployment, education, and health they were closer to Labour, while they were nearer to the Conservatives on trade unions and inflation.

It might be argued that these items are subject to the problem of rationalization, that is, those who intend to vote Conservative

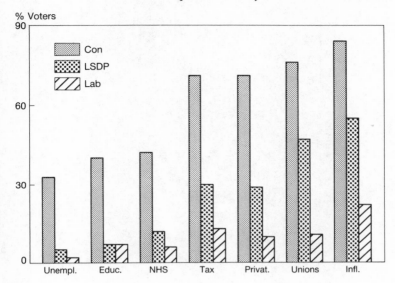

Fig. 9.10. Approval of the government's performance

(for whatever reason) are expressing support of the government while opposition voters are expressing blanket disapproval. The direction of causation rests upon theoretical considerations rather than the measures of association, but this potential criticism is weakened by the clear distinction which people drew between the government's performance on different issues. Voters from all parties gave credit to the government for their performance on inflation, where the record shows that the economy improved substantially during Mrs Thatcher's second administration, while remaining fairly critical of their performance on unemployment and education. Further, these results were replicated where identical items were available in the series of BBC 'Newsnight' constituency surveys, with a total sample of over six thousand respondents (see Table 9.8). The association between mediated government approval and voting choice proved statistically significant and consistent. The most salient issues in the surveys—unemployment, education, and the National Health Service—also tended to serve as the strongest predictors of voting choice.

Table 9.8.   *Evaluations of government performance by constituency voting choice (coefficient of association)*[a]

Issue	Fulh.	Rye.	W. Derb.	Dudley W.	Welwyn & Hat.	Bolt. W.	Mitcham	Bristol	Bath	Cov. SW	Hal.	Twi.
Unempl.	.78	.80	.79	.67	.78	.70	.66	.81	.85	.80	.76	.79
Educ.	.64	.78	.70	.57	.76	.69	.71	.64	.68	.71	.54	.69
NHS	.70	.58	.57	.68	.64	.72	.74	.81	.74	.43	.59	.58
Tax	.60	.54	.53	na	na	na	na	na	.60	.33	.34	.37
Privat.	.53	.58	.62	na	na	na	na	na	na	na	na	na
T. Unions	.49	.45	.32	.63	.39	.49	.67	.47	.32	.25	.35	.40
Inflat.	.37	.55	.35	.55	.41	.30	.54	.37	.29	.35	.42	.41
Defence	na	na	na	.66	.53	.51	.67	.68	.42	.46	.51	.54
N. Energy	na	na	na	.55	.51	.52	.55	.65	na	na	na	na
N.	632	423	498	533	508	569	511	761	523	520	522	484

Notes: Q. Do you approve or disapprove of the way the government has handled — ?
a. Gamma coefficient of association. All reported association proved significant ($p > .05$).
See Table 9.7 for details of the categories employed.
na = not available.

Source: BBC 'Newsnight' surveys 3, 4, 5, 6, 7, 8, 9, 14, 15, 16, 20, 21 as listed in Appendix.

PROSPECTIVE ISSUES

Yet we need to consider the relative importance of retrospective evaluations compared with other influences on voting choice, notably prospective issues, social structural variables, and partisan identification. As mentioned earlier the assumption of the prospective model of voting is that people vote according to their preferences for future party policies, selecting instrumentally from manifesto promises in the political market-place. To measure prospective issues the surveys included a series of questions, replicating items in the British General Election Studies, which were found in previous work to reflect enduring issues which divided the Labour and Conservative parties, and which acted as strong predictors of voting choice (Heath, Jowell, and Curtice 1985: 107–12). People were asked whether income and wealth should be redistributed, whether Britain should bring back the death penalty, whether the government should spend less on defence, and whether the government should continue with policies of privatizing state industry and services. In addition voters were asked whether they favoured increased government services even if it meant some rise in taxes, whether things should be left as they are, or whether taxes should be cut even if it meant some reductions in government services. The results in the Fulham, Ryedale, and West Derbyshire by-elections suggest that these prospective items proved statistically significant but weaker predictors of party vote (see Table 9.9).

Table 9.9. *Prospective issues (% votes agree)*

Issue	Con. voters	LSDP voters	Lab. assoc.	Coeff. of.
Re-introduce death penalty	73	54	40	.25 *
Continue privatization	71	25	12	.40 **
Cut defence spending	28	59	76	.30 **
Extend services	32	60	67	.35 **
Redistribute income & wealth	37	67	85	.41 **

Note: See text for details.
Source: BBC 'Newsnight' Surveys, Fulham, Ryedale, W. Derbyshire, Mar. 1986, N. 1,936.

THE INFLUENCE OF SOCIAL LOCATION VARIABLES

In the traditional model we would expect a strong relationship between voting choice and the major social cleavages in British politics: divisions of occupational class, housing tenure, and region, along with other structural variables such as age, gender, and education. The nature of the relationship between social class and voting choice has proved highly controversial in recent years; some see evidence of class dealignment since the early seventies while others have argued that production and consumption cleavages continue to exert a major influence on British politics (see, for example, Sarlvik and Crewe 1983; Robertson 1984; Franklin 1985; Rose and McAllister 1986; Heath, Jowell, and Curtice 1985, 1987; Dunleavy and Husbands 1985). Controversy surrounds not just the substantive findings, but also the most appropriate conceptual definitions, and operational measures, of social class (Crewe 1986; Heath, Jowell, and Curtice 1987; Dunleavy 1987). To investigate the influence of social class in by-elections the BBC 'Newsnight' surveys used a limited threefold occupational classification which collapsed the seventeen categories of socio-economic groups in the 1981 census. Social groups were classified into professional and managerial, other non-manual, and manual groups on the basis of the respondent's own occupation.

The results of this analysis suggest that social class was only weakly associated with voting choice in these by-elections (Gamma coefficient = .07) (see Table 9.10). During the campaign, among the professional and managerial group, just under half (46%) said they intended to vote Conservative, compared with a third (32%) who supported the Alliance, and a fifth (22%) Labour. Nor were voters sharply polarized by age group, gender, education, and employment status, although all these factors produced some variance in party support. As other studies have found, the Alliance vote was remarkably consistent across all social groups, although they attracted slightly stronger support among women, the early middle-aged, and graduates.

The strongest social division proved to be associated with housing tenure; there was a 40% difference in Labour support between council tenants and owner-occupiers, compared with a 24% difference between manual and professional groups. The significance of housing tenure on voting choice persists even after controlling for social

Table 9.10. *Social groups and voting choice*

	Con.	LSDP	Lab.	Coeff of. assoc.[a]
ALL	38	30	32	
Age group				
Young (18–25)	32	26	42	
Early middle (26–45)	34	33	32	
Late middle (46–64)	46	27.8	26	
Elderly (65+)	44	27	28	.10*
Gender				
Men	37	27	35	
Women	39	33	27.5	.04
Socio-economic group				
Professional/managerial	46	32	21	
Other non-manual	35	36	29	
Manual	28	26	46	.07
Employment status				
Employed	37	32	31	
Unemployed	21	29	50	
Student	23	29	48	
Housewife	49	29	21	
Housing tenure				
Owner-occupier	47	34	19	
Private tenant	31	26	43	
Council tenant	19	23	58	.13*
Educational qualifications				
Graduate	36	35	29	
Non-graduate	39	29	32	.07

Note: The Gamma coefficient measures the association between social group and voting choice for the major parties. *Sig. .05

Source: BBC 'Newsnight' Constituency Surveys, Fulham, Ryedale, W. Derbyshire, Mar. 1986.

class, which tends to confirm the pattern evident in the 1983 and 1987 British General Election Studies (see Heath, Jowell, and Curtice 1985: 45; Norris 1990). This was replicated in the series of BBC polls from Tyne Bridge to Truro where few social cleavages proved to be significantly related to party support (see Table 9.11). The measures of social class are limited but overall the results suggest that in by-elections social structural variables have less direct influence upon voting choice than evaluations of the government performance.

Table 9.11.　*Association between social group, location, and voting choice*[a]

	Tyne Br.	Fulham	Ryedale	W. Derby	Knows.	Green.	Truro
Age							
group	.07	.03	.02	.12	.11	.01	.09
Housing	.07	.18*	.02	.02	.04	.07	.09
Gender	.08	.07	.19*	.19	.20*	.01	.01
SEG	.03	.11	.06	.03	.05	.11	.25*

Note: For details of the categories employed see Table 9.10.

a. Gamma coefficients of association between social group and voting choice for the major parties. *Sig. *p.* > .01.

Table 9.12.　*Partisan identification by vote*

Partisan identification	Con.	LSDP	Lab.	Coeff. of assoc.[a]
Conservative	74	8	2	
Liberal/Social Democratic	5	78	3	
Labour	3	7	81	
Other/None/Don't know	10	8	16	.76

Notes: Q. Would you say you generally think of yourself as Conservative, Labour, Liberal, SDP or what? (Alliance responses combined).

a. Gamma coefficients of association between vote and partisan identification.

Source: BBC 'Newsnight' Constituency Surveys, Fulham, Ryedale, and W. Derbyshire, Mar. 1986.

But it can be suggested there might be an indirect relationship between social factors and electoral choice, which operates through voters' partisan identification. The results confirm that party loyalties continue to be strongly related to voting choice: 74% of Conservative identifiers, 78% of Alliance identifiers, and 81% of Labour identifiers voted for their respective parties (see Table 9.12). Yet as we have discussed the concept of partisan identification is open to an affective or instrumental interpretation. If, as Fiorina suggests, partisan loyalties are seen as a cumulative summary evaluation of each party's performance over time then the association between partisan identification and voting choice is not inconsistent with retrospective theory.

To compare the relative influence of these factors on voting choice we can develop a multivariate analysis, using ordinary least squared

Table 9.13. *Multivariate analysis of government support*

	Standardized Beta coefficients	Adjusted R^2
Social location		
Housing tenure	.15 *	
Socio-economic group	.08 *	
Gender	.05	
Education	.02	
Age	.02	.11
Prospective issues		
Privatization	.25 **	
Taxes v. services	.18 **	
Captial punishment	.11 **	
Redistribution of income	.05	
Defence spending	.03	.20
Government performance		
Trade Unions	.28 **	
Taxation	.20 **	
Unemployment	.15 **	
Privatization	.13 **	
Health Service	.13 **	
Inflation	.10*	
Education	.07	.34

Source: BBC 'Newsnight' Constituency Survey, Fulham, Ryedale, and W. Derbyshire, Mar. 1986.

regression with stepwise entry, with vote for the government transformed into a dummy variable. The results suggest that overall retrospective evaluations proved the strongest indicator of voting choice, explaining 34% of variance in the voting choice. The approval for government performance on trade unions, taxation, and unemployment proved particularly strong indicators. In contrast prospective issues and social location variables proved significant but less strongly related to voting choice.

CONCLUSIONS

To summarize the analysis presented in this chapter, we have established that in by-elections there is a systematic tendency for third parties to gain support at the expense of the party in government. The analysis of constituency results suggests that to a large extent the first stage of the shift in by-elections is associated with approval of the government's record. Under conditions of partisan dealignment, where electors are dissatisfied with the government's performance, some will temporarily defect. In a by-election this suggests that voters feel free to express a protest vote for another party or to stay at home on polling day, safe in the knowledge that a single by-election will rarely affect the government's overall majority. The extent of the swing-backs from the by-election to the subsequent general election indicates that the change represents a temporary disaffection rather than a long-term erosion of government support. Evidence from aggregate results is replicated at the level of the individual voter, where evaluations of the government's record are found to be more strongly related to voting choice than traditional social cleavages including occupational class. This provides initial support for the retrospective model of by-elections, yet so far we have only touched on the second-stage shift, the changes which occur within the campaign. We need to turn to the campaign-specific factors to explore how these factors influence the shifts, not just from the government to the opposition, but from one opposition party to another.

10

The Impact of Candidates and Party Organizations

IN general elections the local campaign is usually considered largely irrelevant to the outcome. 'The constituency campaign has come to be regarded by most observers as little more than a ritual. The anachronistic local rites of canvassing and public meetings are performed at each election, but are not thought to have any bearing on the results.' (Butler and Kavanagh 1988: 211). Yet we would expect by-elections to be different: voters are choosing one MP rather than a government; individual candidates are subject to greater public attention; parties invest greater organizational resources at constituency level to mobilize their supporters; the national media subject the local campaign to intense scrutiny. We would expect the weaker partisan loyalties evident in recent years to leave greater room for the influence of short-term considerations. Therefore we need to examine the role of campaign-specific factors—local party organizations, the selection of candidates, the media coverage of the campaign, and the use of opinion polls—to consider their potential impact.

LOCAL PARTY ORGANIZATIONS

Party leaders and managers believe the local campaign matters, irrespective of conventional psephological wisdom, as demonstrated by their committment of resources to these contests. Officers from national headquarters are drafted into the constituency, to work full-time alongside local agents for the duration of the campaign. Campaign managers organize the day-to-day grassroots operation including planning the canvass, deploying volunteers, co-ordinating photo-opportunities, and arranging daily press conferences for the candidate, party 'minder', and visiting celebrities. In by-elections like Crosby over a thousand Alliance activists were mobilized from around the country for the final weekend.

Recently new developments in campaign techniques have been introduced; party central offices, learning from campaigns in the United States, have started to import computers into the constituency. These are mostly employed for routine work, to prepare canvass cards and monitor the results, with a copy of the electoral register on disk. Campaign managers have also started to deploy targeted direct mail shots, for example in Fulham the elderly were sent letters stressing Labour policy on pensions while teachers were sent personalized messages about Labour plans for education. Nevertheless these innovations should not be exaggerated; even in high-tech Fulham volunteer MPs were to be seen in the constituency headquarters stuffing letters into envelopes. At the grass roots most traditional electioneering in Britain has remained virtually unchanged over the years. The local campaign still revolves around volunteers knocking on doors in target wards to deliver election leaflets, monitor support, and reinforce waverers.

THE EFFECT OF PARTY ORGANIZATION

It is easier to describe party campaign organizations than to assess the potential effect this has on the outcome. Most energy is devoted to the canvass, so that potential support can be mobilized on election day, although whether this is an effective use of resources is open to question. One detailed study of the canvassing operation in a Greenwich ward concluded that when canvassing is done well, on a large enough scale, in a well resourced campaign, it proved a fairly efficient way of identifying party opponents and, to a lesser extent, party supporters (Swaddle 1988). Based on recorded canvass returns the study estimated that over 90% of the registered electors in one ward were contacted during the campaign (Swaddle 1988).

This level of canvassing activity can be confirmed for the whole constituency. During the last week of the Greenwich campaign, according to the BBC survey, about three quarters of the electors said a party worker had called (see Table 10.1)[1] and nearly all (94%) had received some campaign leaflets at home. This compares

[1] The difference between the 'Newsnight' survey estimate of 80% contacted and the 90% estimate provided on the basis of canvass returns by Swaddle may be due to interviewers who only talk to one member of a household, yet record voting intentions for husbands, wives, or other members of the family based on this information.

with under a third who had seen any candidate in person, and only one in ten who had heard any candidate at a political meeting. Canvassing is therefore one of the most visible activities in the campaign, with a high level of penetration. As expected, canvassing was found to be more intensive during the Greenwich by-election than

Table 10.1. *Campaign activity (%)*

	Greenwich by-election[a]	1987 general election	
		Marginals[b]	All seats[c]
Received campaign leaflet	94	90	—
Visit by party worker	77	45	47
Seen candidate in person	36	—	—
Been to political meeting	9	—	3

Note: Q. So far during the by-election campaign ... has a party worker called at your home to talk to you? Have you received any campaign leaflets at home? Have you seen any candidates in person? Have you heard any candidate at a political meeting?

Sources: a. BBC 'Newsnight' Greenwich Survey, 21 Feb. 1987, N. 914.
 b. MORI General Election poll 3–4 June 1987, N. 1,305, quoted in Swaddle (1988).
 c. British General Election study June 1987, N. 3,812.

is common in other contests; in the 1987 general election only a third of voters said they were canvassed by a party worker (see Table 10.1). Given its high profile Greenwich cannot be considered representative of all by-elections, but this tends to confirm that the local campaign can be far more important in these contests.

One function of the canvass is to give campaign managers an idea of their electoral strengths and weaknesses, so they know where to concentrate their efforts. Yet this strategy can prove misleading as canvass returns, like public meetings, exaggerate support. Canvassing operations should not be treated as though they were opinion polls, irrespective of their size, as they do not attempt to draw on a balanced sample of the electorate. Parties concentrate the canvass where it will do most good, in their areas of greatest strength. In Greenwich, Labour started with the high-rise council estates, not the Edwardian semis. Partisan volunteers are not trained interviewers: they may give an over-optimistic interpretation of ambiguous replies. In addition some electors marked on the canvass in Vanburgh were not actually seen, some electors could be expected to be less than frank to party workers, and some could be expected to change their voting intentions during the campaign (Swaddle

1988). As a result not surprisingly each party estimated they were ahead in the Vanburgh ward.

The danger of treating partisan canvass returns as representative opinion polls can be shown by the results of the Social and Liberal Democrats canvass in the 1988 Kensington by-election. Based on interviews with 15,000 people, or a third of the electorate, the SLD announced the day before polling that their support was 20%, compared with 11% who actually voted for them the following day. This canvass estimated Conservative support as 48% (actually 42%), Labour 26% (actually 38%), and SDP as 3% (actually 5%). In the absence of opinion polls these estimates were widely, if sceptically, reported in the press. If evaluated by the criteria of an opinion poll this estimate would have produced unacceptably high average error (7%).

Whether the canvass achieves its primary objectives, to mobilize potential support, is more difficult to judge. To some extent canvassing is employed because it has always been done that way; volunteers and voters expect it; it keeps the troops occupied; it probably does no harm, and, particularly in marginal seats, it may do some good. Campaign managers, candidates, and activists tend to believe that the effort has an electoral pay-off and, without more convincing evidence, it is difficult to gainsay them. But the campaign organization is probably more important for the credibility of third party challengers, who are trying to mobilize a bandwagon by converting floaters, than for established incumbents who are trying to reinforce supporters. An efficient, well-run campaign may increase media and public perceptions that the party is competent, unified, and well-organized. Yet as Labour found in the 1987 general election, the most effective and co-ordinated campaign failed to deliver the goods. Based on limited evidence we can conclude that probably few additional by-election votes turn on party organization alone, although these may be the decisive few.

THE SELECTION OF CANDIDATES

In by-elections such as Bermondsey, Glasgow Govan, and Greenwich commentators have frequently blamed the selection of particular candidates for spectacular defeats. Was the choice of candidates decisive? If so, should the party leadership seek to control the selection process more directly? We need to consider four issues concerning the role of candidates in by-elections: selection procedures within the Conservative and Labour parties, the outcome of the process in terms of the composition of Parliament, the impact of candidate selection on by-election results, and the role of minor-party and fringe candidates.

There have been three main kinds of procedural changes in candidate selection in recent decades. First there has been a greater democratization of the selection process with increasing participation by local party members. This tendency has most recently been manifest in the Labour Conference decision in 1987 to select its candidates via a 'one member one vote' system which will operate through an electoral college. There has also been a trend towards greater central scrutiny, often using regional agents, as parties have sought to control the quality of their candidates. Lastly there has been a widely noted increase in the competition for seats, caused in part by the declining number of marginals (see Curtice and Steed 1986). The major parties differ in their selection procedures.

CONSERVATIVE SELECTION

Current Conservative selection procedures were devised at the beginning of the 1970s and made more rigorous ten years later (for details of the process see Lovenduski and Norris 1989). Following demands for a democratization of the party the Chelmer committee was established in 1969, which led to the adoption of new model rules for constituency selection (Rush 1986). Although the decision remains firmly local, most Conservative selection takes place using an approved list of candidates which is compiled at Central Office. Assessment for inclusion on the approved list is rigorous and highly selective. Applicants complete a standard form including references from three sponsors—ideally including an MP and a constituency chairman. The vice chair in charge of candidate selection assesses this information and interviews all applicants. Those who pass this stage are invited to a residential weekend selection board in which applicants are assessed by a team for their intellectual, practical, social, and political abilities. At the end of the process assessors make a recommendation to a senior party committee, the Standing Advisory Committee on Candidates. About half of those attending the residential boards are accepted for the approved candidates list, which just prior to the 1987 election included about 750 names. Local selectors reserve the right to choose candidates who are not on the Central Office list (subject to Central Office ratification); but such selections are increasingly rare (7% in 1987).

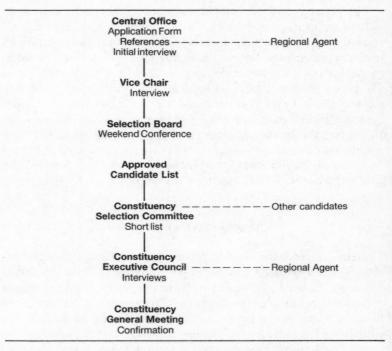

FIG. 10.1.   The selection process in the Conservative Party

Once past these hurdles Conservative candidates face the selection process at the constituency level (see Fig. 10.1). Since the early 1970s the practice has been that vacancies are notified to all persons on the approved list of candidates. Interested individuals then notify the party vice-chair in charge of candidates, who passes their names and biographical details to the particular constituency. There is considerable competition for the most winnable seats. There may well be over a hundred applicants which the selection committee, if it is following the new model rules, will reduce to between sixteen to twenty individuals who will then meet the committee which will short-list four candidates. These will be invited to attend a meeting of the executive committee, whose decision is formally confirmed by the Constituency General Meeting. For most by-elections the Regional Agent or Deputy Regional Agents supervise every stage of the process to ensure that the required procedures are followed. Therefore in the Conservative Party Central Office plays a major role at the start of the process, only seeking later to recommend certain potential candidates to constituency organizations.

SELECTION IN THE LABOUR PARTY

Until recently the process of candidate selection in by-elections was largely determined by the constituency Labour party but recently this principle has been eroded, with direct intervention by Labour's National Executive Committee (NEC). Labour's selection procedures reflect the party's federal structure and have been a target of the general movement to democratize the party since the early 1970s. Like the Conservatives, the Labour Party maintains national candidates lists, the 'A' list of trade union-sponsored candidates, and the 'B' list. Constituency organizations, including party branches, women's sections, trade union branches, and Young Socialists, are invited to nominate candidates. They may select from either national list, or they are free to nominate other candidates. The constituency executive considers these nominations and draws up a short-list by exhaustive ballot, which is presented to the constituency management committee.

Once short-listed, candidates are invited to meet party branches in a fairly protracted process which may involve speaking engagements every evening for two or three weeks. Finally candidates are invited to a formal presentation before the General Management Committee. After voting by exhaustive ballot a candidate is selected who must then be endorsed by the National Executive Committee. In most cases when presented with the local choice as a *fait accompli* NEC endorsement follows, although there have been some problematic cases. Under Michael Foot the party leadership opposed the selection of Peter Tatchell in Bermondsey, and the conflict which ensued within the party provided meat and drink to the opposition, with rumours that the Labour leadership wanted to lose the contest

(Tatchell 1983). In Greenwich the party leadership failed to influence the selection process, although Neil Kinnock was known to prefer the moderate candidate, Glenys Thornton, to Deirdre Woods.

The NEC has been reluctant to intervene in the past since this tactic sometimes backfired, most notably with the loss of Leyton in 1965. In recent years intervention has been employed more successfully, as discussed earlier, in Knowsley North. The resulting conflict, in which the local party refused to help with the campaign,

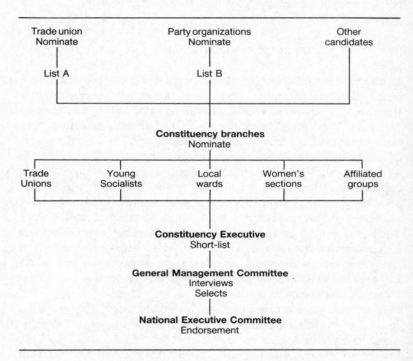

FIG. 10.2. The selection process in the Labour Party

and even the absence of the candidate during the campaign, did not seem to have any damaging effect on Labour's final result (for details see Chapter 6). Following their spectacular defeat at Glasgow Govan in 1988 the NEC revised the candidate selection procedure for by-elections, with representatives from the NEC attending the early selection meetings at Vauxhall, and successfully imposing the selection of Kate Hoey.

THE OUTCOME OF CANDIDATE SELECTION

What is the result of this process? As one might expect, by-election candidates for the major parties are similar in most social characteristics to those selected in general elections. There has been a gradual drift towards more middle-class candidates in all the parties, with fewer Tories from the traditional landed estates and fewer Labour members with a trade union/manual occupational background. Over the years Parliament has become more socially homogeneous, but some important distinctions between the parties remain. Labour are rather more likely to select public sector employees such as teachers, local government officers, social workers, and public servants. Labour is also the only party to select almost a third of their MPs from the manual working class. The Conservatives tend to come from the private sector and self-employed professions, such as business managers, company executives, lawyers, accountants and farmers. During the 1980s the Alliance candidates were middle-middle-class, as were the Liberals during the 1970s.

Reflecting the general shift towards middle-class occupations over the years, an increasing proportion of candidates are university-educated; in 1970 only about half of all candidates were graduates compared with more than two-thirds in 1987. Over the last thirty years there has been a slight fall in the number from public schools although in the 1987 Parliament a high proportion of Conservative members (68%) and Alliance members (over 40%) continue to have been educated privately. Candidates tend to be middle-aged, mostly in their early forties. To summarize, local selectorates tend to choose a fairly standard type of Parliamentary candidate: the middle-aged, well-educated professional man.

Although women continue to be a minority in Parliament, there has been a consistent increase in the number of women standing as candidates for the major British parties in every general election since the mid-sixties; the proportion of women tripled from about 4% in 1966 to nearly 13% in 1987. In the last general election this increase affected all the major parties although the Conservatives lagged slightly behind the others, selecting only 46 female candidates

Table 10.2. *Women candidates in by-elections and general elections (%)*

	Women candidates		Women MPs		
	GE	BE	GE	BE (No./contest)	
1945–50	4.9	4.1	3.8	3.8	(2/47)
1950–51	6.7	2.8	3.4	0.0	(0/14)
1951–55	5.7	7.3	2.7	8.3	(4/44)
1955–59	6.6	8.0	3.8	7.7	(4/49)
1959–64	5.5	2.7	4.0	1.6	(1/61)
1964–66	4.9	4.1	4.6	0.0	(0/13)
1966–70	4.4	7.1	4.1	5.3	(2/37)
1970–74	5.2	5.8	4.1	6.7	(2/30)
1974–74	6.2	0.0	3.6	0.0	(0/1)
1974–79	7.0	9.7	4.3	3.3	(1/30)
1979–83	7.4	8.9	3.0	17.6	(3/17)
1983–87	10.4	11.2	3.5	31.2	(5/16)
1987	12.9	—	6.3	—	
MEAN	6.4	5.9	3.9	6.7	(24/359)

compared with 92 for Labour and 105 for the Liberal–Social Democratic Alliance (see Table 10.2). The increased opportunities for women candidates may be attributed to recent changes in the selection procedures although equally this could be explained by an increase in the number of women coming forward to pursue a Parliamentary career.

Yet until recently the increase in female candidates in general elections did not lead to a parallel rise in the number of women entering Parliament; there remained fewer than thirty women MPs until 1987, when the number of women in the Commons increased to forty-one. The reasons why the proportion of women candidates has risen at a faster rate than the proportion of women MPs can be explained in large part by the type of constituencies for which women were standing: few were selected for potentially winnable seats (Vallance 1988; Lovenduski and Norris 1989).

Yet women are relatively successful in by-elections; twenty-four women entered Parliament through post-war by-elections, or 6.7% of the total contests, compared with only 3.9% of candidates in general elections (see Table 10.2). During Mrs Thatcher's second administration women made up a third of the MPs returned in a by-election: Mrs Ann Clwyd for Cynon Valley; Mrs Virginia Bottomley for Surrey South-West; Elizabeth Shields for Ryedale; Llin

Goulding for Newcastle under Lyme; Rosie Barnes for Greenwich. As a result the number of women in Parliament increased from twenty-three in 1983 to twenty-eight at the time of dissolution. With so few cases it is difficult to explain the reasons for the greater success of women candidates in by-elections, but clearly special circumstances played a part in some contests. One study found that the causes are not related to the electorate. Based on his study of women candidates, using aggregate by-election results from 1923 to 1972, Rasmussen (1981*b*: 23) concluded: 'the British electorate at the macro level appears to believe that women as a group are no different than men as candidates for Parliament; the electorate does not react to them in contrasting fashion.'

Instead it can be suggested that the success for women is related to the more open nature of these contests. In general elections the decline in the number of marginals has resulted in fewer winnable seats open to non-incumbents (Curtice and Steed 1982; 1986). By-election volatility, and the absence of an incumbent, provides greater opportunities for new (female) candidates to break into Parliament. The problem for female representation has not been the number of candidates willing to come forward, as there has been a marked increase in recent years, but the difficulty of getting a winnable seat.

THE EFFECT OF CANDIDATES ON VOTING CHOICE

The issue which remains to be assessed is the impact candidates have on the results. Whether candidates can make a difference in a general election is open to dispute. On the one hand many studies have tended to conclude that in a national campaign the influence of prospective Parliamentary candidates on constituency results is fairly minimal: 'They are mere bearers of party labels, the anonymous footsoldiers in a battle waged far away in the television studios' (Criddle 1988). The conventional wisdom is that, despite the efforts of grassroots organizations, the campaign is fought primarily at the national level, and few can hold out against national and regional party swings. One Labour MP expressed the common view about safe seats: 'You could put a monkey up, and he'd get in if he was Labour' (quoted in Cain, Ferejohn, and Fiorina 1987: 84).

In support of this view Butler and Stokes found that between elections few voters were aware of their representative and few could

little effect on the outcome. In Croydon North-West the relatively unknown Bill Pitt achieved a swing which was close to that for Shirley Williams at Crosby, and greater than Roy Jenkins achieved in Glasgow. In Greenwich, despite all the media hoo-ha about the seat being lost by the 'loony Lesbian London left' represented by Deirdre Woods, the Labour share of the vote fell by only 4%. Journalists treated Chesterfield as a referendum on the left-wing candidature of Tony Benn, analogous to Bermondsey, but the Labour vote was almost unchanged.

In the absence of more convincing evidence, therefore, we can conclude that candidates are likely to have more impact in by-elections than in general elections, given the intense media focus on personality politics, resulting in higher levels of candidate recognition in these contests. Further the choice of candidates is likely to have become more important in recent years, under conditions of partisan dealignment, with the decline of stable by-elections. Nevertheless on balance the media probably tends to place greater weight on the influence of candidates than seems warranted by the evidence. The focus on personalities makes for a good story, but except in exceptional circumstances the choice of candidates is rarely decisive by itself, unless the choice of candidate highlights wider issues, such as general divisions within the party.

MINOR AND FRINGE PARTY CANDIDATES

We have to consider the effects, not just of the major candidates, but also the wide range of minor party and fringe candidates attracted to these contests (see Table 10.4). In the fifties a scattering of independents stood in by-elections, but by the eighties there were often about 8 candidates, in some cases more; Bermondsey and Chesterfield attracted 17 candidates, Fulham 14, and Kensington 15. We can distinguish three different groups: the minor party, fringe, and single-issue candidates. The first group are those from the minor parties with serious political concerns but no Parliamentary representation, such as the National Front, the Green Party, the International Marxist Group, the Workers Revolutionary Party, the New Britain Party, the Communists, and the British Movement. Marxist parties and the National Front became particularly active during

Table 10.4. *Minor and fringe candidates in by-elections*

	Com.	ILP	NF	Oth.	Total	No.BE	Av. per contest
1945–50	3	4	—	19	26	47	0.5
1950–51	1	2	—	2	5	14	0.3
1951–55	1	0	—	4	5	44	0.1
1955–59	1	3	—	12	16	49	0.3
1959–64	6	1	—	37	44	61	0.7
1964–66	0	0	—	10	10	13	0.8
1966–70	6	0	1	25	32	37	0.9
1970–74	1	0	5	30	36	30	1.2
1974–74	0	0	1	1	2	1	2.0
1974–79	1	0	18	65	84	30	2.8
1979–83	1	0	6	78	85	17	5.0
1983–87	2	0	2	117	121	16	7.6
1945–87	23	10	33	400	466	359	1.3

Note: Minor and fringe parties include all except the Conservative and Unionist, Labour/Co-op, Liberal, Social Democrat, Scottish Nationalist, and Plaid Cymru, excluding parties in Northern Ireland. Com = Communist, ILP = Independent Labour Party, NF = National Front.

the late seventies, with violent clashes in some campaigns, although this died down in the eighties.

Secondly there are the fringe candidates, following the long tradition of British eccentricity, led by the veteran Lord David Sutch for the Monster Raving Loony Party and George Weiss for Captain Rainbow Universal Party, long-standing veterans of the process hardened to lost deposits. Fringe candidates include those out to entertain (Woy Jenkins' Student grant's Doubled party, the 'Prisoner: I am not a number' party, the 'Reclassify Sun Newspaper as a Comic' party. Others wish to attract publicity (Cynthia Payne's Payne and Pleasure Party), while others are purely commercial ventures ('Buy your Chesterfield in Thame' party, the 'Connoisseur Wine' party). In between there are the single-issue candidates, which may be serious or frivolous, such as the 'Free Trade Anti-Common Market' party, the 'Death off the Roads: Freight on Rail' party, the 'England Demands Repatriation' party, the 'London Class War' party, the 'Independent Janata' party, the 'Turkish Troops out of Cyprus' party, the 'Yoga and Meditation' party, and the like.

This development has only a marginal effect on the outcome: most minor candidates attract less than a hundred votes. We can divide contests into those with minor party withdrawals (where a minor party candidate contested only the previous contests); minor interventions (where a minor party candidate contested only the by-election); and minor consistents (where a minor party candidate

Table 10.5.   *Minor party share of the vote (%)*

		No.	GF	BE	Change
Minor withdrawals	(GE only)	15	2.6	—	−2.6
Minor consistents	(GE & BE)	52	6.2	6.5	+0.3
Minor interventions	(BE only)	91	—	4.4	+4.4

Note: For a definition of these categories see text. 'Minor parties' includes the total vote for all independent and fringe candidates excluding Conservative, Labour, Liberal, SDP, SNP, and PC candidates.

Table 10.6.   *Lost deposits*

	General Election		By-Election	
	Total no.	% of opposed candidates	Total no.	% of opposed candidates
1945–50	182	10.8	35	24.3
1950–51	461	24.7	5	14.3
1951–55	96	7.0	14	13.2
1955–59	100	7.1	17	12.3
1959–64	116	7.6	61	27.0
1964–66	186	10.6	16	32.7
1966–70	237	13.9	48	34.0
1970–74	408	22.2	49	40.8
1974–74	321	15.0	3	60.0
1974–79	442	19.6	106	60.2
1979–83	1001	38.9	101	67.3
1983–87	—	—	81	50.9
TOTAL	3550	17.4	536	36.4

Source: Craig, (1987).

contested both the previous general election and the by-election). As shown in Table 10.5, minor interventions increased their total share of the vote by less than 5%. Therefore the main change has been in the number of minor candidates, rather than their level of electoral support.

The Representation of the People Act, 1985 attempted to limit the number of frivolous candidates, without unduly restricting minor parties such as the Greens. It was argued that some candidates were running simply for the publicity and commercial gain, notably the free delivery of the electoral address to all households, which lowered the tone of by-elections. For the first time since 1918 Parliament raised the costs of a lost deposit, from £150 to £500, while simultaneously lowering the minimum threshold from 12.5% to 5% of the valid vote (See Table 10.6). This reduced the number of independent and minor party candidates in the 1987 general election but so far it has not acted as a major deterrent in by-elections; from May 1983 to October 1985 there were about eight candidates per contest, while from November 1985 to June 1987 there were seven. Therefore minor and fringe candidates will probably come forward so long as by-elections continue to attract media publicity. On this basis we need to go on to consider the impact of other campaign-specific factors, notably the indirect effect of the media and opinion polls on voting choice.

11

The Role of the Media and Opinion Polls

IN recent years there has been a substantial increase in the number of opinion polls being commissioned, and the amount of media attention devoted to campaigns. In the quiet by-elections of the fifties and sixties press coverage was minimal and opinion polls were the exception rather than the rule; there was only one poll even in such well-known contests as Rochdale in 1958 or Orpington in 1962. Polls became more regular features of by-elections in the seventies but the turning-point came with Warrington. During the more dramatic contests in the eighties there developed an avalanche of polls; during the campaign eight polls were published in Darlington and Croydon North-West, nine in Crosby, ten in Fulham, thirteen in Greenwich, sixteen in Chesterfield, and seventeen in Glasgow Hillhead alone. In a small seat such as Glasgow Hillhead over 10,000 voters were polled in total by different companies, which represents one in five of the electorate. We seem to have reached the stage where opinion polls are not simply recording what is happening in the campaign; they are events in the campaign themselves. This growth reflects broader trends. In the 1987 general election there were 73 nation-wide polls during the campaign, not including at least a hundred constituency polls and eighteen surveys of marginal seats: 'all these extra surveys made 1987, by a considerable margin, the most exhaustively polled election in British history' (Butler and Kavanagh 1988). No wonder that this situation has been referred to as 'saturation polling' (Crewe 1986). In the light of this development we need in this chapter to consider three issues: the role of the media in the campaign, the record of by-election polls, and lastly the indirect effect of these factors on voting choice.

THE ROLE OF THE MEDIA

Media coverage of by-elections has been transformed over the years. In the late forties and fifties, given the predictable outcome, there was minimal attention in the national press; *The Times* would briefly note the reason for the by-election, the moving of the writ, the nomination of the candidates, and the final result, with a few other stories in exceptional circumstances. Television coverage of the campaign started in the late fifties, breaking new ground with the Rochdale by-election in 1958. Press attention gradually increased during the seventies but the early eighties saw a quantum leap in media interest, for example in Warrington there were almost eighty articles in *The Times* and the *Sunday Times* alone, from June to mid-July, not counting correspondence and leading articles.

The content of media coverage can be divided into three broad categories: the 'horse-race', the candidates, and the campaign issues. The 'horse-race' aspect of by-elections tends to dominate the national press, especially in the closing stages, with polls and canvass returns reinforcing speculation about who is ahead. The horse-race has an immediate impact, with individual standard-bearers dramatizing conflict between, or within, the parties, which is difficult to achieve when covering complex party policies, particular local issues, or political speeches (Stovall and Solomon 1984; Broh 1980; Mendelsohn and Crespi 1970; Worcester 1980). Given this focus, to an increasing extent in by-elections opinion polls do not just reflect the campaign events, they are the news. Polls in the public domain act as the handmaidens of journalism, providing an answer to the question preoccupying reporters, campaign agents, party activists, and candidates: 'who will win?'

In the early stages of the campaign press coverage tends to focus on the candidates, their political experience, background, and performance in daily press conferences. Well-known national politicians receive extensive scrutiny, as do those like Peter Tatchell who could be seen to personify internal party divisions. Lastly the press also covers a diverse range of campaign 'issues', broadly interpreted, such as local unemployment in Tyne Bridge, housing conditions in Greenwich, the role of the Militant Tendency in Knowsley North, anti-CND sentiment in Portsmouth South, Scottish nationalism and the poll tax in Glasgow Govan, the activity of black members of the Labour Party in Vauxhall, protests about health service reforms in the Vale of Glamorgan, and so on. In covering these issues journalists often treat by-election features as an opportunity to test public reaction to events in the national news.

Any attempt to assess the effect this media coverage has on the campaign, and on voting behaviour, raises complex and difficult theoretical issues. Journalists often feel that the media play a decisive role in shaping expectations of the race, perceptions of the candidates, and images of the parties, but the evidence is not clear-cut. On the one hand there are contests like Chesterfield where the press mobilized in force; from the initial announcement on 13 November 1983 to the by-election on 1 March *The Times* and the *Sunday Times* ran over seventy stories on the contest, not including correspondence or leading articles. The by-election was high priority: nineteen stories were front-page, while fifty-six stories were on the front or second page. Sixteen polls were commissioned. Yet in Chesterfield according to opinion polls there was little overall change in the position of the parties during the campaign. The media hoop-la had no discernible effect on the flow of the vote.

On the other hand there are contests like Portsmouth South which are relatively quiet in terms of media coverage. In *The Times* and the *Sunday Times* there were nineteen fairly minor articles throughout the race, none treated as front-page news, not even the final result. Only one poll was commissioned. Yet the SDP won Portsmouth South from the Tories. Similarly in Penrith, with minimal press coverage and no published polls, the Alliance increased their vote by 16.7% to come within 1.4 percentage points of taking the seat from the Conservatives. This suggests, not surprisingly, that we can be sceptical about simple theories of media influence which attribute a linear relationship between electoral change and the amount of press coverage devoted to a campaign. Instead we need to explore the conditions under which media coverage, particularly the publicity given to opinion polls, can influence certain types of voter in certain types of campaign.

THE RECORD OF OPINION POLLS

Serious professional polling was started in the mid-thirties in the United States by Gallup, Roper, and Crossley. The first Gallup survey published in Britain concerned the 1938 West Fulham by-election. As the organizer, Dr Henry Durant, recalled the event: 'Edith Summerskill was the Labour candidate. It was a Conservative seat and she upset the Conservatives, as I had forecast, and by a miracle I got it on the nose within one per cent; beginner's luck' (Durant quoted in Worcester 1983: 100).

Gallup went on to predict a Labour victory in the 1945 general election and to establish regular political polling as a feature of British political commentary. Over the years other major companies have expanded the field and continue to provide regular by-election surveys for newspaper clients. Among them National Opinion Polls (NOP) was founded in 1957, Opinion Research Centre (ORC) in 1965, Marplan in 1968 (later International Communications and Marketing Research, ICM), Harris Research in 1968, and Market and Opinion Research International (MORI) in 1969. (For a history see Clemens 1983; Teer and Spence 1973; Hodder-Williams 1970; Kavanagh 1982; Rose 1984.)

The focus on opinion polls in by-elections has increased substantially over the years, with more polls being commissioned and stronger criticisms being voiced about their possible abuse. As a result a number of Private Member's bills have been introduced to ban the publication of polls, or control their activities more tightly, during the period of the campaign. Given this debate there is clearly a need to look carefully at the role of the polls in election campaigns. The major polling companies can justifiably claim a reasonable level of accuracy in predicting the outcome of general elections over the years. There have been certain exceptions, notably in 1970, but usually their estimated results in general elections have been within the accepted standards of sampling error. In contrast the performance of the polls as predictors of by-elections and constituency results has proved more variable, with problems experienced at some stage by all the major companies; MORI at Brecon and Radnor, Gallup at Glasgow Hillhead; Audience Selection at Bermondsey; Marplan at Chesterfield; and BBC 'Newsnight' at Tyne Bridge. But the problem is not just one of particular companies in particular campaigns, for that could be explained as the result of inadequate fieldwork or sample bias. Instead the evidence suggests there is a systematic source of bias; the record of by-election surveys by all the major companies shows a consistent tendency to overestimate support for Labour at the expense of the Alliance; error is not random.

Four basic types of polls are used in British by-elections: cross-sectional surveys, panel surveys, exit polls, and qualitative groups. Cross-sectional surveys are the most common type, usually involving face-to-face interviews with a representative quota sample of 600 to 1,000 respondents, with fieldwork carried out in a constituency over one or two days. The media often treat these polls as predictions of the final result, rather than a snapshot of voting intentions at one moment of time, which can prove misleading since in by-elections there are often sudden shifts in support, even in the last few days. The results of cross-sectional polls should be interpreted dynamically, as part of voting trends rather than as static predictions.

Panel surveys track changes in voter preference over time by repeated waves of interviews. These should provide the most accurate indicator of voting trends, but they suffer from three problems. First, there is likely to be a differential refusal rate, due to the difficulty of recontacting the original respondents, and insuring their continued co-operation, over a series of interviews. Secondly, the sample can become 'corrupted' by repeated contacts; the interview process may heighten respondents' awareness of the campaign and therefore make them unrepresentative of the electorate as a whole. Lastly any undetected flaws in the original sample are repeated in subsequent re-interviews, with no opportunities for correction.

Exit polls, commissioned for television, record how people have voted as they leave the polling station. Exit polls have certain advantages over pre-election surveys; the problem of non-voters, late shifters or the undecideds does not arise since they are carried out on the day of the election amongst a stratified area random sample of voters leaving the polling station. They are usually restricted in scope, asking only a limited number of questions to predict, rather than explain, voting patterns. Nevertheless the possibility of error remains concerning differential refusal rates and the selection and weighting of polling stations.

Lastly, small 'qualitative' focus groups have been used to give detailed comments about how voters are reacting to the campaign. This approach can be useful for probing the values and attitudes of small groups of voters in depth, and it was used for this purpose by the advisers to Tory Central Office in the 1987 election (Tyler 1987). For newspapers, in the tradition of *'vox pop'* interviews, this approach can provide useful journalistic copy. The danger of such groups is to treat the results as though they were based on a large-scale sample. For example in Darlington a panel of thirty-five 'politically representative' members was used by *The Times. The Times* confidently predicted mid-way through the campaign, on the basis of this group, that the Alliance 'were firmly on the road to victory' in Darlington since sixteen members were planning to vote SDP. With qualitative research there is a temptation to 'count heads' as though a small group can provide insights into shifts across the whole constituency.

The principles of sampling for cross-sectional and panel surveys are generally agreed although polling companies differ in their exact methods. Statistically probability samples are the most reliable, with a known margin of error, but in recent years they have been superseded in British polling companies by quota samples. For elections quota samples have practical advantages in terms of speed, and therefore closeness to the final result (Worcester 1984). As John Barton, the head of National Opinion Polls (NOP), remarked apropos by-election polls: 'The lesson all of us have learned over the years is that it's really more important to go on asking questions to the very last minute than it is to worry about the fine points of sampling—although by all means worry about sampling if you can' (Barton 1982: 75).

This method selects respondents who fit certain quota controls, which reflect social divisions within the population (for example in a constituency if a third of the electorate is under thirty, then a third of all interviews are drawn from this age group). The major companies employ slightly different fieldwork procedures: Gallup send their interviewers to a random selection of streets, covering between 50 to 100 sampling points in the constituency, then restrict their quota controls to age and gender. National Opinion Polls (NOP) use interlocking quotas based on age, gender, and (Market Research) social class, with the addition of employment status for women. Harris Research prefer to use housing tenure rather than social class, giving their interviewers considerable discretion about where they contact voters within each ward. In quota samples fieldworkers are assigned to representative sampling points within the constituency, but have discretion to select people for interview who fulfil their quota controls. In random surveys interviewers are not allowed to substitute from a list of individual names drawn by chance from the electoral register. Quota samples avoid the need for repeated call-backs but the element of discretion may introduce interviewer bias, if they avoid contacting those who might appear more difficult or uncooperative, such as ethnic minorities, the very old, and the young unemployed.

To gauge the accuracy of opinion polls based on these methods we can employ three measures: predicted winner, average error, and systematic error. First we can use the criteria common to journalists, politicians, and the public: do the polls predict the correct winner? This guideline is straightforward but limited; a poll might be accurate within the accepted standards of sampling error but call the wrong winner in a close race. Or they might predict the successful party but overestimate their lead. It is therefore preferable to compare the 'average error' per party, the mean of the differences between the predicted percentage and the actual vote percentage, ignoring the sign. This indicates the size of the error but conceals the direction of any bias. Lastly there is 'systematic error', which takes account of biases by comparing the mean error of the predicted versus actual vote taking account of the sign (see Table 11.1).

In presenting the results the media often fail to emphasize sufficiently that errors can arise from various sources. All surveys are subject to sampling errors, the extent to which the results from a sample may differ from those that would have been obtained if all voters in the constituency had been interviewed. In the theory of probability due to sampling error at best we would expect surveys to be accurate to within (+ or −) 3% on the average random sample of about 1,000 respondents at the accepted 95% confidence level (that is 95 times out of a 100). Clustering within a constituency, through a limited range of sampling points, would increase this chance of error. Where the size of sample is down to 750 or 600, not uncommon in constituency surveys, then we would expect the level of sampling error to increase to (+ or −) 4% or 5%. For example if a survey of 750 voters found that 30% intended to vote Conservative, we would expect that very probably (95 times out of a 100) samplings would be somewhere between 26% and 34%. This wide margin is frequently ignored, or at least understated, by the media, with the aim of a simple prediction.

Yet sampling error, although the most frequently quoted, is not necessarily the most common source of error. Polling is both an art and a science. The spurious precision of the commonly quoted '(+ or −) 3% sampling error' statement often serves to disguise the way in which other factors, such as the way in which an item is phrased, may have a major impact on the results. Different company practices, such as the order of the voting intentions questions, and whether a 'leaning' question is introduced to squeeze the proportion of undecideds and refusals, may influence estimates of the party share of the vote.

Even with a large enough sample to minimize sampling error,

to estimate voting intentions the pollster has to cope with the apathetic who will not vote, the belligerent who will not say, and the undecided who do not know. Pollsters have to carry out the interviews close enough to election day to minimize last-minute swings in voting intentions. As suggested by Paul Perry, head of Gallup in the United States, polling appears straightforward enough but really it is not very easy to do any of these things (Perry 1979). Given the limitations of survey methods, contests such as West Derbyshire or Brecon and Radnor, where only a few hundred votes separates the winners from the losers, are strictly too close to call. As one of the founders of Gallup polls in Britain, Dr Henry Durant, remarked: 'The surprise is not that we should get it wrong, the wonder is that we get it right at all' (quoted in Worcester 1983).

GENERAL ELECTION POLLS

Yet if we examine the general election surveys taken closest to polling day, they often do get it right to within a couple of percentage points, with certain notable exceptions such as in 1970 when nearly all the polling organizations were way off mark. If we look at the record of commercial survey organizations in British general elections since the war two-thirds of the final polls have proved accurate within the (+ or −) 2% margin of average error usually taken as the accepted standard of sampling tolerance. Of the remaining third only three have average errors above 3%, including two by Marplan in the early seventies and one by the *Daily Express*, although all faced problems in 1951 and 1970 (see Tables 11.1 and 11.2). There is no evidence that the polls have become significantly more, or less accurate, over the years, despite technological changes in survey techniques. Nor do the results suggest that there are any systematic differences by polling company; Gallup, with the longest experience, has an excellent record but in the 1979 General Election they produced the least accurate of the predictions while Marplan, the least successful in the early seventies, produced the closest result.

Over the years systematic error has provided some difficulties; from 1966 to 1983 there was a consistent tendency for most of the final polls to overestimate the share of the vote of the party which had previously been in government. Why this should be the case is not clear. If this was a methodological problem it was one shared

Table 11.1. *Accuracy of final general election polls*

Year	Mean error on Con.lead over Lab. (%)	Average error per party (%)	Number of final polls	Total no. of campaign polls
1945	3.5	1.6	1	1
1950	3.2	1.5	2	2
1951	6.0	2.6	3	3
1955	1.1	0.7	2	2
1959	1.0	1.0	3	21
1964	1.8	1.3	4	23
1966	3.9	1.7	4	26
1970	6.6	2.6	5	25
1974 (Feb.)	2.4	1.6	5	22
1974 (Oct.)	4.2	1.3	4	23
1979	1.7	0.9	4	28
1983	4.2	1.2	6	47
1987	3.0	1.1	7	39

Note: General election polls published by the major companies excluding surveys of individual and marginal constituencies.

Source: Worcester (1984); Crewe (1983).

by all the polls. If this was due to last-minute shifts in voting intentions in the last few days it is not apparent why this would be in the anti-government direction. In 1987, contrary to trends, there was a slight tendency for five out of the final seven polls to underestimate the government's share of the vote, and overestimate Labour's. Whatever the reason, this seems to support the conclusions of William Buchanan's general assessment of the accuracy of polls (1986): 'Whenever the polls are wrong, they are all wrong.'

BY-ELECTION POLLS

Compared with nation-wide polls, those in by-elections have a mixed record in recent years. The major organizations operating throughout the mid-fifties were Gallup and NOP, whose by-election polls were within the accepted margin of error. In the thirty-six by-elections where NOP or Gallup made predictions, from 1957 to 1966, the polls called the wrong winner on only four occasions: South Dorset and Middlesbrough West in 1962, which turned out to be unexpected Labour gains: Devizes in 1964, which the Tories retained with a

Table 11.2. *Accuracy of final general election polls by company*

Year	Poll	Systematic error			Pty.		Av. error
		Con.	LSDP	Lab.	lead		per party
1945	Gallup	+1.6	+1.3	−1.8	Lab.	1.6	1.6
1950	Gallup	+0.5	+1.3	−1.8	Lab.	1.2	
	D. Exp.	+1.5	+1.3	−2.8	Con.	1.9	1.5
1951	Gallup	+1.5	+0.5	−1.8	Con.	1.3	
	RSL	−2.0	+3.8	−5.8	Con.	3.9	2.4
	D. Exp.	+2.0	+1.0	−2.8	Con.	1.9	
1955	Gallup	+1.3	−1.5	+1.1	Con.	1.3	
	D. Exp.	+0.3	−0.5	+0.9	Con.	0.6	1.0
1959	Gallup	−0.3	−1.6	+1.9	Con.	1.3	
	NOP	−0.8	+2.4	−0.5	Con.	1.2	1.1
	D.Exp.	+0.3	−1.1	+0.8	Con.	0.7	
1964	RSL	+2.1	−3.3	+1.2	Lab.	2.2	
	NOP	+1.4	−4.0	+2.6	Lab.	2.7	
	Gallup	−0.4	−0.8	+1.2	Lab.	0.8	2.3
	D.Exp.	+1.6	+0.5	−1.1	Con.	1.1	
1966	RS	+0.2	−1.2	+1.0	Lab.	0.8	
	D.Exp.	−4.0	−1.4	+5.4	Lab.	3.6	
	NOP	+0.2	−2.1	+1.9	Lab.	1.4	1.8
	Gallup	−1.4	−0.9	+2.3	Lab.	1.5	
1970	ORC	+0.3	−2.0	+1.7	Con.	1.3	
	Harris	−0.2	−4.0	+4.2	Lab.	2.8	
	NOP	−2.2	−2.1	+4.3	Lab.	2.9	2.9
	Gallup	−4.2	−1.0	+5.2	Lab.	3.5	
	Marplan	−4.7	−1.6	+6.3	Lab.	4.2	
1974	ORC	+0.9	+5.1	−1.3	Con.	2.4	
(Feb.)	Harris	+1.4	+1.4	−2.8	Con.	1.8	
	NOP	+0.7	+2.4	−2.5	Con.	1.9	2.2
	Gallup	+0.7	+1.8	−0.5	Con.	1.0	
	Marplan	−2.3	+5.8	−3.5	Con.	3.9	
1974	ORC	−2.3	+0.7	+1.6	Lab.	1.5	
(Oct.)	Harris	−2.1	−0.7	+2.8	Lab.	1.9	
	Gallup	−0.7	−0.6	+1.3	Lab.	0.9	1.7
	Marplan	−3.4	−0.2	+3.6	Lab.	2.4	
1979	Gallup	−1.9	−0.6	+3.3	Con.	1.9	
	Marplan	−0.1	−0.6	+0.8	Con.	0.5	
	NOP	+1.1	−1.6	+1.3	Con.	1.3	1.1
	MORI	+0.1	+0.9	−0.7	Con.	0.6	

Table 11.2. *continued*

Year	Poll	Systematic error			Pty. lead	Av. Error per party
		Con.	LSDP	Lab.		
1983	AS	+1.0	+3.0	−5.0	Con. 3.0	
	Harris	+3.0	—	−3.0	Con. 2.0	
	Gallup	+1.5	—	−1.5	Con. 1.0	
	Marplan	+2.0	—	−2.0	Con. 1.3	1.5
	NOP	+3.0	—	−3.0	Con. 2.0	
	MORI	—	—	—	Con. 0.0	
1987	AS	−0.3	+2.5	−2.7	Con. 1.3	
	Harris	−1.3	+3.5	−2.7	Con. 2.0	
	Gallup	−2.3	+2.5	−0.2	Con. 1.5	
	Marplan	−1.3	+3.5	−2.7	Con. 2.0	1.6
	NOP	−1.3	+3.5	−2.7	Con. 2.0	
	MORI	+0.7	+0.5	−1.7	Con. 0.7	
AVERAGE		−0.1	−0.1	+0.4	1.9	

Note: AS = Audience Selection.

Source: Calculated from Worcester (1984); Crewe (1983); *The Times* (1987).

highly marginal majority; and Leyton West with the greatest margin of polling error, which the Conservatives gained in 1965. There were only sporadic polls throughout 1957 to 1962, but the successful prediction by NOP of the Liberal victory in Orpington (despite underestimating the Liberal vote by 11%) led to a flurry of polling activity in subsequent contests throughout 1962–64. The average margin of error for all the polls during this period was 2.6 percentage points, with a slight tendency to overestimate the vote for the two main parties at the expense of the Liberals and others (see Table 11.3).

Table 11.3. *Average error in NOP and Gallup by-election polls (%)*

	No.	Con.	Lab.	LSDP	Others	All
1957–66	44	+0.5	+1.1	−0.5	−1.0	2.6
1966–79	32	+1.2	+1.5	−1.3	−2.1	2.8
1979–87	37	+1.7	+5.9	−6.9	−0.2	5.4

Note: Where two polls have been taken by the same company only final poll is included in the above result.

Source: Teer and Spence (1973).

Since the mid-sixties, despite the greater experience of polling organizations, refinements of technique and technological developments, the accuracy of by-election predictions has fallen (see Table 11.3). In recent years Gallup and NOP polls have tended to overestimate the Conservative and Labour vote at the expense of the Liberals (subsequently the Alliance) (Tables 11.4 and 11.5). Only the NOP polls at Glasgow Hillhead and Croydon North-West, and the Gallup poll at Fulham, approached the margin of error achieved during the mid-fifties.

Table 11.4. *Average error in NOP by-election polls, 1979–1987 (%)*

	Con.	Lab.	LSDP	Others	Av.	Days to BE	N.
Bermondsey	+5.5	+10.9	−32.4	−0.4	16.4	8	994
Warrington	+2.9	+11.6	−13.4		9.3	7	739
Portsm'th S.	+8.4	+8.8	−12.5	—	7.7	4	723
Chesterfield	−1.1	+8.5	−6.7	−0.7	4.3	3	1038
Brecon/Rad.	−4.7	+7.7	−2.8	−0.2	3.9	4	873
Darlington	−6.9	+1.5	+6.5	−1.1	4.0	2	—
Croydon NW	+1.5	+5.0	−5.0	−1.5	3.3	3	732
Fulham	−0.9	−4.4	+6.2	−0.9	3.1	15	732
Crosby	−4.8	+4.5	+0.9	−0.6	2.7	2	748
G'gow H'd	−2.6	+2.1	+0.3	−0.2	1.3	1	1048
AVERAGE	−0.2	+5.6	−5.9	+1.1	5.6	5	847

Note: The percentage point error is the difference between the predicted and actual result. Where there are alternative NOP polls the one closest to the election date is included in the above.

Not all these by-election polls should be taken as predictive, since strictly speaking only polls with fieldwork carried out within three or four days of the election can be seen as providing a forecast of the result. Nevertheless if we take the benchmark used by journalists and politicians, of whether these polls would have got the winner right, one or both failed in Bermondsey, Portsmouth South, Brecon and Radnor, Croydon North-West, and Glasgow Hillhead. Of course Brecon and Radnor was something of an elephant's graveyard for all pollsters, with MORI predicting an 18 percentage point Labour lead in a poll published in the *Daily Mail* the day before

Table 11.5.   *Average error in Gallup by-election polls, 1979–1987 (%)*

	Con.	Lab.	LSDP	Others	Av.	Days to BE	N.
Warrington	+2.0	+13.6	−14.9	—	10.2	12	1,001
Chesterfield	+14.4	—	−10.7	−3.7	7.2	40	1,000
G'gow Hill'd	+0.4	+7.6	−7.4	+1.5	4.2	3	943
Ryedale	−2.3	+5.6	−3.3	—	3.7	5	—
W. Derb.	−0.5	+7.2	−5.4	—	3.5	5	—
Mitcham	−0.1	+6.1	−4.9	−1.3	3.1	2	—
Croydon NW	+2.0	+1.5	−3.0	−0.5	1.8	2	1,010
Fulham	+1.6	−0.9	+1.7	−1.4	1.4	20	740
AVERAGE	+2.2	+5.1	−6.0	−1.1	4.2	11	939

Note: The Gallup poll closest to the election date is included in the above.

the result, which showed a 2% lead for the Alliance. But MORI is not alone: every company has had its equivalent where it was out of line with trends in the other polls or the final results: for NOP it was Chesterfield, for Gallup it was Glasgow Hillhead, for BBC exit polls it was Tyne Bridge.

It could be suggested that the margin of error has increased over the years owing to changes in methodology, such as that NOP and Gallup were completing fieldwork earlier in the campaign, or using smaller samples. Yet this explanation can be discounted; what is notable in recent years is the consistency of the error by all the major polling organizations over a series of contests (see Table 11.6). The final by-election polls by all the major companies show a systematic tendency to overestimate the Labour vote, producing an average error of 3.3 percentage points.

We would expect that exit polls would prove highly accurate, given that they do not have to cope with the abstainers, the undecided, and the last-minute switchers, and the record of the BBC 'Newsnight' surveys shows this to be so, despite exceptional cases such as Tyne Bridge (see Table 11.7).

We can therefore conclude that over the years, as the number of by-election polls has increased, the record of accuracy amongst all the major companies has decreased. Why? Is this due to changes in polling methodology or changes in the electorate? On the one hand it could be the result of the expansion in the number of polls undertaken, with more constituency surveys being carried out by

Table 11.6.   *Average error in final by-election polls, 1979–1987 (%)*

	Days before BE	Con.	Lab.	LSDP	Others	Av.	Polling company
Bermondsey	1	+0.5	+5.9	−15.4	+12.4	8.6	AS
Brecon/Rad.	1	−4.0	+12.0	−8.0	—	5.9	MORI
Chesterfield	1	−1.1	+8.5	−6.7	−0.7	4.3	NOP
Darlington	2	−6.9	+1.5	+6.5	−1.1	4.0	NOP
Croydon NW	1	−2.5	+4.0	−4.0	−2.5	3.3	MORI
Darlington	2	−0.9	−3.5	+4.5	−0.1	2.2	POP
Crosby	1	−3.8	+1.5	−0.1	+2.4	1.7	MORI
G'gow Hillhead	1	−2.6	+2.1	+0.6	—	1.3	NOP
G'gow Hillhead	1	−5.6	+0.1	−0.4	+1.0	1.8	MORI
Fulham	6	−1.9	+0.6	+1.2	+0.1	0.9	Harris
AVERAGE		−2.2	+3.2	−2.0	+0.8	3.3	

Note: Polls with fieldwork in the last two days of the campaign are included in the above, excluding exit polls on the day.
   AS = Audience Selection; POP = Political & Opinion Polls.

Table 11.7.   *Average error in BBC 'Newsnight' exit polls (%)*

	Con.	Lab.	LSDP	Others	Av.
Tyne Bridge	+2.0	−7.8	+7.3	—	5.7
G'gow Hillhead	−4.6	+3.1	+2.6	−1.0	3.4
Croydon NW	+2.5	+4.0	−4.0	−2.5	3.3
Chesterfield	+3.4	+0.4	−3.1	−1.7	2.3
Knowsley N.	−0.4	+3.8	−2.0	—	2.2
Crosby	−2.9	+3.5	—	−0.6	1.8
Fulham	−0.9	−2.4	+3.2	+0.1	1.7
Brecon/Radnor	−2.4	−0.8	+3.3	−0.2	1.6
Greenwich	+3.0	−1.0	+2.0	—	1.5
Bermondsey	−0.5	+2.9	−0.7	−1.7	1.4
W. Derbyshire	−1.6	+0.2	+1.6	—	1.1
Darlington	+0.4	+0.6	−1.9	+0.9	0.9
MEAN	0.0	−0.5	+0.7	−0.7	2.2

Source: Payne, Brown, and Hanna (1986).

market research companies without previous experience of political fieldwork. Yet smaller and less experienced companies may get closer to the results than the established organizations; in Brecon and Radnor, for example, Beaufort Research had the lowest margin of error. In addition this cannot explain why organizations with the reputation and experience of Gallup and NOP consistently have results with higher levels of average error in by-elections than in general elections.

It could be suggested that this is caused partly by the change from random to quota methods, since at the constituency level it is more difficult to establish the accurate demographic information necessary for quotas. Often annual or quarterly government statistics which are available nationally, regionally, or by county are not released by constituency. Yet although quota sampling poses particular difficulties at the constituency level, with sufficient care these problems are not insurmountable.

Others have suggested that polling companies tend to concentrate their resources in too limited a range of sampling points within a constituency, or to reduce sample sizes beyond the minimum acceptable, or to use imported fieldworkers who are unfamiliar with the area. In difficult constituencies (the sprawl of Ryedale, or the social divisions within Fulham, for example, may cause problems) polling methods and organizational resources may prove inadequate. Yet these practical problems, whilst they might produce inaccuracies, should not produce the sort of systematic bias which we have observed where most major polling organizations have a consistent tendency to underestimate support for the Liberals (and Alliance).

To explain these systematic trends therefore we have to turn to changes in the electorate. The problem is that in by-elections, with a more volatile electorate, polling methods are inadequate to the task expected of them by journalists and the public. Polls can document trends in different stages of the campaign, as shown by the consistency of many of the polls with each other. But it is difficult for polls to predict the final outcome, given the last-minute shifts of support characteristic of many by-elections. All cross-sectional polls can give is a snapshot in time of voter intentions, and a series of polls provides an indication of trends. Where by-elections are stable, as during many contests in the fifties and early sixties, then the polls will be more in line with the actual result. Where by-elections are volatile then polls can monitor, but not predict, change. As Richard Rose remarked in the light of the failure of the polls to get near the Brecon and Radnor result:

There is no alternative to opinion polls if we want to know how the electorate is moving. But they suffer because their audience is either too credulous or too sceptical ... More than at any time since 1923 Britain faces a three-party race. An increasingly volatile electorate can move in many ways and falsify predictions. (Rose 1986.)

In this respect by-elections can be seen as similar to primaries in the United States, where the polls also have a poor record of prediction; it has been found that a lot can happen in the the closing days, if not the closing hours, of a campaign (Mendelsohn and Crespi 1970). Given reasonable sampling techniques the core voters, with stable voting preferences, do not pose a major problem to pollsters. The main difficulty lies in estimating the voting intentions of other groups, including the abstainers who will not turn out, the tacticals who may change their vote depending on the position of the parties, and the floaters who are undecided. We therefore need to go on to understand the types of voter which cause this volatility.

12

Abstainers, Tacticals, and Floating Voters

To understand changes in by-elections we can distinguish four main groups in the electorate according to the certainty and stability of their vote. By certainty we mean whether voters are open to change their minds during the course of the campaign or whether they feel committed to their choice. The more voters are willing to reconsider the alternatives, the greater the potential for dramatic shifts in support in the last few days before polling. By stability we mean whether voters are consistent over a series of elections. We can outline these concepts and then examine the empirical basis of this classification.

Core voters can be seen as the most certain and stable in their electoral choice; at an early stage of the campaign they have decided how they are going to vote, and they would not consider switching even if their candidate had no chance of winning the seat. These are the bedrock supporters, the 'stand-patters', voting consistently over two or three successive elections. Core voters can be expected to have developed a general party loyalty, understood as an instrumental evaluation of government performance over time, and therefore to be concentrated amongst older voters who have experience of successive governments. Electoral outcomes can be viewed as short-term deviations around a stable baseline of core voters, the normal vote of the electorate. Given trends in partisan dealignment since the mid-sixties we need to see how many voters remain in this category in by-elections.

Tactical voters can be seen as less certain and stable in their electoral choice; at an early stage of the campaign they have decided who they would like to support as their first choice, but they would consider switching to their second choice, if it would keep out the party they most dislike. There has been considerable speculation about the effect of tactical voting in campaigns like Greenwich and Ryedale, but there have been few systematic studies of the conditions necessary to generate this shift.

The third group within the electorate consists of *floating* voters, those who intend to vote but remain unsure which party to support. Floaters may be totally undecided, or they may be leaning or swither-

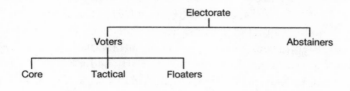

FIG. 12.1.   Typology of the electorate

ing (to use Miller's term) between two possible preferences (W. L. Miller *et al.* 1990).[1] A Conservative dissatisfied with the government's mid-term performance may be leaning towards the Social and Liberal Democrats; or a traditional Labour voter in Glasgow, disenchanted with party policy, may be considering the Scottish Nationalists; or in the absence of a Green candidate an environmentalist might consider the Democrats.

Lastly there are the *abstainers*, who will not participate, one of the largest groups in by-elections. Where there is differential abstention this can have a dramatic effect on the outcome. We therefore need to explore how many voters fall into these categories in by-elections. Who are the tacticals? What distinguishes floating voters? To simplify the presentation, the detailed analysis will focus on the 1986 surveys in Fulham, Ryedale, and West Derbyshire, noting where this differs, if at all, with the results in the other surveys.

CORE VOTERS IN GENERAL ELECTIONS

Panel studies indicate that between successive pairs of general elections about two-thirds of the electorate can be considered core voters, consistently voting for the major parties, or consistently

---

[1] Rose and McAllister (1986) draw the distinction between stable voters, who do not change their behaviour from one election to the next; mobile voters, who in turn can be classified as those who move in and out of the ranks of voters; floating voters, who have moved between parties in the immediate past; and wobbling voters, who are unsure whether to vote the same or float to another party. Heath, Jowell, and Curtice (1985) define floating voters as those who reportedly made up their minds during the campaign, while party loyalists were those who made up their minds a long time ago.

abstaining; the proportion was 66% for 1966–70, 59% for 1970–Feb. 1974, 65% for Oct. 1974–1979 and 61% for 1983–7 (Heath, Jowell and Curtice 1987; Crewe 1985). This general pattern shows no consistent trends towards greater volatility over the last twenty years. Studies found the Conservative Party had a higher retention rate than Labour, while the Liberal/Alliance vote has proved the softest. If we exclude the abstainers, from 1959 to 1983 about half the electorate provided the parties with consistent support over successive pairs of elections (Rose and McAllister 1986).

Yet over more than two successive general elections we would expect a decline in the proportion of stable voters. In a longitudinal panel study covering six general elections, from 1959 to 1979, Himmelweit *et al.* found consistency to be the exception; only 30% of the electorate came to the same decision throughout the period, with the most frequent switch from voter to abstention, and vice versa. In each general election Himmelweit and colleagues found considerable movement to and from the Liberals, who acted as a half-way house between the major parties. Further Himmelweit *et al.* (1985) found that when voters switched parties this was not due to apathy; rather they disliked some aspect of the party they had previously supported, or were positively drawn towards the other side.

If we turn to panel-survey estimates of volatility *within*, rather than between, general elections, most sources suggest that between 20% and 30% of the electorate change their voting intentions from the start to the end of the campaign, depending on the particular election. The most detailed panel study of the 1987 general election (W. L. Miller *et al*, 1990), suggested that during the campaign one in five (21%) changed their voting intention during the campaign, including 13% who switched party, and 8% who did not have a preference for one party above all others at the start. This confirms the estimates of the BBC 'Newsnight' general election panel where 21% were found to change their voting intentions during the 1987 campaign (see Table 12.1). In the BBC panel Labour and the Conservatives were particularly successful in retaining over 90% of their original supporters, while the Alliance vote proved softer (Norris 1987a:464). A similar pattern was found in the MORI panel for

Table 12.1. *Changes in voting intentions during the 1987 general election campaign (%)*

| | POLL II | | | | | | | |
	Con.	Lab.	LSDP	Other	DK	Ref.	Ab.	%
POLL I								
Con.	94.5	1.5	3.2	—	0.8	—	—	100
Lab.	2.7	92.0	3.6	0.4	1.1	—	0.4	100
LSDP	3.1	9.3	80.9	0.7	2.4	—	0.2	100
Other	9.5	19.0	19.0	52.3	—	—	—	100
DK	21.2	32.2	21.2	1.6	17.5	4.1	1.6	100
Ref.	23.9	16.4	13.4	—	14.9	31.3	—	100
Ab.	—	10.0	30.0	—	—	—	60.0	100

Note: For survey details see Appendix.

Source: BBC 'Newsnight' Panel Survey Poll I, 14–17 May 1987; Poll II, 7–8 June 1987, N. 1,977.

the *Sunday Times* where 17% changed during the campaign, including 9% who switched parties.[2] The extent of electoral change was often under-estimated, as the nation-wide opinion polls seemed fairly stable throughout the campaign. The flux of the vote had little impact on the outcome because the change was in multiple directions, rather than flowing consistently towards Labour or the Alliance.

In terms of trends over time the evidence from the British General Election Studies suggests that volatility within campaigns shows some increase during the seventies, reaching a peak in 1979, before falling back slightly during the eighties. The proportion of respondents who reported deciding during the campaign averaged 14% from 1964 to 1970, increasing to 22% in the 1974 elections, 28% in 1979, before falling back to 22% in 1983 and 21% in 1987. The proportion who 'seriously thought of voting for another party dur-

[2] See Appendix for details. It should be noted that the BBC 'Newsnight' panel seems likely to have underestimated Conservative support, which puts into question the accuracy of the overall *level* of party support, but this should not affect the estimate of *change* during the campaign.

MORI used a nationally representative panel of 1,521 respondents first established 11–14 May 1987, then recontacted on three successive occasions. The final MORI panel on 27–28 May included 1,188 interviews (77% response rate). In both panels the data for the final wave were weighted so that they remained representative of voting intentions in the first wave.

ing the campaign' averaged about 22% from 1964 to October 1974, increasing to 31% in 1979, 25% in 1983, and 27% in 1987.

From what we have already established we would expect less stable voting behaviour during by-election campaigns, although it is difficult to make direct comparisons with the available data. In the series of BBC 'Newsnight' surveys there was a fairly consistent pattern across all constituencies: we can estimate that on average about 37% of electors can be seen as *core*, defined as those with a voting intention which they were unwilling to change (see Table 12.2). Almost as many were *potential tacticals* (30%) who would

Table 12.2.   *Types of voters in the electorate (%)*

Constituency	Core	Tactical	Floating	Abst.	N.
Ryedale II	35	31	12	22	784
W. Derbyshire II	36	24	10	30	690
Bolton W.	37	34	6	23	655
Bristol W.	37	35	5	23	761
Welwyn/Hatfield	41	35	7	17	598
Knowsley N. I	37	33	13	17	736
Mitcham/Morden	37	28	5	29	620
Dudley West	33	29	9	29	656
Greenwich I	37	25	10	28	671
Truro I	38	23	10	29	632
Average above	37	30	9	24	6,803
GE I	39	37	9	15	2,401

Note: Identical questions on tactical voting and abstention were not available in the first six BBC 'Newsnight' constituency surveys. See Appendix for details of surveys.

Source: BBC 'Newsnight' Surveys.

consider switching to keep out the party they most disliked, although we would expect many of these to vote for their party of first choice unless the necessary conditions were met to mobilize the potential tactical shift. We can estimate that about 9% of the electorate were floaters, who did not know who they would choose during the course of the campaign. The proportion of floaters was slightly higher in the by-election than the marginal constituency surveys, which is consistent with the theory that in lower-salience by-elections voters may be more willing to consider deviating from their habitual voting patterns. Lastly about a quarter (24%) said they intended to abstain, although this figure probably represents an underestimate of those who will actually abstain on the day. These proportions are relatively similar to the results of the BBC Newsnight General Election panel except that there were slightly fewer non-voters, as we might expect given the lower turn-out characteristic of by-elections.

ABSTAINERS

One of the most predictable features of these contests is the decline in electoral participation, evident in all but twenty-three post-war by-elections. In most by-elections about two-thirds (62%) of the electorate participate, a decline of about 14% from the previous general election, (see Fig. 12.1 and Table 12.3). There are substantial

Table 12.3.   *By-election turn-out 1945–1987 (%)*

	Abstainers	Voters	Decline GE to BE
Lab. 1945	38	62	−9
Lab. 1950	31	69	−16
Con. 1951	41	59	−22
Con. 1955	36	64	−12
Con. 1959	36	64	−15
Lab. 1964	36	64	−12
Lab. 1966	38	62	−13
Con. 1970	44	56	−12
Lab. 1974	44	57	−13
Con. 1979	44	56	−15
Con. 1983	37	64	−10
MEAN	39	62	−14

differences between constituencies; turn-out has been lowest among Labour inner-city seats, particularly in London; fewer than one in three voters turned out in by-elections such as Shoreditch in 1958, Newham South in 1974, and Islington North in 1969, while fewer than one in four voted in Southwark and Peckham in 1982, Tyne Bridge in 1985, and Glasgow Central in 1980.

Constituency turn-out can be explained by a range of factors;

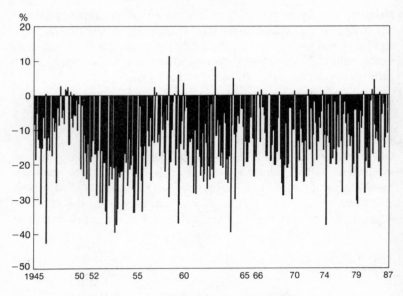

Fig. 12.2.　Change in by-election turn-out, 1945–1987

the perceived closeness of the race, the extent of media coverage, the accuracy of the electoral register, the number of minor party candidates, the effectiveness of local party organizations and the timing of the by-election (for a detailed discussion see Mughan 1986*a*). Regression analysis indicates that by-election turn-out is significantly related to whether a constituency changed hands, the marginality in the seat in the previous general election, and interventions by third parties (see Table 12.4). We would expect participation to increase in close contests where electors had greater incentives to vote, and where interest is likely to be stimulated by extensive media coverage and more intensive canvassing drives by parties to identify and mobilize support. Minor party competition may stimulate turn-out by increasing the choice available to electors; nationalist parties seem particularly successful in mobilising supporters who would otherwise abstain.

Where equal numbers of supporters from all parties fail to participate this will have little effect on the outcome, but commentators suggest that differential turn-out may have played a decisive role

Table 12.4. *Association between by-election turn-out and constituency factors*

	Pearson correlation (*r*)	Stand. Betas	Sig. *T*	Multiple *R*	Adj. *R²*
Turn-out GE	.61 **	.58	.000		
Seat change	.20 **	.12	.003		
Majority in GE	.17 **	.12	.007		
Third party inter.	.16 *	.10	.011	.64	.40

Note: The Standardized Betas are produced using multiple regression, ordinary least squared analysis with step-wise entry.
**Sig. $p = .01$, *Sig. $p = .05$.

in certain contests, with Labour experiencing difficulties mobilizing its potential support in Newcastle under Lyme in 1986, and Ashfield in 1977, while the Conservatives had problems at Penrith in 1983. Differential turn-out is likely because a series of studies have established that political participation is strongly related to demographic factors, notably education, social class, home ownership, ethnicity, and age (see, for example, Wolfinger and Rosenstone 1980; Milbrath 1966; Verba and Nie 1972). This pattern was confirmed in the BBC by-election surveys; manual workers were almost twice as likely to abstain as those in the professional and managerial socio-economic group (see Table 12.5). Education was strongly related to voting; 33% of non-graduates abstained compared with 18% of graduates. As other studies have found, there were strong variations by age group; young voters were more than twice as likely to abstain as the elderly, indeed younger voters were almost evenly divided between voters and abstainers. Younger voters are likely to be more geographically mobile, and have weaker ties with the constituency. As shown in Table 12.5, this social bias was higher in by-elections than general elections, since greater numbers of occasional voters drop out in these low-stimulus contests.

Therefore one factor leading to Labour's relatively poor by-election performance is that much of their potential support is concentrated in the groups most likely to abstain: manual workers, council tenants, the unemployed, and the young. Even if the Labour Party developed the most effective grassroots organization to get out the vote, they face greater difficulties in mobilizing their potential vote. In contrast the Alliance support has been found to be particularly

Table 12.5.   *Abstainers and voters by social group (%)*

	By-elections 1986[a]		General election 1983[b]	
	Voters	Abstainers	Voters	Abstainers
All	69	31	83	17
Education				
College	83	18	91	9
Non-College	67	33	83	17
Socio-economic group				
Prof./manag.	81	19	87	13
Other non-manual	70	30	86	14
Manual	65	36	81	19
Age group				
18–24	52	48	73	27
25–49	68	32	84	16
50–64	75	25	88	16
65+	78	22	84	16
Gender				
Men	71	29	83	18
Women	67	33	84	16
Employment status				
Employed	71	30		
Unemployed	55	45		
Students	63	37		
Housing tenure				
Owner-occ.	72	28	85	15
Private tenant	67	33	81	19
Council tenant	62	38	80	20
N.	1,330	599	3,295	660

Notes: a. Voting intentions Ryedale, West Derbyshire, and Fulham, Mar. 1986.
    b. Recalled vote.
Sources: British General Elections Study 1983; BBC 'Newsnight' constituency surveys.

strong among the public sector professionals, with higher levels of education (Heath, Jowell and Curtice 1985). The strong relationship between education and political participation would help to explain why the Alliance were more successful than the Labour Party in mobilizing their potential by-election support. This also helps to explain why by-election opinion polls which report voting intentions, without taking into account probable turn-out are likely to overestimate Labour at the expense of the Alliance.

TACTICAL VOTERS

Tactical voting has often been treated as a new phenomenon but it is a long-established feature of British voting behaviour, evident in some form in every general election since 1959 (Curtice and Steed 1988: 335–41). Traditionally in general elections the Liberals have often suffered from the third party squeeze; they have had to convince the electorate that supporting the Liberals was not merely a 'wasted' vote. Tactical voting was the subject of extensive speculation in the 1987 campaign, with supporting articles from Eric Hobsbawm in *Marxism Today*, Stuart Weir in *New Socialist*, Colin Crouch and Hugo Young in the *Guardian*, and the foundation of campaign groups such as TV '87 to encourage the practice (see Butler and Kavanagh 1988: 97–8). Proponents argued that the only hope of challenging the government lay in supporting the party in a constituency which was thought to have the best chance of ousting the Conservatives. In the event the amount of new tactical voting disappointed the hopes of those who believed it would allow an opposition breakthrough, although there is evidence that tactical voting had some impact; Labour performed somewhat more strongly in Conservative marginals where they started second, while the Alliance performed slightly more strongly where they started second to the Conservatives (Curtice and Steed 1988; Norris 1987*b*).

Tactical voters can be seen as calculating gamblers; if they believe their first choice cannot win they will vote for the next best alternative. As defined tactical voting is essentially negative in character, it represents a form of protest voting against the party in the lead, with dissatisfaction triggered by such factors as the selection of particular candidates, divisions within the party, or the unpopularity of the government. Yet certain conditions need to be met for the potential tactical shift to be mobilized: first, voters need information about party prospects, from past performance in general or local elections, opinion polls, published canvass returns, or informed speculation in the press, so they can calculate whether it is worthwhile switching their vote.

Secondly, this information has to suggest that the parties are in a distinct rank order, to calculate the most probable winner in their constituency. As a result of these conditions, according to the polls, any tactical switch is often mobilized late in the campaign. Last-minute tactical shifts are most likely in by-elections where there is sufficient information for voters to evaluate party prospects, where the parties are seen in a distinct rank order, and where enough voters are motivated by strong negative feelings against the party in the lead to switch to their second choice.

There are difficulties about measuring the necessary conditions for tactical voting: there can be problems using nation-wide surveys to measure constituency-specific shifts; tactical voting often requires a series of fairly complex items; and post-election surveys are open to the problem of rationalization.[3]

In BBC 'Newsnight' constituency surveys during the campaign people were asked to nominate their first and second voting choice. Voters were then asked, if their first choice had no chance of winning, whether they would seriously consider voting for another, to keep out the party they most disliked. On this basis it is possible to classify groups of potential tacticals, for example Conservative–Liberals, or Labour–Nationalists. Lastly voters were asked to rank which party they thought would win, or come second, in the constituency.

In terms of social background we would expect higher levels of tactical voting among the younger population, since party loyalties can be expected to increase with experience of successive parties in government, and indeed this proved to be the case. In the by-election surveys half of the elderly were core voters, compared with a third who were potential tacticals and only 16% who were floaters. In contrast among the under-30 age bracket the largest group (45%) were potential tacticals, willing to consider switching in the right

---

[3] In May 1983 Gallup polls asked respondents the following in an attempt to assess tactical voting: 'If the opinion polls in a general election said that a party you disliked most was going to win, with your party in third place, but that the party in second place stood a good chance of winning, would you stick to voting for your own party, seriously think of voting for the party in second place, or decide not to vote?' The question was repeated in terms of a hypothetical by-election. The responses to questions about general-election voting strategy were (with responses in terms of a by-election in parentheses): stick to own party, 77% (75%); think of other party, 14% (14%); decide not to vote, 4% (5%); don't know, 5% (6%).

Gallup also used the following, equally complex, question: Here are two views about voting. Which one comes closest to your own view, assuming just for a moment that your party has little chance of winning?

You should stick by your party through thick and thin. Stick to your principles and vote for them even when they haven't much chance to win. (72%).

Second choice is better than third choice. Wasting a vote on a party bound to lose is fine if you don't feel strongly about the other parties. But if the party is unacceptable, voting to keep them out is sensible. (19%).

Don't know (9%).

circumstances, while slightly fewer (40%) were core voters (see Table 12.6). Retrospective theory suggests that those with experience of successive governments will tend to develop a general party loyalty based on party performance over the years. Without this anchor younger voters will tend to be more open to the influence of short-term evaluations.

Table 12.6. *Social characteristics of types of voters (%)*

	Core All	Tacticals All	Floaters
All voters	43	40	16
Age group			
18–29	40	45	14
30–49	42	43	15
50–64	43	37	20
65+	51	34	15
Socio-economic group			
Prof./manag.	49	40	11
Other non-manual	42	43	15
Manual	42	43	16
Housing tenure			
Owner-occ.	46	37	16
Private tenant	38	47	15
Council tenant	38	45	17
Gender			
Men	44	44	12
Women	44	36	20
Employment status			
Employed	42	42	15
Unemployed	36	51	12

Note: Percentage of all voters excluding abstainers.

Source: BBC 'Newsnight' constituency surveys, Ryedale and West Derbyshire, Apr. 1986.

Tacticals proved consistently less positive towards their first-choice party: when asked to evaluate party performance across a series of issues, from unemployment to nuclear energy, fewer tactical voters nominated their own party (Table 12.7). Tacticals also proved less stable in their vote over time; a higher proportion recalled having changed parties in the past. Further, if we consider the direction of the switch, it is apparent why third parties are often the main beneficiaries of new tactical voting in by-elections; in Greenwich the Alliance was the second choice of over 90% of Labour and Conservative voters who would consider switching (see Fig. 12.3). In contrast Alliance voters split their second preference between the major parties, with about two-thirds (64%) going to Labour and one-third (36%) to the Tories.

Table 12.7. *Percentage positively evaluating own party*

Issue		Tactical	Core	Difference
Unemployment	Con.	75.7	87.8	−12.1
	Lab.	84.9	88.4	−3.5
	LSDP	64.5	86.1	−21.6
Inflation	Con.	54.2	67.0	−12.8
	Lab.	88.4	96.0	−7.6
	LSDP	60.0	69.0	−9.0
Defence	Con.	60.0	66.7	−6.7
	Lab.	87.9	95.4	−7.5
	LSDP	60.7	73.5	−12.5
Education	Con.	73.9	81.4	−7.5
	Lab.	85.1	90.4	−5.3
	LSDP	62.5	80.0	−17.5
NHS	Con.	81.3	90.5	−9.2
	Lab	77.9	85.2	−7.3
	LSDP	58.3	82.4	−24.1
Trade unions	Con.	66.2	66.7	−0.5
	Lab.	77.8	88.6	−10.8
	LSDP	60.9	81.8	−20.9
Nuc. energy	Con.	70.6	71.8	−1.2
	Lab.	82.0	94.8	−12.8
	LSDP	55.9	71.0	−15.1

Note: Q. Which party do you think would be most likely to take the right decisions on the following matters ...

Source: BBC 'Newsnight' Survey Greenwich I, 31 Jan.–1 Feb. 1987, N. 671.

FLOATING VOTERS

Certain characteristics distinguish floaters from tacticals: floaters are more uncertain at the start of the campaign whom to support,

Fig. 12.3. Second choice amongst tacticals

1st choice vote	2nd choice vote		
	Con.	LSDP	Lab.
Con.	CORE	96.0	4.0
LSDP	36.4	CORE	63.5
Lab.	6.3	93.7	CORE

Note: The second choice of tacticals who would consider switching.
Source: BBC 'Newsnight' Survey, Greenwich I, 31 Jan.–1 Feb. 1987.

saying that they are undecided rather than being able to nominate a party preference. Secondly voting is not based on tactical criteria: floaters are not deciding based on information about the rank order of the parties. Floaters can be seen as the least attached of the electorate, the 'softest' vote, and therefore the most open to the effect of short-term factors, including campaign events, the selection of candidates, media coverage and the influence of party activists. For this reason the parties may wish to target their campaign on the floating voters, if they can be identified.

In the traditional view floaters are seen as undecided at a relatively late stage in the campaign as they have low levels of political involvement and minimal interest in the campaign. In this view floaters are essentially apathetic, wavering back and forth between parties through lack of political interest. Yet in contrast others suggest that floaters are deciding at a later stage because they are more concerned about the campaign issues (Himmelweit *et al.* 1985: 41). Himmelweit and colleagues suggest that floating voters are responding to genuine political concerns, shifting rationally on the basis of changes in party policies.

The BBC surveys found that the essential characteristic of the floating voter was their greater political uncertainty; they consistently tended to avoid expressing an opinion across a series of items, from their evaluations of the government to their judgement of party leadership, party policies, and party images. The indecision which floaters displayed towards their voting choice was therefore consistent with their general political attitudes. This lends support to the traditional perspective; in by-elections most floaters are vacillating in their political choice because they are less committed, less interested, and less involved in the political process, rather than because they are conscientiously weighing up the policy alternatives during the campaign.

EXPLANATIONS OF ELECTORAL CHANGE

On this basis we can suggest that the type of by-election campaign depends on the balance amongst these groups. In the stable by-elections characteristic of the late forties and early fifties, there was minimal electoral change with the main direction of movement from core Labour or Conservative supporters to abstention. In contrast since the mid-sixties under conditions of partisan dealignment increasing numbers of tactical and floating voters have led to more volatile by-elections, with the greater capacity for short-term change within the campaign. This development has significant implications for the electoral strategies adopted by the parties, who can use by-election campaigns for three primary functions: reinforcement, recruitment, and conversion.

In terms of reinforcement parties aim to build on their areas of greatest strength, fighting 'on their own turf' to consolidate their core support. Parties seek to set the campaign agenda with traditional consensus issues where they have a long-standing lead—the health service for Labour, law and order for the Conservatives, electoral reform for the Liberals, independence for Scotland for the SNP. Through this strategy parties are essentially preaching to the converted to reinforce their stable base. Candidates with a strong by-election lead may attempt to use reinforcement to get their established voters to the polling station, although it is insufficient for parties seeking to generate new support. In terms of recruitment parties aim to win over the the tacticals and the floaters for the duration of the campaign. Party strategists try to mobilize tacticals by using negative campaigning against the party in the lead, and publicizing favourable canvass returns and opinion polls which suggest they are the main challenger. In low-stimulus by-elections party strategists have problems attracting the floaters, the most detached voters, who are characterized by low levels of political interest.

The most difficult and rewarding task for parties is *conversion*, switching core and tactical voters who started the campaign with another party preference. Here the political market-place is uncertain, and to switch core voters parties may need to develop new, possibly divisive, issues rather than emphasizing traditional areas of strength. Unfortunately for parties the reinforcement and conversion strategies may conflict, especially if there are deep-rooted divisions in party support; in Bermondsey Labour may have alienated some traditional working-class supporters by trying to attract the radical-left, pacifist, or gay vote, while in Vauxhall Labour may have lost black votes by aiming to present a moderate image. In the Vale of Glamorgan the Conservatives may have lost support by emphasizing party divisions on the issue of government aid for regional development. Given the nature of these contests, generating short-term shifts of tacticals and floaters may prove easier for parties in a by-election than in a general election, but, as minor parties have often found, under conditions of partisan dealignment campaign recruitment should not be mistaken for long-term conversions.

13
The Comparative Context: Australia and Canada

BY-ELECTIONS are used world-wide to fill legislative seats which fall vacant between regular elections. Sixty-four countries, with diverse political systems, use by-elections for all Parliamentary vacancies; they range from China to Poland, to New Zealand, Malta, South Africa, and Iran. Another thirty use by-elections to fill vacancies in the lower chamber, either commonly or in special circumstances such as the absence of any substitute candidates; these include Canada, Australia, the United Kingdom, and the United States. Only thirty-five countries employ substitute lists or legislative appointments rather than by-elections; these include Israel, Norway, Italy, and the Netherlands.

In earlier chapters we observed certain systematic features characteristic of by-elections in Britain: notably the increased volatility over time, the cyclical decline in government support, the remarkable gains for third parties, and the consistent fall in turn-out. To examine this further we can consider whether these trends are evident elsewhere, comparing Britain with Australia and Canada. These countries are chosen for comparison as socially, culturally, and politically they are relatively similar, based on the legacy of the Old Commonwealth. All are well-established representative democracies with a bi-cameral legislature dominated by two major, and at least one 'minor', parties. These countries use single-member constituencies and an electoral system based on variants of the Westminster model. There are differences: in their elections to the lower chamber Canada and Britain use first-past-the-post systems while Australia uses the alternative vote, but in practice these electoral systems operate in relatively similar ways (Butler 1984). These countries are therefore relatively similar politically although they also provide significant contrasts in terms of partisan change.

PARTY SYSTEMS IN AUSTRALIA, BRITAIN, AND CANADA

Since the war Australia has commonly been ruled by a Liberal–Country Party coalition or by the Australian Labour Party (ALP)

(1946–9, 1972–5, and 1983–). Labour is the oldest political party in Australia, aiming at democratic socialism with an emphasis on improved social services and close links with the trade unions. The party has been particularly successful since 1983 under the leadership of Bob Hawke. The Liberals were founded by Sir Robert Menzies in 1945 as a conservative and private enterprise party. Third parties, especially the National (previously Country) Party, have commonly been represented in the Australian Parliament. The National (Country) Party has a strongly rural and conservative base. Since this party is consistently in coalition with the Liberals, it is somewhat difficult to describe it as a conventional third party, even though they are a free-standing organization in the extra-Parliamentary sense and have been in Parliament since the 1919 election.

Occasionally other third parties have also appeared in the Australian Parliament, notably the Democratic Labour Party (DLP) which contested elections throughout the sixties, although such parties are rarely successful. In the last decade only the Australian Democrats (AD; a former Liberal Party faction) could be termed a consistent dissident party. Founded in 1977, the Australian Democrats seek to exploit the middle ground, advocating consensus politics and individualism within the welfare state, under the dominant leadership of former Liberal Party Minister Donald Chipp (Edwards 1985; Reynolds 1977). Jupp (1982:193) suggests that the Australian Democrats and the DLP achieve their greatest influence first by holding the balance of power in the Senate as well as by affecting outcomes for the House through the distribution of second preferences. We focus in this chapter only on elections to the lower chamber, the House of Representatives, since there are no by-elections to the upper chamber. Third parties do better in the Australian Senate owing to the system of proportional representation, achieved through multi-member constituencies in concert with the single transferable (Hare/Clarke) system of preferential voting. By contrast, a preferential vote system is used in House elections, but the presence of single-member districts militates against a significant third party presence.

Studies of partisanship by Aitken (1982), Kemp (1978), and others have suggested that trends towards partisan dealignment detected in other countries in the seventies are not evident in Australia. The broad consensus of electoral studies is that Labour and the Liberal/Country parties continue to attract the enduring loyalties of stable groups of supporters. As Edwards (1985) characterized the situation, since 1977 the Australian Democrats have developed a relatively weak base in electoral support, founded in large part on the personality of their leader, which has failed to threaten the established two-party system. Studies have suggested that although there have been some shifts in the traditional bases of party support, with changes in social cleavages, nevertheless party allegiances continue to exert a strong stabilizing force on the Australian party system. As Aitken concluded from his study of Australian voters from 1967 to 1979, 'the extent to which the electorate accepted a partisan label varied hardly at all over twelve years.' (1982; see also Kemp 1978). Hence the changes in electoral consistency noted in Britain and Canada have not occurred in Australia, and the 'habit of voting' appears to be remarkably strong (Brugger and Jaensch, 1982).

The Canadian party system has been characterized by a high degree of stability in several senses. The Liberals have ruled for long periods in the post-war period (1945–57, 1963–1979, 1980–4). Three of the five elections they lost (1957, 1962, 1979) were to minority governments of the Progressive Conservatives. On the other hand, their defeats of 1958 and 1984 were of the landslide variety, as the Tories captured roughly three-quarters of the seats in the Commons in those contests. An unusual feature of the Canadian party system has been the extent to which two minor parties have been institutionalized. On the left of the political spectrum, the Cooperative Commonwealth Federation (CCF), renamed the New Democratic Party in 1961, was first represented in the Commons as a result of the 1935 elections, and has been there ever since, averaging about 20% of all seats. In this sense, it is the most successful of the third parties in the three countries under study. Social Credit (Socreds), also first appearing in 1935, has been both more and less successful than the CCF/NDP, initially concentrating its efforts in the western provinces and then experiencing difficulties as it expanded to the East (Cairns, 1968). By way of contrast with the CCF/NDP, the Socreds have been absent from Commons as the result of three national elections (1958, 1980, 1984). As an electoral force they have all but disappeared in recent years, contesting only 133 of the 564 seats up for election in 1980 and 1984, and 3 of the 17 by-elections in this time (Feigert 1989).

With these two relatively institutionalized third parties, there is normally a plenitude of third parties, loosely defined, as ballot access is rather open in Canada. In 1984, for instance, there were eight other 'parties' (including Independents) which more often than not consisted of single candidates. Additionally, candidates have not, in recent years, been required to declare a party identification, and there is often a surfeit of non-party candidacies in general elections if not in by-elections. The Canadian electorate has been seen as having a relatively low level of partisan attachments, compared with Britain and Australia (Irvine 1981). More recent studies have concluded that even over a relatively brief time-span such as between the 1979 and 1980 elections, partisan instability characterized a large segment of the Canadian electorate (Clarke and Stewart 1985).

TRENDS IN BY-ELECTION VOLATILITY

We can examine whether national trends in partisan change are consistent with by-election results by comparing the results of almost 60 contested by-elections in Australia, Britain, and Canada since the war.[1] Since 1945, Australia has had 17 general and 61 by-elections, Britain has had 13 general and 359 by-elections, and Canada has had 14 general and 154 by-elections. In line with the previous analysis, certain exceptional cases such as uncontested contests are excluded.[2]

Table 13.1. *By-election changes of seat by country (%)*

	Australia		Britain		Canada	
	No change	Change	No change	Change	No change	Change
1945/49	—	—	97.9	2.1	57.1	42.9
1950s	93.3	6.7	92.5	7.5	65.2	34.8
1960s	86.4	13.6	77.1	22.0	75.0	25.0
1970s	87.5	12.5	73.8	26.2	58.3	41.7
1980s	92.3	7.7	64.5	35.5	64.7	35.3
ALL	88.5	11.5	82.7	17.0	64.0	36.0
No.	54	7	297	61	119	67

[1] Unless otherwise noted data are derived from the following sources: Craig (1987); *Commonwealth By-Elections 1901–82* (Australian Electoral Office, Canberra, 1983); *Election Statistics Commonwealth By-Elections 1983–84* (Australian Electoral Commission, 1986); *Reports of the Chief Electoral Officer* (Ottawa, 1945–87).

[2] Excluded are for Australia one uncontested 1956 by-election and for Canada two uncontested by-elections in 1950 and 1957.

As Table 13.1 shows, fairly consistent with all we would predict in terms of partisanship, Australia has the lowest proportion of seat changes and shows no consistent trends over time. In the post-war years, only seven seats changed hands out of sixty-one by-elections. In contrast, Canada consistently has the highest level of seat-changing, more than a third of all by-elections showing this result. Britain shows the clearest developments over time. In the immediate post-war decade there was exceptional stability but in the 1980s British by-elections have become as unstable as those of Canada.

Alternatively to summarize trends we can develop a simple classification of by-elections according to the extent of the change in the vote (see Table 13.2). In line with the previous analysis volatile by-elections are classified as those with more than a 15% change in the share of the vote for any party from the previous general

Table 13.2.   *By-elections classified by change of vote*

	Australia		Britain		Canada	
	Stable	Volatile	Stable	Volatile	Stable	Volatile
1945–9	—	—	80.9	19.1	35.7	64.3
1950s	86.7	13.3	87.9	12.1	71.7	28.3
1960s	95.5	4.5	59.6	40.4	67.9	32.1
1970s	100.0	0.0	61.5	38.5	69.4	30.6
1980s	76.9	23.1	48.4	51.6	41.2	58.8
ALL	85.2	14.8	70.2	29.8	58.6	41.4

Note: A volatile by-election is classified as one where there is a change of more than 15% in the share of the vote for any party.Figures represent the change in the share of the vote for each party from the previous general election to the by-election, including minor party interventions and withdrawals.

election. If we look at these trends, it is apparent that there are cross-national contrasts similar to those shown in the previous table. That is, Australia proves highly stable, Canada is relatively volatile, while Britain changes over time from stable to unstable. By the eighties over half of all by-elections in Britain and Canada can be classified by this measure as volatile compared with under a quarter of Australian contests.

A consistent feature of by-elections already noted for Britain is the systematic decline in government support. Further evidence

along these lines, in cross-national perspective, is found in Table
13.3. During every decade the parties in government have experienced a decline in their mean share of support in by-elections,

Table 13.3.   *Comparative change in the share of the vote*

| | Australia | | Britain | | Canada | |
	Govt.	Opp.	Govt.	Opp.	Govt.	Opp.
1945–9	—	--	−3.9	+3.9	−1.5	−6.7
1950s	−10.3	+5.1	−4.5	+1.0	−6.1	+4.8
1960s	−6.8	−0.4	−13.6	+1.3	−4.6	+1.0
1970s	−1.9	−4.9	−9.8	+2.5	−5.3	+2.9
1980s	−6.1	−1.2	−12.7	−5.4	−15.1	+8.4
ALL	−5.9	+0.7	−8.9	+1.2	−5.4	+2.2

Note: Figures represent the mean change in the share of the vote for the parties
in government and in opposition from the previous general election to the by-election.
Figures are excluded where there are fewer than four cases.

although the extent of the loss varies substantially. Governing parties have lost support in roughly two-thirds of all by-elections in
Canada (63.4%) and Australia (68.8%), while the proportion is even
higher in Britain (83.6%). While the government consistently loses
votes, the major opposition parties in Britain and Canada frequently
make limited gains.

But as Table 13.4 shows, the main beneficiaries of by-elections
in Britain and Canada are minor parties, although here we need
to control for the number of seats contested. Some change in the
minor party share of the vote is due to minor party interventions
and withdrawals from the general election to the by-election. These
parties may have sufficient organizational resources for a local by-
election without being able to contest all seats in a national election.
In these by-elections change in the minor party share of the vote
can be attributed to the relative strength of local party organizations
as much as to underlying shifts in popular support. On the other
hand there is change in the share of the vote where minor parties
contest both the previous general election and the by-election, which
can be directly attributed to shifts in the level of electoral support.

On the basis of these distinctions it is apparent that in Britain
and Canada minor parties, with the exception of Social Credit, tend
to increase their level of support whether we control for third party

Table 13.4.   *Comparative change in the minor parties' vote (%)*

	All contests[a]		GE & BE only[b]	
	Change	No. contests	Change	No.contests
Australia				
NP/CP	+3.7	13	−3.3	7
DLP	−0.6	29	+0.3	15
AD	−0.3	15	−0.6	11
Britain				
LSDP	+5.0	234	+5.1	135
SNP	+6.1	53	+8.7	13
PC	+11.7	17	+12.7	12
Oth.	+1.1	158	+0.3	52
Canada				
CCF/NDP	+2.8	122	+4.3	105
SC	−1.1	68	−1.4	27
Oth.	+1.5	103	+4.3	50

Notes: There are too few cases to subdivide satisfactorily by decade.
a. The change in the share of the vote where minor parties contested either the by-election, or the previous general election, or both.
b. The change in the share of the vote where minor parties contested both the previous general election and the by-election.

interventions and withdrawals or not. That indicates that the increase in the vote reflects genuine popular support rather than organizational resources. In Canada the decline in support for Social Credit reflects their nationally weakening performance (in seats, since 1962, and in votes, since 1963). In contrast in Australia there tends to be minimal change in support for the Democratic Labour Party and the Australian Democrats, with the National (Country) party tending to lose support when in coalition with the Liberal government.

Lastly, as shown in Table 13.5, cross-national trends show a consistent tendency for turn-out to decline from the previous general election to the by-election. This decline is minimized in Australia, which can be attributed to the system of compulsory voting, which also produces a relatively high level of by-election turn-out. The results provide no evidence for consistent trends towards a greater decline in turn-out over time.

The question which remains to be considered is whether the trends in by-elections indicate less dealignment than a long-term realign-

Table 13.5.   *Comparative change in turn-out (%)*

	Australia		Britain		Canada	
	Change/No. contests		Change/No. contests		Change/No. contests	
1945/9	—		−9.2		−12.7	
1950s	−6.9		−16.9		−8.6	
1960s	−7.0		−13.7		−13.8	
1970s	−8.2		−13.0		−8.7	
1980s	−6.8		−11.2		−11.0	
ALL	−7.3	(61)	−13.7	(356)	−10.5	(153)

Note: Figures are excluded where there are fewer than four cases.

ment in party loyalties towards third parties. So far we have considered the extent of by-election volatility, but not the direction of change. If minor parties make a consistent series of by-election gains which are retained in subsequent general elections, this might suggest that at least in these contests third parties are capable of mounting an effective challenge to the two-party system. Realignment requires the establishment of a long-term base of core identifiers who will support the Alliance over successive elections. On the other hand if support for the third parties proves ephemeral, swinging back in general elections, this would suggest partisan dealignment.

To examine realignment we look at swing-backs from third parties who may pose a serious challenge to the two-party system. To test this in the Australian case we analysed swing-backs in sixteen by-elections since the founding of the Australian Democrats in 1977; in Britain this involves support for the Alliance in sixteen by-elections since the 1983 general election; and in Canada we can analyse support for the New Democrats in forty-three by-elections from 1970 to 1984. We use 1970 since this date serves as baseline for the NDP, having started to contest most seats in this time, and coming under the leadership of Ed Broadbent, its present leader, until the last general election in 1984.

As we found earlier, an analysis of the swing-back from the previous by-election to the following general election (Table 13.6) suggests that support mobilized for third parties in British by-elections proves largely, although not wholly, ephemeral. Yet there was some residual positive effect for the Liberal–Social Democratic Alliance.

Table 13.6.   *Comparative by-election swings and swing-backs*

	Australia Aust. Democrats	Britain Lib./SDP	Canada New Democrats
Change in seats			
Number of BE	16	16	43
Swing GE to BE	0	+4	+4
Swing-back BE to GE	0	−2	−1
Net change	0	+2	+3
Change in mean vote			
GE to BE	−1.2	+12.3	+2.4
BE to GE	−0.2	−8.8	+0.2
Net change	−1.4	+3.5	+2.6

Therefore on balance this suggests a situation of dealignment: some voters who switch to third parties in a by-election are retained for the subsequent general election, but for most the change only represents a temporary defection.

By contrast in Australia there is minimal change in third party support: the share of the vote for the Australian Democrats remains remarkably stable from the previous general election to the by-election, and from the by-election, to the subsequent general election. In Canada the NDP shows a marked tendency to win seats in by-elections and, for the most part, to hold on to them. Their net gain in both seats and votes is not unlike that of the Liberal–Social Democratic Alliance in Britain.

CONCLUSIONS

On balance we can conclude there is little convincing evidence from the analysis of British, Canadian, and Australian by-elections for partisan *realignment*, a complex long-term process in which new social cleavages and issues lead to a fundamental change in the enduring loyalties of groups of the electorate. Instead the evidence is consistent with the theory that in general elections stable alignments continue to dominate Australia, stable dealignment persists in Canada, while Britain has experienced a shift from one to the other.

In Australia, the theory of partisan identification helps to explain the stable by-election results common there. If habitual party loyalties guided voting choice, then we would expect little deviation from general elections to by-elections. Long-term bed-rock levels of party support in each constituency could be expected to prove more influential in by-elections than campaign-specific factors, such as the particular candidate or local issues.

In Canada, the outcome of by-elections is in line with the model of stable partisan dealignment which has been found to characterize its general elections. The government party, not unexpectedly, tend to lose both votes and seats to the opposition and to third parties. A fairly well institutionalized third party environment in Canada, in which two of them were, for so long, able to maintain a parliamentary presence, has made it possible for one of those third parties, the NDP, to provide a haven for temporary defectors and to retain some marginal gains. However, these are not sufficient to threaten the overall systemic stability of the Canadian polity. Gains of this sort, most recently the by-elections of 1987 in the Yukon and St John's East (Newfoundland) gave rise to speculation that the NDP could, if not form a government on its own, be developing to the point where they would be either the official opposition or a necessary part of a ruling coalition. On the basis of our analysis of previous by-election gains, a more cautious assessment might be appropriate regarding the prospects for Canadian third party success.

Lastly for Britain the comparative evidence serves to reinforce the model of by-election change presented earlier. The results of by-elections in Britain confirm the model of stable partisan alignments during the 1950s and the transition to stable dealignments in the 1970s. This suggests that party loyalties play a weaker role in most British by-elections, which leaves greater room for short-term factors to influence voting choice, including the particular candidates, campaign events, or local party organizations. The loosening of traditional party loyalties increases the potential for short-term electoral change.

Conclusions: The Volatile Electorate

As we have seen, two main viewpoints have dominated our understanding of by-elections: the campaign-specific and the referendum models. On the basis of the material which has been presented we can return to the questions posed at the start of the book: can the results of particular by-elections be treated as alternatives to public opinion polls, reliable indicators of national party popularity? Do by-elections represent a public referendum on the performance of the government? Or, instead, are by-elections idiosyncratic contests reflecting a variety of complex campaign-specific factors, deserving study for their intrinsic interest but indicating little beyond the specific circumstances of the contest?

The argument which has been presented here suggests that by itself neither perspective is entirely satisfactory. A broad overview reveals that each campaign is not *sui generis*, there are systematic trends, notably the consistent tendency for minor parties to gain at the expense of the party in government. The evidence confirms that the results of a series of by-elections are associated with long-term cycles in government popularity, which are related to evaluations of the government's performance. We have demonstrated that under conditions of partisan dealignment by-elections have become increasingly volatile over time; during the late forties and early fifties by-election results proved highly stable, reflecting the quiescent period of dominant two-party politics. From the early sixties these contests started to reflect the growing Labour challenge to the Macmillan government, with a string of Labour gains before the return of the Wilson administration in 1964. During the late sixties increased electoral volatility produced the series of Tory victories, preceding Edward Heath's return in 1970. During periods of revival the strength the Liberals and Nationalists demonstrated in the early seventies, from Rochdale to Glasgow Govan, presaged their performance in the 1974 general election. In the early eighties by-elections, from Warrington to Greenwich, proved crucial to the fortunes of the Liberal–Social Democratic Alliance, providing the oxygen of publicity, increasing party morale, and establishing electoral credibility.

But at the same time it cannot be stressed strongly enough that journalists, editorial writers, party leaders, and political scientists should be highly cautious about reading too much into individual results. Commentators seeking to interpret the electoral runes should be particularly circumspect in the mid-term period. Administrations consistently tend to experience a decline in support in their second or third years in office, with the 'mid-term blues', at which time there may be dramatic government losses to third parties, but some governments manage to recover their popularity, while others do not. It follows that mid-term by-elections, like mid-term polls, are a highly unreliable guide to long-term party fortunes.

Therefore we can conclude that particular by-elections should not be treated as indicating the outcome of a forthcoming general election, or, indeed, even of the next by-election: Bermondsey could not be used to predict Darlington, Fulham could not predict Ryedale, Knowsley North could not predict Greenwich. These contests should not be treated as substitutes for nation-wide opinion polls, as in by-elections voters face a different logic of choice; voters are selecting a particular representative, not choosing a party for government. In each particular constituency the combination of campaign-specific factors—the choice of candidate, the tactical situation, or the local party organization—may prove important. We have shown that in by-elections over the last decades weakening party loyalties have led to the development of the volatile electorate; core voters may remain fairly constant, but the tacticals, floaters and abstainers may shift unpredictably within the few weeks of a campaign. As a result there have been classic third party victories, but support quickly gained may be just as quickly lost; temporary recruitment during a campaign, under conditions of partisan dealignment, should not be mistaken by contemporary observers as evidence for long-term partisan realignment.

Appendix
Post-War By-Election Results for Major Parties

Key: * Change of seat.
Bold type: Winner.
Year's average: 12 months from date of GE.

LAB. GOVT. 1945	Date	Maj. GE	Turn-out (%) GE	Turn-out (%) BE	Turn-out (%) Change	Con. vote (%) GE	Con. vote (%) BE	Con. vote (%) Change	Lab. vote (%) GE	Lab. vote (%) BE	Lab. vote (%) Change	Lib. vote (%) GE	Lib. vote (%) BE	Lib. vote (%) Change
GENERAL ELECTION	5.7.45		72.8			39.6			48.0			9.0		
1 Smethwick	1.10.45	6.5	72.4	65.4	−7.0	34.1	31.2	−2.9	65.9	68.8	2.9	—	—	—
2 Ashton u. Lyme	2.10.45	12.8	78.6	70.5	−8.1	43.6	35.0	−8.6	56.4	54.1	−2.3	—	10.9	10.9
3 Edinburgh E.	3.10.45	19.1	69.4	51.0	−18.4	37.3	38.4	1.1	56.4	61.6	5.2	—	—	—
4 Monmouth	30.10.45	3.8	72.0	66.7	−5.3	51.9	52.7	0.8	48.1	47.3	−0.8	—	—	—
5 City of London	31.10.45	67.8	63.9	51.6	−12.3	78.8	75.0	−3.8	—	—	0.0	11.0	25.0	14.0
6 Bromley	14.11.45	10.9	70.9	60.6	−10.3	45.0	49.6	4.6	34.1	39.1	5.0	20.9	11.3	−9.6
7 Bournemouth	15.11.45	33.8	71.2	56.5	−14.7	55.5	46.8	−8.7	21.7	33.7	12.0	22.8	19.5	−3.3
8 Kensington S.	20.11.45	50.9	67.9	36.8	−31.1	69.8	81.7	11.9	18.9		−18.9	11.3	18.3	7.0
9 Tottenham N.	13.12.45	43.6	70.3	39.5	−30.8	28.2	36.4	8.2	71.8	63.6	−8.2	—	—	—
10 Preston	31.1.46	4.5	80.2	64.9	−15.3	41.8	44.4	2.6	46.3	55.6	9.3	6.1		−6.1
11 S. Ayrshire	7.2.46	22.6	75.0	69.0	−6.0	38.7	36.4	−2.3	61.3	63.6	2.3	—	—	—
12 G'gow, Cathcart	12.2.46	17.6	67.6	55.6	−12.0	58.8	52.5	−6.3	41.2	37.1	−4.1	—	—	—
13 Lancs., Heywood/Radcliffe	21.2.46	2.0	76.4	75.6	−0.8	49.0	49.5	0.5	51.0	50.5	−0.5	—	—	—
14 Yks., Hemsworth	22.2.46	62.8	80.8	—	—	18.6	—	—	81.4	Unopp.		—	—	—
15* Eng. Universities[a,b]	13.3.46	—	50.0	42.1	−7.9	—	**30.0**	—	—	—		—	—	—
16 Glam., Ogmore	4.6.46	58.4	75.6	33.1	−42.5	18.0	—	−18.0	76.4	70.6	−5.8	—	—	—
17 Bexley	22.7.46	27.1	76.7	61.2	−15.5	29.8	47.5	17.7	56.9	52.5	−4.4	13.3	13.3	13.3
18 Mon., Pontypool	23.7.46	54.6	77.0	64.8	−12.2	22.7	26.8	4.1	77.3	73.2	−4.1	—	—	—
19 Battersea N.	25.7.46	47.8	70.9	55.4	−15.5	26.1	29.6	3.5	73.9	68.9	−5.0	—	—	—
20 G'gow Bridgeton	29.8.46	33.6	58.2	53.3	−4.9	33.6	21.6	−12.0	—	28.0	+28.0	14.2	17.0	−0.1
YEAR'S AVERAGE		28.2	71.3	56.5	−14.2	43.1	45.5	−0.7	55.2	54.3	0.6	14.2	17.0	−0.1
21 Bermondsey/Rotherhithe	19.11.46	58.2	68.1	50.9	−17.2	20.9	9.7	−11.2	79.1	65.0	−14.1	—	25.3	25.3
22 Paddington N.	20.11.46	24.1	71.0	53.9	−17.1	37.1	43.2	6.1	61.2	55.6	−5.6	—	—	—
23* Scot. Universities[a,b]	22.11.46		51.6	50.7	−0.9	—	**68.2**	—	—	11.5	11.5	8.0	8.0	

		Turn-out (%)				Con. vote (%)			Lab. vote (%)			Lib. vote (%)		
LAB. GOVT. 1945	Date	Maj. GE	GE	BE	Change	GE	BE	Change	GE	BE	Change	GE	BE	Change
25 Aberdare/Merthyr Tydfil	5.12.46	68.6	76.1	65.7	−10.4	15.7	11.7	−4.0	84.3	68.3	−16.0	—	—	—
26 Ayrshire, Kilmarnock	5.12.46	18.8	76.1	68.4	7.7	40.6	32.5	−8.1	59.4	59.7	0.3	—	—	—
27 Yks., Normanton	11.2.47	68.6	79.9	54.6	−15.3	15.7	17.8	2.1	84.3	79.8	−4.5	—	—	—
28 Durham, Jarrow	7.5.47	32.0	76.0	73.4	−2.6	34.0	37.5	3.5	66.0	59.3	−6.7	—	—	—
29 L'pool, Edge Hill	11.9.47	29.8	66.1	62.7	−3.4	35.1	42.6	7.5	64.9	52.1	−12.8	—	4.4	4.4
30 Islington W.	25.9.47	47.6	60.1	51.4	−8.7	26.2	26.6	0.4	73.8	57.2	−16.6	—	16.0	16.0
YEAR'S AVERAGE		39.1	69.7	59.7	−10.0	30.2	34.5	7.3	68.4	55.4	−6.2	10.9	13.4	8.6
31 Kent, Gravesend	26.11.47	17.2	74.5	77.3	2.8	35.3	48.2	12.9	52.5	51.8	−0.7	12.2	—	−12.2
32 Yks., Howdenshire	27.11.47	26.8	71.1	67.0	−4.1	56.0	64.0	8.0	29.2	25.5	−3.7	14.8	10.5	−4.3
33 Edinburgh E.	27.11.47	19.1	69.4	63.0	−6.4	37.3	34.3	−3.0	56.4	50.6	−5.8	—	10.1	10.1
34 Surrey, Epsom	4.12.47	12.2	74.6	70.5	−4.1	50.0	61.0	11.0	37.8	31.5	−6.3	12.2	7.5	−4.7
35* G'gow, Camlachie^c	28.1.48	15.4	65.0	56.8	−8.2	42.3	43.7	1.4	57.7	42.1	−15.6	—	1.2	1.2
36 Paisley	18.2.48	22.9	73.9	76.0	2.1	32.7	43.2	10.5	55.6	56.8	1.2	10.0	—	−10.0
37 Wigan	4.3.48	36.4	80.4	81.4	1.0	31.8	35.7	3.9	68.2	59.0	−9.2	—	—	—
38 Croydon N.	11.3.48	1.0	73.2	74.8	1.6	41.1	54.0	12.9	40.1	36.6	−3.5	18.8	9.4	−9.4
39 Lincs, Brigg	24.3.48	17.8	74.6	77.1	2.5	41.1	45.4	4.3	58.9	54.6	−4.3	—	—	—
40 Southwark C.	29.4.48	43.8	62.6	48.7	−13.9	28.1	34.6	6.5	71.9	65.4	−6.5	—	—	—
41 G'gow, Gorbals	30.9.48	60.0	56.8	50.0	−6.8	20.0	28.6	8.6	80.0	54.5	−25.5	—	—	—
YEAR'S AVERAGE		25.7	70.6	67.5	−3.0	37.8	44.8	7.0	55.1	48.0	−2.0	13.6	7.7	−4.2
42 Stirling/Falkirk	7.10.48	12.2	71.5	72.9	1.4	43.9	42.8	−1.1	56.1	49.0	−7.1	—	—	—
43 Edmonton	13.11.48	39.2	69.0	62.7	−6.3	29.0	46.6	17.6	68.2	53.4	−14.8	—	—	—
44 G'gow, Hillhead	25.11.48	24.9	65.8	56.7	−9.1	58.5	68.4	9.9	33.6	31.6	−2.0	7.9	—	−7.9
45 Batley/Morley	17.2.49	29.7	80.7	81.3	0.6	28.4	40.7	12.3	58.1	59.3	1.2	13.5	—	−13.5
46 Hammersmith S.	24.2.49	16.0	65.7	60.6	−5.1	42.0	47.2	5.2	58.0	52.8	−5.2	—	—	—
47 St Pancras N.	10.3.49	29.1	71.0	65.1	−5.9	34.7	39.5	4.8	63.8	57.5	−6.3	—	—	—
48 Yks., Sowerby	16.3.49	19.9	81.9	80.7	−1.2	30.9	46.9	16.0	50.8	53.1	2.3	18.3	—	−18.3
49 Leeds W.	21.7.49	31.5	75.2	65.1	−10.1	27.6	44.8	17.2	59.1	55.2	−3.9	13.3	—	−13.3
50 Bradford S.	8.12.49	19.4	76.7	74.4	−2.3	33.1	42.4	9.3	52.5	51.3	−1.2	14.4	—	−14.4
YEAR'S AVERAGE		24.7	73.1	68.8	−4.2	36.5	46.6	10.1	55.6	51.5	−4.1	13.5	—	−13.5
PARLT. AVERAGE			71.1	61.9	−9.0	38.2	43.2	4.8	58.0	52.5	−2.3	13.5	12.7	−1.9

^a Con. gain from Ind.

^b GE figures omitted as the elections were conducted by Single Transferable Vote.

^c Con. gain from Ind. Lab.

LAB. GOVT. 1950	Date	Maj. GE	Turn-out (%)			Con. vote (%)			Lab. vote (%)			Lib. vote (%)		
			GE	BE	Change	GE	BE	Change	GE	BE	Change	GE	BE	Change
GENERAL ELECTION	23.2.50		83.9			43.4			46.1			9.1		
1 Sheffield Neepsend	5.4.50	45.6	83.8	62.9	−20.9	27.2	26.8	−0.4	72.8	70.9	−1.9	—	—	—
2 Dunbartonshire W.	25.4.50	1.5	85.5	83.4	−2.1	47.8	49.6	1.8	49.3	50.4	1.1	—	—	—
3 Brighouse/Spenborough	4.5.50	4.4	88.0	85.4	−2.6	47.8	49.5	1.7	52.2	50.5	−1.7	—	—	—
4 Leicester NE	28.9.50	23.2	85.8	63.0	−22.8	33.3	42.1	8.8	56.5	57.9	1.4	9.5	—	−9.5
5 Glasgow Scotstoun	25.10.50	0.5	84.6	73.7	−10.9	46.5	50.8	4.3	46.0	47.3	1.3	4.9	—	−4.9
6 Oxford	2.11.50	6.2	84.9	69.3	−15.6	46.9	57.5	10.6	40.7	42.5	1.8	11.6	—	−11.6
7 B'ham Handsworth	16.11.50	11.3	83.1	63.2	−19.9	50.5	60.7	10.2	39.2	38.1	−1.1	10.3	—	−10.3
8 Bristol SE	30.11.50	35.8	85.0	61.1	−23.9	26.8	35.2	8.4	62.6	56.7	−5.9	9.5	8.1	−1.4
9 Mon., Abertillery	30.11.50	74.2	84.6	71.1	−13.5	12.9	13.5	0.6	87.1	86.5	−0.6	—	—	—
10 Bristol W.	15.2.51	28.9	82.4	53.6	−28.8	58.9	81.4	22.5	30.0	18.6	−11.4	11.1	—	11.1
YEAR'S AVERAGE		23.2	84.8	68.7	−16.1	39.9	46.7	6.9	53.6	51.9	−1.7	9.2	9.6	−8.1
11 Lancs., Ormskirk	5.4.51	32.6	83.9	64.7	−19.2	66.3	71.5	5.2	33.7	26.5	−7.2	—	—	—
12 Harrow W.	21.4.51	29.1	86.7	68.0	−18.7	58.6	72.0	13.4	29.5	28.0	−1.5	11.9	—	−11.9
13 Woolwich E.	14.6.51	28.5	83.3	66.8	−16.5	33.0	39.3	6.3	61.5	60.7	−0.8	3.5	—	−3.5
14 Lancs. Westhoughton	21.6.51	24.6	88.2	76.5	−11.7	37.7	39.6	1.9	62.3	60.4	−1.9	—	—	—
YEAR'S AVERAGE		28.7	85.5	69.0	−16.5	48.9	55.6	6.7	46.8	43.9	−2.9	7.7	—	−7.7
PARLT. AVERAGE		24.6	85.0	68.8	−16.2	42.3	49.1	6.8	51.8	49.8	−2.0	8.8	9.6	−8.0

CON. GOVT. 1951	Date	Maj. GE	Turn-out (%)			Con. vote (%)			Lab. vote (%)			Lib. vote (%)		
			GE	BE	Change	GE	BE	Change	GE	BE	Change	GE	BE	Change
GENERAL ELECTION	15.9.51		82.6			48.0			48.8			2.6		
1 B'mouth E./Christchurch	6.2.52	38.2	80.8	63.8	−17.0	63.3	61.8	−1.5	25.1	23.4	−1.7	11.6	10.1	−1.5
2 Southport	6.2.52	35.4	77.7	61.0	−16.7	60.2	62.0	1.8	24.8	28.5	3.7	15.0	9.5	−5.5
3 Leeds SE	7.2.52	21.0	84.4	55.7	−28.7	39.5	36.8	−2.7	60.5	63.2	2.7	—	—	—
4 Dundee E.	17.7.52	7.6	87.2	71.5	−15.7	46.2	35.6	−10.6	53.8	56.3	2.5	—	—	—
YEAR'S AVERAGE		25.6	82.5	63.0	−19.5	52.3	49.1	−3.3	41.1	42.9	1.8	13.3	9.8	−3.5
5 Yks., Cleveland	23.10.52	9.6	85.1	71.4	−13.7	45.2	45.9	0.7	54.8	54.1	−0.7	—	—	—
6 Bucks., Wycombe	4.11.52	3.4	86.2	83.9	−2.3	51.7	52.0	0.3	48.3	48.0	−0.3	—	—	—
7 Birmingham Small Heath	27.11.52	32.5	77.2	46.6	−30.6	30.9	33.0	2.1	63.4	67.0	3.6	5.7	—	−5.7
8 Lancs., Farnworth	27.11.52	18.4	86.8	71.0	−15.8	40.8	40.1	−0.7	59.2	59.9	0.7	—	—	—
9 Kent, Canterbury	12.2.53	30.1	80.1	49.2	−30.9	61.1	67.1	6.0	31.0	32.9	1.9	7.9	—	−7.9
10 Kent, Isle of Thanet	12.3.53	23.2	78.0	58.7	−19.3	61.6	61.3	−0.3	38.4	38.7	0.3	—	—	—
11 Barnsley	31.3.53	52.4	77.2	57.9	−19.3	17.3	27.1	9.8	69.7	72.9	3.2	13.0	—	−13.0
12 Stoke-on-Trent N.	31.3.53	42.8	83.8	50.5	−33.3	28.6	24.5	−4.1	71.4	75.5	4.1	—	—	—
13 Hayes/Harlington	1.4.53	29.6	82.2	45.0	−37.2	35.2	36.1	0.9	64.8	63.9	−0.9	—	—	—
14* Sunderland S.	13.5.53	0.6	82.2	72.7	−9.5	49.7	48.6	−1.1	50.3	46.1	−4.2	—	5.3	5.3
15 Berks., Abingdon	30.6.53	11.0	80.0	75.9	−4.1	55.5	53.2	−2.3	44.5	39.7	−4.8	—	7.1	7.1
16 Birmingham Edgbaston	2.7.53	28.6	76.1	50.2	−25.9	64.3	67.6	3.3	35.7	32.4	−3.3	—	—	—
17 Notts., Broxtowe	17.9.53	45.4	84.1	63.5	−20.6	27.3	25.9	−1.4	72.7	74.1	1.4	—	—	—
YEAR'S AVERAGE		25.2	81.5	61.3	−20.2	43.8	44.8	1.0	54.2	54.2	0.1	8.9	6.2	−2.8
18 Crosby	12.11.53	41.8	79.8	62.5	−17.3	70.9	68.1	−2.8	29.1	27.6	−1.5	—	—	—
19 Lancs., Ormskirk	12.11.53	34.8	78.7	54.1	−24.6	67.4	65.4	−2.0	32.6	34.6	2.0	—	—	—
20 Holborn/St Pancras S.	19.11.53	4.4	73.7	56.2	−17.5	45.8	45.6	−0.2	50.2	52.1	1.9	4.0	2.3	−1.7
21 Paddington N.	3.12.53	11.4	81.0	60.3	−20.7	44.3	45.3	1.0	55.7	53.8	−1.9	—	—	—
22 Ilford N.	3.2.54	17.5	84.8	45.4	−39.4	55.5	59.8	4.3	38.0	32.3	−5.7	6.5	7.9	1.4
23 Essex, Harwich	11.2.54	17.8	78.8	58.8	−20.0	58.9	59.1	0.2	41.1	40.9	−0.2	—	—	—
24 Haltemprice/Kingston u. Hull	11.2.54	16.2	82.8	45.7	−37.1	58.1	61.8	3.7	41.9	38.2	−3.7	—	—	—
25 Bournemouth W.	18.2.54	31.0	77.7	45.1	−32.6	65.5	69.7	4.2	34.5	30.3	−4.2	—	—	—
26 Sussex, Arundel/Shoreham	9.3.54	34.8	78.0	54.2	−23.8	67.4	68.5	1.1	32.6	31.5	−1.1	—	—	—
27 Yks., Harrogate	11.3.54	41.2	78.7	55.3	−23.4	70.6	70.8	0.2	29.4	29.2	−0.2	—	—	—

CON. GOVT. 1951	Date	Maj. GE	Turn-out (%)			Con. vote (%)			Lab. vote (%)			Lib. vote (%)		
			GE	BE	Change	GE	BE	Change	GE	BE	Change	GE	BE	Change
28. Edinburgh E.	8.4.54	8.2	83.8	61.8	−22.0	45.9	42.4	−3.5	54.1	57.6	3.5	—	—	—
29. Lanarks., Motherwell	14.4.54	14.6	84.7	70.5	−14.2	42.7	39.3	−3.4	57.3	56.4	−0.9	—	—	—
YEAR'S AVERAGE		22.8	80.2	55.8	−24.4	57.8	58.0	0.2	41.4	40.4	−1.0	5.3	5.1	−0.2
30. Croydon E.	30.9.54	17.6	84.2	57.5	−26.7	58.8	56.6	−2.2	41.2	35.4	−5.8	—	8.0	8.0
31. Shoreditch/Finsbury	21.10.54	45.2	73.2	40.7	−32.5	27.4	21.8	−5.6	72.6	78.2	5.6	—	—	—
32. Wakefield	21.10.54	16.6	85.3	68.6	−16.7	41.7	41.9	0.2	58.3	58.1	−0.2	—	—	—
33. Hants., Aldershot	28.10.54	20.6	77.8	58.7	−19.1	60.3	60.1	−0.2	39.7	39.9	0.2	—	—	—
34. Aberdare	28.10.54	63.1	86.1	69.7	−16.4	15.4	14.5	−0.9	78.5	69.5	−9.0	—	—	—
35. Sutton/Cheam	4.11.54	25.6	81.7	55.6	−26.1	62.8	66.5	3.7	37.2	33.5	−3.7	—	—	—
36. N'land, Morpeth	4.11.54	43.8	85.5	73.0	−12.5	28.1	28.7	0.6	71.9	71.3	−0.6	—	—	—
37. Liverpool West Derby	18.11.54	3.2	80.3	58.9	−21.4	51.6	53.2	1.6	48.4	46.8	−1.6	—	—	—
38. Inverness	21.12.54	29.0	69.3	49.2	−20.1	64.5	41.4	−23.1	35.5	22.6	−12.9	—	36.0	36.0
39. Norfolk S.	13.1.55	9.0	82.4	66.6	−15.8	54.5	51.5	−3.0	45.5	48.5	3.0	—	—	—
40. Kent, Orpington	20.1.55	25.4	82.0	55.4	−26.6	62.7	65.8	3.1	37.3	34.2	−3.1	—	—	—
41. Twickenham	25.1.55	24.2	81.3	47.3	−34.0	62.1	64.0	1.9	37.9	36.0	−1.9	—	—	—
42. Edinburgh N.	27.1.55	17.6	80.0	46.4	−33.6	58.8	59.4	0.6	41.2	40.6	−0.6	—	—	—
43. Stockport S.	3.2.55	8.4	84.2	64.6	−19.6	54.2	54.3	0.1	45.8	45.7	−0.1	3.6	—	—
44. Denbighs., Wrexham	17.3.55	26.8	84.8	62.4	−22.4	34.8	30.8	−4.0	61.6	57.9	−3.7	3.6	11.3	7.7
YEAR'S AVERAGE		25.1	81.2	58.3	−22.9	49.2	47.4	−1.8	50.2	47.9	−2.3		18.4	17.2
PARLT. AVERAGE			81.1	59.0	−22.1	50.3	49.7	−0.6	48.0	47.2	−0.8	8.6	9.9	1.6

	CON. GOVT. 1955	Date	Maj. GE	Turn-out (%)			Con. vote (%)			Lab. vote (%)			Lib. vote (%)		
				GE	BE	Change	GE	BE	Change	GE	BE	Change	GE	BE	Change
	GENERAL ELECTION	25.5.55		76.8			49.7			46.4			2.7		
1	Gateshead W.	7.12.55	30.6	72.5	42.3	−30.2	34.7	33.5	−1.2	65.3	66.5	1.2	—	—	—
2	Greenock	8.12.55	2.8	77.9	75.3	−2.6	48.6	46.3	−2.3	51.4	53.7	2.3	—	—	—
3	Torquay	15.12.55	35.0	75.5	62.6	−12.9	60.4	51.0	−9.4	25.4	25.2	−0.2	14.2	23.8	9.6
4	Durham, Blaydon	2.2.56	33.0	80.7	56.5	−24.2	33.5	30.1	−3.4	66.5	69.9	3.4	—	—	—
5	Leeds NE	9.2.56	22.8	73.1	39.9	−33.2	61.4	63.2	1.8	38.6	36.8	−1.8	—	—	—
6	Herefords., Hereford	14.2.56	28.4	78.8	61.5	−17.3	51.8	44.3	−7.5	23.4	19.3	−4.1	24.8	36.4	11.6
7	Lincs., Gainsborough	14.2.56	11.6	76.8	61.9	−14.9	55.8	40.8	−15.0	44.2	37.6	−6.6	—	21.6	21.6
8	Som., Taunton	14.2.56	12.6	85.5	75.0	−10.5	52.1	50.8	−1.3	39.5	49.2	9.7	8.4	—	−8.4
9	Walthamstow W.	1.3.56	31.4	72.5	52.0	−20.5	34.3	20.2	−14.1	65.7	64.7	−1.0	—	14.7	14.7
	YEAR'S AVERAGE		23.1	77.0	58.6	−18.5	48.1	42.2	−5.8	46.7	47.0	0.3	15.8	24.1	9.8
10	Kent, Tonbridge	7.6.56	20.8	75.5	75.5	0.0	60.4	52.0	−8.4	39.6	48.0	8.4	—	—	—
11	Newport	6.7.56	7.4	81.6	72.1	−9.5	46.3	39.9	−6.4	53.7	56.3	2.6	—	—	—
12	Chester le Street	27.9.56	52.6	79.6	64.9	−14.7	23.7	19.2	−4.5	76.3	80.8	4.5	—	—	—
13	Chester, City	15.11.56	25.1	77.9	71.5	−6.4	56.7	51.7	−5.0	31.6	36.2	4.6	11.7	12.1	0.4
14	Leics., Melton	19.12.56	21.8	80.9	56.5	−24.4	60.9	53.3	−7.6	39.1	46.7	7.6	—	—	—
15*	Lewisham N.	14.2.57	8.0	77.9	70.8	−7.1	54.0	46.5	−7.5	46.0	49.5	3.5	—	—	—
16	Wednesbury	28.2.57	20.8	72.9	60.0	−12.9	39.6	28.0	−11.6	60.4	62.1	1.7	—	—	—
17*	Carmarthen	28.2.57	6.8	85.1	87.5	2.4	—	—	—	42.7	47.3	4.6	49.5	41.2	—
18	Bristol W.	7.3.57	50.6	74.6	61.1	−13.5	75.3	70.2	−5.1	24.7	29.8	5.1	—	—	—
19	Warwick/Leamington	7.3.57	29.0	78.8	77.9	−0.9	64.5	52.3	−12.2	35.5	47.7	12.2	—	—	—
20	Beckenham	21.3.57	38.0	76.5	64.7	−11.8	69.0	62.9	−6.1	31.0	37.1	6.1	—	—	—
21	Ncl. u. Tyne N.	21.3.57	27.6	77.6	64.1	−13.5	63.8	60.2	−3.6	36.2	39.8	3.6	—	—	—
	YEAR'S AVERAGE		25.7	78.2	68.9	−9.4	55.8	48.7	−7.1	43.1	48.4	5.4	30.6	26.7	0.9
22	Edinburgh S.	29.5.57	35.0	77.2	65.8	−11.4	67.5	45.6	−21.9	32.5	30.9	−1.6	—	23.5	23.5
23	East Ham N.	30.5.57	18.2	74.9	57.3	−17.6	40.9	29.4	−11.5	59.1	56.3	−2.8	—	—	—
24	Hornsey	30.5.57	23.0	76.3	63.0	−13.3	60.2	53.5	−6.7	37.2	46.5	9.3	—	—	—
25	Dorset N.	27.6.57	19.7	82.2	75.8	−6.4	52.1	45.1	−7.0	15.5	18.3	2.8	32.4	36.1	3.7
26	Gloucester	12.9.57	1.8	80.9	71.0	−9.9	49.1	28.6	−20.5	50.9	51.3	0.4	—	20.1	20.1
27	Ipswich	24.10.57	5.8	80.5	75.6	−4.9	47.1	32.7	−14.4	52.9	45.8	−7.1	—	21.5	21.5

CON. GOVT. 1955	Date	Maj. GE	Turn-out (%)			Con. vote (%)			Lab. vote (%)			Lib. vote (%)		
			GE	BE	Change	GE	BE	Change	GE	BE	Change	GE	BE	Change
28 Leicester SE	28.11.57	28.4	78.5	56.4	-22.1	64.2	61.0	-3.2	35.8	39.0	3.2	—	—	—
29* Garston L'pool[a]	5.12.57	27.0	71.0	49.7	-21.3	63.5	**49.2**	-14.3	36.5	35.6	-0.9	—	15.2	15.2
30* Rochdale	12.2.58	3.0	82.8	80.2	-2.6	51.5	19.8	-31.7	48.5	**44.7**	-3.8	—	35.5	35.5
31* G'gow Kelvingrove	13.3.58	10.8	67.6	60.5	-7.1	55.4	41.6	-13.8	44.6	**48.0**	3.4	—	—	—
32* Devon, Torrington	27.3.58	30.2	69.2	80.6	11.4	65.1	37.4	-27.7	34.9	24.6	-10.3	—	**38.0**	38.0
33 Islington N.	15.5.1958	20.6	64.7	35.6	-29.1	39.7	29.3	-10.4	60.3	67.7	7.4	—	—	—
YEAR'S AVERAGE		18.6	75.5	64.3	-11.2	54.7	39.4	-15.3	42.4	42.4	0.0	32.4	27.1	19.7
34* Ealing S.[a]	12.6.58	28.6	77.9	64.5	-13.4	59.5	**50.3**	-9.2	30.9	32.5	1.6	9.6	17.2	7.6
35 St Helens	12.6.58	28.6	73.5	54.6	-18.9	35.7	35.3	-0.4	64.3	64.7	0.4	—	—	—
36 Wigan	12.6.58	32.2	80.3	70.3	-10.0	32.2	26.5	-5.7	64.4	71.0	6.6	—	—	—
37 Weston super Mare	12.6.58	25.4	73.8	72.2	-1.6	62.7	49.3	-13.4	37.3	26.2	-11.1	—	24.5	24.5
38 Argyll	12.6.58	35.2	66.6	67.1	0.5	67.6	46.8	-20.8	32.4	25.7	-6.7	—	27.5	27.5
39 Morecambe/Lonsdale	6.11.58	42.4	74.4	63.8	-10.6	71.2	65.3	-5.9	28.8	34.7	5.9	—	—	—
40 Sussex, Chichester	6.11.58	41.6	71.8	51.7	-20.1	70.8	70.9	0.1	29.2	29.1	-0.1	—	—	—
41 Pontypool	10.11.58	45.8	77.1	61.7	-15.4	27.1	21.5	-5.6	72.9	68.5	-4.4	—	—	—
42 Aberdeenshire E.	20.11.58	37.0	59.8	65.9	6.1	68.5	48.6	-19.9	31.5	27.1	-4.4	—	24.3	24.3
43 Shoreditch/Finsbury	27.11.58	47.0	61.6	24.9	-36.7	26.5	24.0	-2.5	73.5	76.0	2.5	—	—	—
44 Southend W.	29.1.59	43.4	74.1	42.9	-31.2	64.2	55.6	-8.6	20.8	20.2	-0.6	15.0	24.2	9.2
45 Harrow E.	19.3.59	8.8	82.6	68.9	-13.7	54.4	52.8	-1.6	45.6	46.2	0.6	—	—	—
46 Norfolk SW	25.3.59	0.6	82.6	75.2	-7.4	49.7	46.4	-3.3	50.3	51.0	0.7	—	—	—
47 Kircudbrights., Galloway	9.4.59	33.8	69.1	72.7	3.6	66.9	50.4	-16.5	33.1	23.9	-9.2	—	—	—
48 Yks., Penistone	11.6.59	24.6	80.0	65.0	-15.0	37.7	35.9	-1.8	62.3	64.1	1.8	—	25.7	25.7
49 Cumb., Whitehaven	18.6.59	16.0	83.8	79.2	-4.6	42.0	41.4	-0.6	58.0	58.6	0.6	—	—	—
YEAR'S AVERAGE		30.7	74.3	62.5	-11.8	52.3	45.1	-7.2	46.0	45.0	-1.0	12.3	23.9	18.3
PARLT. AVERAGE		25.0	76.1	63.8	-12.3	52.8	44.0	-8.9	44.5	45.6	1.0	19.1	25.4	12.8

[a] Con. gain from Con. Ind.

CON. GOVT. 1959	Date	Maj. GE	Turn-out (%)			Con. vote (%)			Lab. vote (%)			Lib. vote (%)		
			GE	BE	Change	GE	BE	Change	GE	BE	Change	GE	BE	Change
GENERAL ELECTION	8.9.59		78.7			49.4			43.8			5.9		
1* Brighouse/Spenborough	17.3.60	0.2	85.5	82.4	-3.1	49.9	50.8	0.9	50.1	49.2	-0.9			
2 Harrow W.	17.3.60	41.8	79.2	61.6	-17.6	70.9	55.7	-15.2	29.1	18.2	-10.9		21.4	21.4
3 Edinburgh N.	19.5.60	28.0	73.9	53.8	-20.1	64.0	54.2	-9.8	36.0	30.3	-5.7		15.5	15.5
YEAR'S AVERAGE		23.3	79.5	65.9	-13.6	61.6	53.6	-8.0	38.4	32.6	-5.8		18.5	18.5
4 Bolton E.	16.11.60	5.6	80.9	68.2	-12.7	52.8	37.8	-15.0	47.2	36.2	-11.0		24.8	24.8
5 Bedfordshire M.	19.11.60	11.4	84.5	71.1	-13.4	46.8	45.4	-1.4	35.4	29.2	-6.2	17.8	24.8	7.0
6 Devon, Tiverton	19.11.60	30.4	80.7	68.4	-12.3	55.6	45.7	-9.9	25.2	17.6	-7.6	19.2	36.7	17.5
7 Hants, Petersfield	19.11.60	39.6	73.6	53.6	-20.0	60.9	54.4	-6.5	21.3	16.6	-4.7	17.8	29.0	11.2
8 Shrops., Ludlow	16.11.60	20.6	76.2	63.6	-12.6	60.3	46.4	-13.9	39.7	26.3	-13.4		27.3	27.3
9 Surrey, Carshalton	19.11.60	23.5	82.5	54.2	-28.3	54.0	51.7	-2.3	30.5	20.7	-9.8	15.5	27.6	12.1
10 Ebbw Vale	17.11.60	62.0	85.8	76.1	-9.7	19.0	12.7	-6.3	81.0	68.8	-12.2		11.5	11.5
11 Blyth	24.11.60	49.2	82.6	54.1	-28.5	25.4	21.6	-3.8	74.6	68.9	-5.7			
12 Worcester	16.3.61	15.4	79.3	64.2	-15.1	57.7	39.7	-18.0	42.3	30.2	-12.1		30.1	30.1
13 Cambridgeshire	16.3.61	15.8	78.0	62.4	-15.6	57.9	45.9	-12.0	42.1	30.1	-12.0		24.0	24.0
14 Derbys., High Peak	16.3.61	12.0	82.7	72.5	-10.2	46.0	37.4	-8.6	34.0	32.1	-1.9	20.0	30.5	10.5
15 Essex, Colchester	16.3.61	15.7	82.4	64.9	-17.5	51.6	47.2	-4.4	35.9	33.1	-2.8	12.5	19.7	7.2
16 B'ham, Small Heath	23.3.61	14.8	65.7	42.6	-23.1	42.6	28.8	-13.8	57.4	59.2	1.8		12.0	12.0
17 Warrington	20.4.61	12.6	76.9	56.7	-20.2	43.7	31.6	-12.1	56.3	55.9	-0.4		12.5	12.5
18 Paisley	20.4.61	14.6	78.9	68.1	-10.8	42.7	13.2	-29.5	57.3	45.4	-11.9		41.4	41.4
19* Bristol SE	4.5.61	12.4	81.4	56.7	-24.7	43.8	30.5	-13.3	56.2	69.5	13.3			
YEAR'S AVERAGE		22.2	79.5	62.3	-17.2	47.6	36.9	-10.7	46.0	40.0	-6.0	17.1	25.1	17.8
20 Manch. Moss Side	7.11.61	24.6	69.2	46.7	-22.5	62.3	41.2	-21.1	37.7	25.8	-11.9		27.8	27.8
21 Fife E.	8.11.61	39.8	75.2	67.3	-7.9	69.9	47.5	-22.4	30.1	26.4	-3.7		26.1	26.1
22 Shrops., Oswestry	8.11.61	27.9	74.2	60.8	-13.4	55.9	40.8	-15.1	28.0	28.0	0.0	16.1	28.4	12.3
23 G'gow, Bridgeton	16.11.61	26.8	68.5	41.9	-26.6	36.6	20.7	-15.9	63.4	57.5	-5.9			
24 Lincoln	8.3.62	10.2	84.2	75.0	-9.2	44.9	30.2	-14.7	55.1	50.5	-4.6		18.2	18.2
25 Blackpool N.	13.3.62	36.2	74.8	55.2	-19.6	57.8	38.3	-19.5	21.6	26.4	4.8	20.6	35.3	14.7
26 Middlesborough E.	14.3.62	23.0	76.2	52.2	-24.0	38.5	14.8	-23.7	61.5	60.5	-1.0		22.9	22.9
27* Kent, Orpington	14.3.62	34.4	82.8	80.3	-2.5	56.6	34.7	-21.9	22.2	12.4	-9.8	21.2	52.9	31.7
28 Pontefract	22.3.62	52.8	84.3	63.3	-21.0	23.6	19.4	-4.2	76.4	77.3	0.9			
29 Stockton-on-Tees	5.4.62	7.4	84.3	81.5	-2.8	46.3	27.8	-18.5	53.7	45.3	-8.4		26.9	26.9
30 Derby N.	17.4.62	2.2	83.9	60.5	-23.4	47.2	22.5	-24.7	52.8	49.4	-3.4		25.4	25.4
31 Montgomeryshire	15.5.62	10.8	76.7	85.1	8.4	31.3	21.9	-9.4	26.6	20.6	-6.0	42.1	51.3	9.2
32* Middlesborough W.	6.6.62	19.5	83.8	72.2	-11.6	54.9	33.7	-21.2	35.4	**39.7**	4.3	9.7	25.8	16.1

CON. GOVT. 1959	Date	Maj. GE	Turn-out (%)			Con. vote (%)			Lab. vote (%)			Lib. vote (%)		
			GE	BE	Change	GE	BE	Change	GE	BE	Change	GE	BE	Change
33 Derbyshire W.	6.6.62	22.6	84.5	79.4	−5.1	61.3	36.1	−25.2	38.7	27.3	−11.4	—	32.5	32.5
34 W. Lothian	14.6.62	20.6	77.9	71.1	−6.8	39.7	11.4	−28.3	60.3	50.9	−9.4	—	10.8	10.8
35 Leicester NE	12.7.62	3.8	78.4	60.8	−17.6	48.1	24.2	−23.9	51.9	41.5	−10.4	—	34.3	34.3
YEAR'S AVERAGE		22.7	78.7	65.8	−12.9	48.4	29.1	−19.4	44.7	40.0	−4.7	21.9	29.9	22.1
36* Dorset S.	22.11.62	15.1	78.8	70.2	−8.6	49.8	31.8	−18.0	34.7	33.5	−1.2	15.5	21.7	6.2
37 Norfolk C.	22.11.62	15.5	79.9	60.2	−19.7	50.3	37.7	−12.6	34.8	37.0	2.2	14.9	22.5	7.6
38 Northamp. S.	22.11.62	14.0	82.7	69.0	−13.7	57.0	41.2	−15.8	43.0	38.6	−4.4	16.9	19.3	19.3
39 Wilts., Chippenham	22.11.62	21.1	80.2	68.0	−12.2	52.1	36.9	−15.2	31.0	29.1	−1.9	7.7	32.5	15.6
40* G'gow, Woodside	22.11.62	6.1	75.2	54.7	−20.5	49.2	30.1	−19.1	43.1	36.1	−7.0	25.8	21.7	14.0
41 Lancs., Colne Valley	21.3.63	14.4	84.1	78.9	−5.2	29.9	15.4	−14.5	44.3	44.4	0.1	—	39.5	13.7
42 Rotherham	28.3.63	25.6	78.9	56.3	−22.6	37.2	28.4	−8.8	62.8	69.3	6.5	—	—	—
43 Swansea E.	28.3.63	45.5	80.1	55.9	−24.2	22.0	7.3	−14.7	67.5	61.2	−6.3	—	15.8	15.8
44 Leeds S.	20.3.63	27.6	79.0	60.5	−18.5	31.0	20.1	−10.9	58.6	63.0	4.4	10.4	14.7	4.3
45 Deptford	4.7.63	23.8	69.3	44.1	−25.2	38.1	19.2	−18.9	61.9	58.3	−3.6	—	22.5	22.5
46 W. Bromwich	4.7.63	14.8	72.5	55.2	−17.3	42.6	23.6	−19.0	57.4	58.8	1.4	—	17.6	17.6
47 Warwicks., Stratford	15.8.63	37.0	76.9	69.4	−7.5	68.5	43.5	−25.0	31.5	34.1	2.6	—	21.0	21.0
48* Bristol SE[a]	20.8.63	12.4	81.4	42.2	−39.2	43.8	—	−43.8	56.2	79.7	23.5	—	—	—
YEAR'S AVERAGE		21.0	78.4	60.4	−18.0	44.0	27.9	−18.2	48.2	49.5	1.3	15.2	22.6	14.3
49* Luton	7.11.63	10.2	82.5	74.0	−8.5	55.1	39.5	−15.6	44.9	48.0	3.1	—	11.4	11.4
50 Perthshire W./Kinross-shire	7.11.63	51.4	71.0	76.1	5.1	68.2	57.4	−10.8	16.8	15.2	−1.6	—	19.5	19.5
51 Dundee W.	21.11.63	1.3	82.9	71.6	−11.3	48.3	39.4	−8.9	49.6	50.6	1.0	—	—	—
52 St Marylebone	5.12.63	40.9	65.5	44.2	−21.3	64.5	54.9	−9.6	23.6	31.8	8.2	11.9	13.3	1.4
53 Manch. Openshaw	5.12.63	20.4	76.0	46.1	−29.9	39.8	29.2	−10.6	60.2	65.9	5.7	—	—	—
54 Suffolk, Sudbury/W'dbr.	5.12.63	20.0	81.1	70.5	−10.6	53.0	49.6	−3.4	33.0	37.0	4.0	14.0	13.4	−0.6
55 Dumfriesshire	12.12.63	43.8	77.4	71.6	−5.8	58.4	40.9	−17.5	14.6	38.5	23.9	—	10.9	10.9
56 Hants, Winchester	14.5.64	43.6	76.7	68.7	−8.0	67.3	52.2	−15.1	23.7	34.6	10.9	—	13.2	13.2
57* Lanarks. Rutherglen	14.5.64	4.2	85.8	82.0	−3.8	52.1	44.5	−7.6	47.9	55.5	7.6	—	—	—
58 Bury St Edmunds	14.5.64	17.4	78.6	74.6	−4.0	58.7	49.0	−9.7	41.3	43.5	2.2	—	7.5	7.5
59 Wilts., Devizes	14.5.64	9.5	79.2	75.8	−3.4	51.4	46.8	−4.6	41.9	42.9	1.0	—	10.3	10.3
60 Kent, Faversham	4.6.64	0.6	83.8	74.8	−9.0	49.7	44.1	−5.6	50.3	55.1	4.8	—	—	—
61 L'pool Scotland	11.6.64	23.6	62.5	42.0	−20.5	38.2	25.7	−12.5	61.8	74.3	12.5	13.0	12.4	9.2
YEAR'S AVERAGE		22.1	77.2	67.1	−10.1	54.2	44.1	−10.1	39.2	45.6	6.4	17.3	23.6	16.9
PARLT. AVERAGE		22.1	78.6	64.0	−14.6	49.1	35.4	−14.3	44.3	42.8	−1.5			

LAB. GOVT. 1964

LAB. GOVT. 1964	Date	Maj. GE	Turn-out (%)			Con. vote (%)			Lab. vote (%)			Lib. vote (%)		
			GE	BE	Change	GE	BE	Change	GE	BE	Change	GE	BE	Change
GENERAL ELECTION	15.9.64		77.1			43.4			44.1			11.2		
1* Leyton	21.1.65	16.8	70.2	57.7	-12.5	33.5	42.8	9.3	50.3	42.4	-7.9	16.2	14.0	-2.2
2 Warwicks., Nuneaton	21.1.65	23.7	80.1	60.8	-19.3	29.1	34.9	5.8	52.8	49.0	-3.8	18.1	16.1	-2.0
3 Altrincham/Sale	4.2.65	18.8	81.2	62.0	-19.2	46.8	50.0	3.2	28.0	29.0	1.0	25.2	19.4	-5.8
4 Sussex, E. Grinstead	4.2.65	26.2	78.0	64.5	-13.5	53.2	55.0	1.8	19.8	13.5	-6.3	27.0	31.5	4.5
5 Salisbury	4.2.65	13.9	78.6	69.1	-9.5	48.3	48.2	-0.1	34.4	37.4	3.0	17.3	12.9	-4.4
6 Essex, Saffron Waldon	23.3.65	12.0	82.4	76.1	-6.3	49.4	48.6	-0.8	37.4	39.5	2.1	13.2	11.9	-1.3
7* Roxburghshire, Selkirkshire, and Peeblesshire	24.3.65	3.9	82.2	82.2	0.0	42.8	38.6	-4.2	15.8	11.3	-4.5	38.9	49.2	10.3
8 Mon., Abertillery	1.4.65	71.8	75.5	63.2	-12.3	14.1	14.3	0.2	85.9	79.0	-6.9	—	—	—
9 B'ham, Hall Green	6.5.65	20.8	75.8	52.4	-23.4	52.6	54.8	2.2	31.8	28.8	-3.0	15.6	16.4	0.8
10 Hove	22.7.65	36.8	69.6	58.5	-11.1	68.4	62.2	-6.2	31.6	20.6	-11.0	—	16.9	16.9
YEAR'S AVERAGE		24.5	77.4	64.7	-12.7	43.8	44.9	1.1	38.8	35.1	-3.7	21.4	20.9	1.7
11 City of London/West.	4.11.65	27.7	59.7	41.8	-17.9	58.3	59.5	1.2	30.6	32.9	2.3	11.1	6.3	-4.8
12 Erith/Crayford	11.11.65	20.6	79.6	72.0	-7.6	32.5	37.4	4.9	53.1	55.4	2.3	14.4	7.2	-7.2
13 Kingston u. Hull N.	27.1.66	2.5	77.2	76.3	-0.9	40.8	40.8	0.0	43.3	52.2	8.9	15.9	6.3	-9.6
YEAR'S AVERAGE		16.9	72.2	63.4	-8.8	43.9	45.9	2.0	42.3	46.8	4.5	13.8	6.6	-7.2
PARLT. AVERAGE		22.9	76.2	64.4	-11.9	43.8	45.1	1.3	39.5	37.6	-2.0	19.5	17.6	-0.2

LAB. GOVT. 1966

LAB. GOVT. 1966	Date	Maj. GE	Turn-out (%)			Con. vote (%)			Lab. vote (%)			Lib. vote (%)		
			GE	BE	Change	GE	BE	Change	GE	BE	Change	GE	BE	Change
GENERAL ELECTION	31.3.66		75.8			41.9			48.0			8.6		
1* Carmarthen[a]	14.7.66	20.1	83.0	74.9	-8.1	11.6	7.1	-4.5	46.2	33.1	-13.1	26.1	20.8	-5.3
2 Warwicks., Nuneaton	9.3.67	22.3	79.7	66.1	-13.6	31.6	32.7	1.1	53.9	42.1	-11.8	14.5	17.6	3.1
3 Rhondda W.	9.3.67	68.3	80.3	82.2	1.9	7.8	4.3	-3.5	76.1	49.0	-27.1	—	—	—
4* G'gow Pollok	9.3.67	4.8	79.0	75.7	-3.3	47.6	36.9	-10.7	52.4	31.2	-21.2	—	1.9	1.9
5 Devon, Honiton	16.3.67	27.8	78.6	72.6	-6.0	54.5	57.0	2.5	26.7	20.4	-6.3	18.8	22.6	3.8
YEAR'S AVERAGE		28.7	80.1	74.3	-5.8	30.6	27.6	-3.0	51.1	35.2	-15.9	19.8	15.7	0.9
6 Staffs., Brierley Hill	27.4.67	2.4	79.0	68.0	-11.0	51.2	53.8	2.6	48.8	36.2	-12.6	—	7.8	7.8
7* Cambridge	21.9.67	2.1	80.0	65.7	-14.3	43.4	51.6	8.2	45.5	36.6	-8.9	10.2	11.8	1.6
8* Walthamstow W.	21.9.67	36.3	71.0	54.0	-17.0	24.8	37.0	12.2	61.1	36.7	-24.4	14.1	22.9	8.8
9* Leicester SW	2.11.67	17.4	74.0	57.5	-16.5	41.3	51.6	10.3	58.7	35.9	-22.8	—	12.5	12.5
10 Gorton Manch.	2.11.67	20.2	72.6	72.4	-0.2	39.9	44.5	4.6	60.1	45.9	-14.2	—	5.9	5.9
11* Lanarks., Hamilton[b]	2.11.67	42.4	73.3	73.7	0.4	28.8	12.5	-16.3	71.2	41.5	-29.7	—	—	—

LAB. GOVT. 1966	Date	Maj. GE	Turn-out (%)			Con. vote (%)			Lab. vote (%)			Lib. vote (%)		
			GE	BE	Change	GE	BE	Change	GE	BE	Change	GE	BE	Change
12 Derbyshire W.	23.11.67	12.4	83.4	64.5	-18.9	49.6	56.6	7.0	37.2	18.4	-18.8	13.2	19.8	6.6
13 Kensington S.	15.3.68	45.3	58.1	40.0	-18.1	65.1	75.4	10.3	19.8	8.6	-11.2	15.1	12.6	-2.5
14* Acton	28.3.68	15.4	73.9	59.7	-14.2	42.3	48.6	6.3	57.7	33.9	-23.8	—	11.4	11.4
15* Dudley	28.3.68	18.2	73.9	63.5	-10.4	40.9	58.1	17.2	59.1	34.0	-25.1	—	7.9	7.9
16* Warwicks., Meriden	28.3.68	7.2	85.7	66.0	-19.7	46.4	64.8	18.4	53.6	35.2	-18.4	—	—	—
17 Warwick/Leamington	28.3.68	15.5	78.9	58.5	-20.4	51.6	68.3	16.7	36.1	16.5	-19.6	12.3	15.2	2.9
YEAR'S AVERAGE		19.6	75.3	62.0	-13.4	43.8	51.9	8.1	50.7	31.6	-19.1	13.0	12.8	6.3
18* Oldham W.	13.6.68	22.4	70.9	54.7	-16.2	38.8	46.5	7.7	61.2	33.6	-27.6	—	6.7	6.7
19 Shef. Brightside	13.6.68	54.6	66.2	49.8	-16.4	21.3	34.8	13.5	75.9	55.1	-20.8	—	—	—
20* Nelson/Colne	27.6.68	12.3	80.9	74.2	-6.7	37.0	48.9	11.9	49.3	38.4	-10.9	—	9.0	9.0
21 Caerphilly	18.7.68	59.7	76.7	75.9	-0.8	14.6	10.4	-4.2	74.3	45.6	-28.7	—	3.6	3.6
22 Notts, Bassetlaw	31.10.68	23.2	73.4	68.0	-5.4	38.4	47.9	9.5	61.6	49.7	-11.9	—	—	—
23 Hants, New Forest	7.11.68	24.5	74.2	55.9	-18.3	51.2	66.3	15.1	26.7	13.8	-12.9	22.1	19.9	-2.2
24 Bright. Pavilion	27.3.69	16.2	70.3	45.1	-25.2	58.1	70.6	12.5	41.9	18.6	-23.3	—	10.8	10.8
25* Walthamstow E.	27.3.69	5.6	80.1	51.2	-28.9	42.3	63.1	20.8	47.9	36.9	-11.0	9.8	—	-9.8
26 Weston s. Mare	27.3.69	23.3	78.5	60.8	-17.7	52.1	65.7	13.6	28.8	14.6	-14.2	19.1	19.7	0.6
YEAR'S AVERAGE		26.9	74.6	59.5	-15.1	39.3	50.5	11.2	52.0	34.0	-17.9	17.0	11.6	2.7
27 Sussex, Chichester	22.5.69	32.1	73.2	53.4	-19.8	57.2	74.2	17.0	25.1	12.2	-12.9	17.7	13.6	-4.1
28* B'ham Ladywood	26.6.69	35.2	59.7	51.9	-7.8	17.4	16.8	-0.6	58.9	25.5	-33.4	23.7	54.3	30.6
29 Islington N.	30.10.69	28.7	54.2	32.8	-21.4	30.7	38.9	8.2	59.4	49.2	-10.2	9.9	10.2	0.3
30 Paddington N.	30.10.69	26.1	66.4	46.3	-20.1	32.3	48.3	16.0	58.4	51.7	-6.7	9.3	—	-9.3
31 Ncl. u. Lyme	30.10.69	23.6	79.9	72.3	-7.6	38.2	43.9	5.7	61.8	46.1	-15.7	—	6.4	6.4
32* Swindon	30.10.69	24.6	73.5	69.8	-3.7	36.7	41.8	5.1	61.3	40.5	-20.8	—	15.3	15.3
33 G'gow Gorbals	30.10.69	50.3	61.7	58.5	-3.2	22.8	18.6	-4.2	73.1	53.4	-19.7	—	—	—
34 Lincs., Louth	4.12.69	9.4	75.0	44.7	-30.3	46.3	57.9	11.6	36.9	19.9	-17.0	16.8	17.8	1.0
35* Northants, Wellingborough	4.12.69	4.8	86.5	69.6	-16.9	47.6	54.4	6.8	52.4	39.8	-12.6	—	—	—
36 Som., Bridgewater	12.3.70	6.3	80.2	70.3	-9.9	44.4	55.5	11.1	38.1	31.9	-6.2	17.5	12.6	-4.9
37 S. Ayrshire/Bute	19.3.70	34.4	75.1	76.3	1.2	32.8	25.6	-7.2	67.2	54.0	-13.2	—	—	—
YEAR'S AVERAGE		25.0	71.4	58.7	-12.7	36.9	43.3	6.3	53.9	38.6	-15.3	15.8	18.6	4.4
PARLT. AVERAGE		24.3	74.8	62.3	-12.5	38.8	45.5	6.7	52.0	34.7	-17.3	16.0	14.4	4.1

a Gain by Plaid Cymru.
b Gain by SNP.

CON. GOVT. 1970	Date	Maj. GE	Turn-out (%)			Con. vote (%)			Lab. vote (%)			Lib. vote (%)		
			GE	BE	Change	GE	BE	Change	GE	BE	Change	GE	BE	Change
GENERAL ELECTION	18.6.70		72.0			46.4			43.1			7.5		
1 St Marylebone	22.10.70	32.8	59.8	35.3	−24.5	62.1	63.4	1.3	29.3	27.0	−2.3	8.6	6.2	−2.4
2 Enfield W.	19.11.70	31.7	71.2	49.9	−21.3	57.9	57.3	−0.6	26.2	26.0	−0.2	12.8	12.3	−0.5
3 L'pool Scotland	1.4.71	49.6	50.7	37.7	−13.0	25.2	18.4	−6.8	74.8	71.3	−3.5	—	—	—
4 Sussex, Arundel/Shoreham	1.4.71	37.9	72.0	53.1	−18.9	60.8	64.1	3.3	22.9	20.9	−2.0	16.3	14.7	−1.6
5 Southampton Itchen	27.5.71	67.2	54.2	50.1	−4.1	—	31.6	31.6	67.2	55.4	−11.8	—	5.4	5.4
6* Worcs., Bromsgrove	27.5.71	17.0	76.6	67.0	−9.6	58.5	48.4	−10.1	41.5	51.6	10.1	—	—	—
7 Yorks., Goole	27.5.71	20.4	69.5	55.6	−13.9	39.8	31.1	−8.7	60.2	68.9	8.7	—	—	—
8 Hayes/Harlington	17.6.71	16.5	67.2	42.3	−24.9	41.2	25.3	−15.9	57.7	74.7	17.0	—	—	—
YEAR'S AVERAGE		34.1	65.2	48.9	−16.3	49.4	42.5	−0.7	47.5	49.5	2.0	12.6	9.7	0.2
9 Greenwich	8.7.71	21.0	64.0	39.2	−24.8	36.3	28.0	−8.3	57.3	66.7	9.4	6.4	—	−6.4
10 Stirling/Falkirk	19.9.71	15.9	73.1	60.0	−13.1	34.8	18.9	−15.9	50.7	46.5	−4.2	—	—	—
11 Lancs., Widnes	23.9.71	15.4	68.8	45.4	−23.4	42.3	30.9	−11.4	57.7	69.1	11.4	—	—	—
12 Ches., Macclesfield	30.9.71	18.8	76.4	75.6	−0.8	52.1	44.7	−7.4	33.3	42.7	9.4	14.6	10.7	−3.9
13* Merthyr Tydfil[a]	13.4.72	23.2	77.9	79.5	1.6	9.8	7.4	−2.4	28.7	48.5	19.8	—	2.4	2.4
14* Southwark	4.5.72	39.1	48.2	32.1	−16.1	28.2	18.1	−10.1	67.3	79.3	12.0	—	—	—
15 Kingston u. Thames	4.5.72	24.9	69.2	53.6	−15.6	56.6	52.3	−4.3	31.7	31.0	−0.7	11.7	11.3	−0.4
YEAR'S AVERAGE		22.5	68.2	55.1	−13.2	37.2	28.6	−8.5	46.7	54.8	8.2	10.9	8.1	−2.1
16* Rochdale	26.10.72	11.2	72.8	69.1	−3.7	28.0	17.7	−10.3	41.6	31.1	−10.5	30.4	**42.3**	11.9
17 Middx., Uxbridge	7.12.72	7.6	74.9	54.3	−20.6	49.3	39.9	−9.4	41.7	36.6	−5.1	9.0	10.3	1.3
18* Sutton/Cheam	7.12.72	30.8	67.6	56.3	−11.3	58.1	31.9	−26.2	27.3	8.7	−18.6	14.6	**53.6**	39.0
19[b] Lincoln	1.3.73	12.0	74.5	72.6	−1.9	39.0	17.5	−21.5	51.0	23.3	−27.7	—	—	—
20 Durham, Chester-le-Street	1.3.73	43.2	73.7	72.3	−1.4	28.4	8.4	−20.0	71.6	53.0	−18.6	—	—	—
21 Dundee E.	1.3.73	5.9	76.1	70.6	−5.5	42.4	25.2	−17.2	48.3	32.7	−15.6	—	—	—
22 W. Bromwich	24.5.73	10.4	62.2	43.6	−18.6	44.8	25.4	−19.4	55.2	53.2	−2.0	—	—	—
23 Lancs., Westhoughton	24.5.73	10.8	76.9	63.4	−13.5	44.6	42.3	−2.3	55.4	57.0	1.6	—	—	—
YEAR'S AVERAGE		16.5	72.3	62.8	−9.6	41.8	26.0	−15.8	49.0	37.0	−12.1	18.0	30.6	19.8
24 Manch. Exchange	27.6.73	40.7	57.0	43.7	−13.3	27.8	7.1	−20.7	68.5	55.3	−13.2	—	36.5	36.5
25* Isle of Ely	26.7.73	19.8	71.9	65.8	−6.1	59.9	35.0	−24.9	40.1	26.7	−13.4	—	**38.3**	38.3

CON. GOVT. 1970	Date	Maj. GE	Turn-out (%)			Con. vote (%)			Lab. vote (%)			Lib. vote (%)		
			GE	BE	Change	GE	BE	Change	GE	BE	Change	GE	BE	Change
26* Yorks., Ripon	26.7.73	34.7	73.7	64.3	−9.4	60.7	40.5	−20.2	26.2	13.9	−12.3	13.1	**43.5**	30.4
27 Hove	8.11.73	37.4	66.8	62.4	−4.4	68.7	47.8	−20.9	31.3	11.6	−19.7	—	37.3	37.3
28* Berwick-u.-Tweed	8.11.73	23.3	73.7	75.0	1.3	50.7	39.7	−11.0	27.4	19.8	−7.6	21.9	**39.9**	18.0
29 Edinburgh N.	8.11.73	15.7	70.1	54.4	−15.7	52.8	38.7	−14.1	37.1	24.0	−13.1	10.1	18.4	8.3
30* Glasgow Govan^c	8.11.73	31.8	63.3	51.7	−11.6	28.2	11.7	−16.5	60.0	38.2	−21.8	—	8.2	8.2
YEAR'S AVERAGE		29.1	68.1	59.6	−8.5	49.8	31.5	−18.3	41.5	27.1	−14.4	15.0	31.7	25.3
PARLT. AVERAGE		25.5	68.5	56.4	−12.0	44.3	32.3	−10.5	46.4	42.6	−3.8	14.1	22.1	11.9

[a] Lab. gain from Ind. Lab.
[b] Dem. Lab. gain from Lab.
[c] SNP gain from Lab.

LAB. GOVT. 1974	Date	Maj. GE	Turn-out (%) GE	BE	Change	Con. vote (%) GE	BE	Change	Lab. vote (%) GE	BE	Change	Lib. vote (%) GE	BE	Change
GENERAL ELECTION	28.2.74		78.8			37.9			37.2			19.3		
1 Newham S.	23.6.74	51.3	63.2	25.9	−37.3	12.2	11.1	−1.1	66.1	62.7	−3.4	14.8	12.5	−2.3
GENERAL ELECTION	10.9.74		72.8			35.8			39.2			18.3		
1* Woolwich W.	26.6.75	8.5	73.9	62.3	−11.6	38.6	**48.8**	10.2	47.1	42.1	−5.0	14.3	5.3	−9.0
2 Coventry N.W.	4.3.76	20.3	75.2	72.9	−2.3	31.6	37.4	5.8	51.9	47.7	−4.2	15.7	11.3	−4.4
3 Carshalton	11.3.76	7.5	74.3	60.5	−13.8	45.4	51.7	6.3	37.9	27.5	−10.4	16.7	15.0	−1.7
4 Wirral	11.3.76	19.2	75.5	55.5	−20.0	50.8	66.8	16.0	31.6	20.3	−11.3	17.6	11.4	−6.2
5 Rotherham	24.6.76	42.5	65.5	46.8	−18.7	22.1	34.7	12.6	64.6	50.7	−13.9	13.3	7.8	−5.5
6 Thurrock	15.7.76	31.2	68.6	54.1	−14.5	24.4	35.4	11.0	55.6	45.3	−10.3	20.0	12.2	−7.8
YEAR'S AVERAGE		24.1	71.8	58.0	−13.9	34.9	45.2	10.3	48.3	38.3	−10.0	16.7	11.5	−5.1
7 Ncl. u. Tyne C.	4.11.76	55.3	58.4	41.0	−17.4	16.5	19.7	3.2	71.8	47.6	−24.2	11.7	29.0	17.3
8* Walsall N.	4.11.76	33.4	66.6	51.5	−15.1	26.1	**43.4**	17.3	59.5	31.6	−27.9	13.4	3.2	−10.2
9* Workington	4.11.76	23.7	75.8	74.2	−1.6	32.3	**48.2**	15.9	56.0	45.6	−10.4	11.7	6.2	−5.5
10 Cambridge	2.12.76	5.2	69.6	49.2	−20.4	41.2	51.0	9.8	36.0	26.0	−10.0	21.1	18.3	−2.8
11 City of London/West. S.	24.2.77	20.8	53.2	39.6	−13.6	51.7	59.1	7.4	30.9	19.7	−11.2	14.9	9.8	−5.1
12* B'ham Stechford	31.3.77	29.8	64.1	58.8	−5.3	27.8	**43.4**	15.6	57.6	38.0	−19.6	14.6	8.0	−6.6
13* Ashfield	28.4.77	41.1	74.7	59.7	−15.0	22.3	**43.1**	20.8	63.4	42.5	−20.9	14.3	9.6	−4.7
14 Grimsby	28.4.77	15.2	69.4	70.2	0.8	31.9	45.7	13.8	47.1	46.9	−0.2	20.6	6.7	−13.9
15 Saffron Walden	7.7.77	13.4	78.1	64.8	−13.3	43.7	55.7	12.0	26.0	14.5	−11.5	30.3	25.2	−5.1
16 B'ham Ladywood	18.8.77	42.4	56.9	42.6	−14.3	22.1	28.4	6.3	64.5	53.1	−11.4	13.4	4.9	−8.5
YEAR'S AVERAGE		28.0	66.7	55.2	−11.5	31.6	43.8	12.2	51.3	36.6	−14.7	16.6	12.1	−4.5
17 Bournemouth E.	24.11.77	26.5	70.5	42.6	−27.9	51.7	63.4	11.7	21.0	15.3	−5.7	25.2	13.4	−11.8
18* Ilford N./Redbridge	2.3.78	1.6	74.5	69.1	−5.4	40.9	**50.3**	9.4	42.5	38.0	−4.5	16.6	5.0	−11.6
19 G'gow Garscadden	13.4.78	38.0	70.8	69.1	−1.7	12.9	18.5	5.6	50.9	45.4	−5.5	5.0	—	−5.0
20 Lambeth C.	20.4.78	33.9	52.6	44.5	−8.1	26.2	34.4	8.2	60.1	49.4	−10.7	12.5	5.3	−7.2
21 Epsom/Ewell	27.4.78	27.5	73.7	54.9	−18.8	54.1	63.6	9.5	19.3	16.5	−2.8	26.6	12.8	−13.8
22 Wycombe	27.4.78	15.5	74.3	59.0	−15.3	46.3	60.0	13.7	30.8	28.5	−2.3	19.4	7.4	−12.0
23 Hamilton	31.6.78	38.0	77.2	72.1	−5.1	9.5	13.0	3.5	47.5	51.0	3.5	4.0	2.6	−1.4

LAB. GOVT. 1974

	Date	Maj. GE	Turn-out (%) GE	BE	Change	Con. vote (%) GE	BE	Change	Lab. vote (%) GE	BE	Change	Lib. vote (%) GE	BE	Change
24 Manch. Moss Side	13.7.78	12.8	62.9	51.6	−11.3	34.3	40.6	6.3	47.1	46.4	−0.7	17.6	9.2	−8.4
25 Penistone	13.7.78	30.2	74.7	59.8	−14.9	24.0	32.9	8.9	54.2	45.5	−8.7	21.8	21.6	−0.2
26 Berwick/E. Lothian	26.9.78	5.7	83.0	71.2	−11.8	37.6	40.2	2.6	43.3	47.4	4.1	5.9	3.6	−2.3
YEAR'S AVERAGE		23.0	71.4	59.4	−12.0	33.8	41.7	7.9	41.7	38.3	−3.3	15.5	9.0	−7.4
27 Pontefract/Castleford	26.11.78	54.2	71.2	48.9	−22.3	16.2	27.3	11.1	70.4	65.8	−4.6	12.3	6.9	−5.4
28 Clitheroe	1.3.79	16.8	78.6	62.8	−15.8	48.0	65.0	17.0	31.2	28.4	−2.8	20.8	6.6	−14.2
29 Knutsford	1.3.79	24.6	76.8	57.2	−19.6	51.0	67.1	16.1	22.6	15.6	−7.0	26.4	15.8	−10.6
30* L'pool Edge Hill	29.3.79	24.6	61.2	57.2	−4.0	20.8	9.4	−11.4	51.9	23.8	−28.1	27.3	**64.1**	36.8
YEAR'S AVERAGE		30.1	72.0	56.5	−15.4	34.0	42.2	8.2	44.0	33.4	−10.6	21.7	23.4	1.7
PARLT. AVERAGE		26.1	69.9	56.5	−13.3	32.9	42.4	9.6	46.9	38.0	−9.1	16.8	12.2	−4.9

CON. GOVT. 1979	Date	Maj. GE	Turn-out (%)			Con. vote (%)			Lab. vote (%)			Lib./SDP vote (%)[a]		
			GE	BE	Change	GE	BE	Change	GE	BE	Change	GE	BE	Change
GENERAL ELECTION	3.5.79		76.0			43.9			36.9			13.8		
1 Manchester C.	27.9.79	48.7	63.7	33.6	−30.1	22.1	12.0	−10.1	70.8	70.7	−0.1	5.3	14.2	8.9
2 Hertfordshire SW	13.12.79	27.0	79.7	48.3	−31.4	54.7	45.9	−8.8	27.7	16.2	−11.5	16.2	23.6	7.4
3 Southend E.	13.3.80	27.0	70.1	62.5	−7.6	56.1	36.8	−19.3	29.1	35.6	6.5	13.1	25.1	12.0
YEAR'S AVERAGE		34.2	71.2	48.1	−23.0	44.3	31.6	−12.7	42.5	40.8	−1.7	11.5	21.0	9.4
4 Glasgow C.	26.6.80	56.1	59.5	42.8	−16.7	16.4	8.8	−7.6	72.5	60.8	−11.7	—	—	—
YEAR'S AVERAGE		56.1	59.5	42.8	−16.7	16.4	8.8	−7.6	72.5	60.8	−11.7	—	—	—
5 Warrington	16.7.81	32.9	71.3	67.0	−4.3	28.8	7.1	−21.7	61.7	48.4	−13.3	9.0	42.4	33.4
6* Croydon NW	22.10.81	9.3	72.5	62.8	−9.7	49.4	30.5	−18.9	40.1	26.0	−14.1	10.5	**40.0**	29.5
7* Crosby	26.11.81	31.5	75.2	69.3	−5.9	56.9	39.8	−17.1	25.4	9.5	−15.9	15.2	**49.0**	34.8
8* G'gow Hillhead	25.3.82	6.6	75.7	76.4	0.7	41.0	26.6	−14.4	34.4	25.9	−8.5	14.4	**33.3**	19.0
YEAR'S AVERAGE		20.1	73.7	68.9	−4.8	44.0	26.0	−18.0	40.4	27.5	−13.0	12.3	41.2	29.2
9 Beaconsfield	27.4.82	41.5	76.2	53.9	−22.3	61.7	61.8	0.1	20.2	10.4	−9.8	17.1	26.8	9.7
10* Merton/Mitcham/Mordern	3.6.82	1.3	76.9	48.5	−28.4	43.9	**43.4**	−0.5	45.2	24.4	−20.8	8.9	24.4	20.5
11 Coatbridge/Airdrie	24.6.82	33.4	75.3	56.3	−19.0	27.5	26.2	−1.3	60.9	55.1	−5.8	—	8.2	8.2
12 Gower	16.9.82	22.7	80.8	65.4	−15.4	30.5	22.1	−8.4	53.2	43.5	−9.3	9.1	25.1	16.0
13 Southwark/Peckham	28.10.82	31.7	57.7	38.0	−19.7	28.1	12.4	−15.7	59.8	50.3	−9.5	7.7	32.2	24.5
14* B'ham Nthfld	28.10.82	0.3	70.6	55.0	−15.6	45.4	35.6	−9.8	45.1	**36.3**	−8.8	8.1	26.1	18.0
15 Glasgow Queen's Park	2.12.82	40.4	68.3	47.0	−21.3	24.1	12.0	−12.1	64.5	56.0	−8.5	—	9.4	9.4
16* Bermondsey/S'wark	24.2.83	38.7	59.3	57.7	−1.6	24.9	5.5	−19.4	63.6	26.1	−37.5	6.8	**57.7**	50.9
17 Darlington	24.3.83	2.1	78.4	80.0	1.6	43.4	34.9	−8.5	45.5	39.5	−6.0	10.2	24.5	14.3
YEAR'S AVERAGE		23.6	71.5	55.8	−15.7	36.6	28.2	−8.4	50.9	38.0	−12.9	9.7	26.0	19.1
PARLT. AVERAGE		28.1	70.8	56.2	−14.6	38.0	26.4	−11.6	48.8	38.2	−10.5	11.0	29.1	19.7

[a] Liberal to 1981, then Liberal–Social Democratic Alliance.

CON. GOVT. 1983	Date	Maj. GE	Turn-out (%)			Con. vote (%)			Lab. vote (%)			Lib./SDP vote (%)		
			GE	BE	Change	GE	BE	Change	GE	BE	Change	GE	BE	Change
GENERAL ELECTION	9.6.83					42.4			27.6			25.4		
1 Penrith & Border	28.6.83	30.9	73.1	55.7	−17.4	58.8	46.0	−12.8	13.3	7.4	−5.9	27.9	44.6	16.7
2 Chesterfield	1.3.84	15.7	81.2	76.9	−4.3	32.4	15.1	−17.3	48.1	46.4	−1.7	19.5	34.6	15.1
3 Cynon Valley	3.4.84	35.4	73.4	65.7	−7.7	14.2	7.4	−6.8	56.0	58.7	2.7	20.6	19.8	−0.8
4 Surrey SW	3.4.84	27.6	74.5	61.7	−12.8	59.7	49.3	−10.4	8.2	6.7	−1.5	32.1	43.3	11.2
5 Stafford	3.4.84	26.5	76.5	65.6	−10.9	51.2	40.3	−10.9	23.7	27.3	3.6	24.7	31.7	7.0
YEAR'S AVERAGE		27.2	75.7	65.1	−10.6	43.3	31.6	−11.6	29.9	29.3	−0.6	25.0	34.8	9.8
6* Portsmouth S.	14.6.84	24.6	67.3	54.5	−12.8	50.0	34.2	−15.8	22.6	26.5	3.9	25.4	37.5	12.1
7 Enfield/Southgate	13.12.84	34.7	69.6	50.6	−19.0	58.1	49.6	−8.5	17.9	11.9	−6.0	23.4	35.6	12.2
YEAR'S AVERAGE		29.7	68.5	52.6	−15.9	54.1	41.9	−12.2	20.3	19.2	−1.1	24.4	36.6	12.2
8* Brecon/Radnor	4.7.85	23.2	80.1	79.4	−0.7	48.2	27.7	−20.5	25.0	34.3	9.3	24.4	35.8	11.4
9 Tyne Bridge	5.12.85	31.3	61.5	38.1	−23.4	25.2	11.1	−14.1	56.5	57.8	1.3	18.3	29.7	11.4
10* Fulham	10.4.86	12.2	76.1	70.8	−5.3	46.2	34.9	−11.3	34.0	44.4	10.4	18.3	18.8	0.5
11* Ryedale	8.5.86	28.7	71.8	67.3	−4.5	59.2	41.3	−17.9	10.3	8.4	−1.9	30.5	50.3	19.8
12 W. Derbyshire	8.5.86	28.8	77.4	71.9	−5.5	55.9	39.5	−16.4	17.1	19.8	2.7	27.1	39.4	12.3
13 Ncl. u. Lyme	17.6.86	5.5	77.3	62.0	−15.3	36.4	19.1	−17.3	41.9	40.7	−1.2	21.6	38.8	17.2
YEAR'S AVERAGE		21.6	74.0	64.9	−9.1	45.2	28.9	−16.3	30.8	34.2	3.4	23.4	35.5	12.1
14 Knowsley N.	13.11.86	44.4	69.5	57.0	−12.5	20.1	8.0	−12.1	64.5	56.3	−8.2	14.8	34.5	19.7
15* Greenwich	26.2.87	3.5	67.7	68.4	0.7	34.8	11.6	−23.2	38.2	33.8	−4.4	25.1	53.0	27.9
16 Truro	12.3.87	19.2	79.6	70.3	−9.3	38.1	31.5	−6.6	4.5	7.1	2.6	57.3	60.4	3.1
YEAR'S AVERAGE		22.4	72.3	65.2	−7.0	31.0	17.0	−14.0	35.7	32.4	−3.3	32.4	49.3	16.9
PARLT. AVERAGE		24.8	73.4	63.1	−10.3	43.7	30.0	−13.8	29.6	30.0	0.4	25.5	37.6	12.2

CON. GOVT. 1987	Date	Maj. GE	Turn-out (%)			Con. vote (%)			Lab. vote (%)			Lib. Dem. vote (%)[a]		
			GE	BE	Change	GE	BE	Change	GE	BE	Change	GE	BE	Change
GENERAL ELECTION	11.6.87		75.3			42.3			30.8			22.6		
1 Kensington	14.7.88	14.3	64.7	51.0	−13.7	47.5	41.6	−5.9	33.2	38.1	4.9	17.2	10.8	−6.4
2* G'gow Govan[b]	10.11.88	52.5	73.4	60.2	−13.2	11.9	7.3	−4.6	64.8	36.9	−27.9	12.3	4.1	−8.2
3 Epping Forest	15.12.88	41.5	76.3	49.0	−27.3	60.9	39.5	−21.4	18.4	18.7	0.3	19.4	25.9	6.5
4 Yorks. Richmond	23.2.89	34.2	72.1	63.4	−8.7	61.2	37.2	−24.0	11.8	4.9	−6.9	27.0	22.0	−5.0
5 Pontypridd	23.2.89	36.8	76.6	62.0	−14.6	19.5	13.5	6.0	56.3	53.4	−3.0	18.9	3.9	−15.0
6* Vale of Glam.	4.5.89	12.1	79.3	—	—	46.8	36.3	−10.5	34.7	48.9	14.2	16.7	4.2	−12.5
7 G'gow C.	15.6.89	51.5	65.6	52.8	−12.8	13.0	7.6	−5.4	64.5	54.6	−9.9	10.5	1.5	−9.0
8 Vauxhall	15.6.89	21.2	64.0	42.0	−22.0	29.0	18.8	−10.2	50.2	52.8	2.6	18.2	17.5	−0.7
YEAR'S AVERAGE		33.0	71.5	54.3	−16.0	36.2	25.2	−9.5	41.7	38.5	−3.2	17.5	11.2	−6.3
9 Mid Staffordshire	23.3.90		79.5	79.1	−0.4	50.6	32.3	−18.3	24.7	49.1	24.4	23.2	11.2	−12.0

[a] Liberal/Social Democratic vote in General Election and Liberal Democrat vote in by-election.
[b] Gain by SNP.

Bibliography

Abramowitz, A. I., Cover, A. D., and Norpath, H. (1986). 'The President's Party in Mid-term Elections: Going from Bad to Worse', *American Journal of Political Science*, 30: pp. 562–76.

Abrams, M. (1970). 'The Opinion Polls and the British Election of 1970', *Public Opinion Quarterly*, 34: 317–24.

Abramson, R. R., Aldrich, J. H., and Rohde, D. W. (1983). *Change and Continuity in the 1980 Elections* (Congressional Quarterly Press, Washington, DC).

Aitken, D. (1982). *Stability and Change in Australian Politics* (St Martin's Press, New York).

Alt, J. E. (1984). 'Dealignment and the Dynamics of Partisanship in Britain', in Dalton, R. J. *et al.* (eds.), *Electoral Change in Advanced Industrial Democracies* (Princeton University Press).

Balsom, D. (1979). [Conference discussion], in Drucker, H. (ed.), *Multi-Party Politics* (Macmillan, London).

Barton, J. (1982). [Conference discussion], in Harrop and Worcester (1982).

Beck, P. (1984). 'The Electoral Cycle and Patterns of American Politics', in Neimi, R. G. and Weisberg, H. F. *Controversies in Voting Behavior* (Congressional Quarterly Press, Washington, DC).

Bochel, J., and Denver, D. (1983). 'Candidate Selection in the Labour Party: What the Selectors Seek', *British Journal of Political Science*, 13: 45–69.

Bogdanor, V. (1983). *Liberal Party Politics* (Oxford University Press).

Bradley, I. (1981). *Breaking the Mould* (Martin Robertson, Oxford).

Brand, J. (1978). *The Nationalist Movement in Scotland* (Routledge and Kegan Paul, London).

Bristow, S. (1980). 'Women Councillors—An Explanation of the Under-representation of Women in Local Government', *Local Government Studies*, 6 (May–June): 73–90.

Broh, A. C. (1980). 'Horse Race Journalism: Reporting the Polls in the 1976 Election', *Public Opinion Quarterly*, 44: 514–29.

Brugger, B., and Jaensch, D. (1982). *Australian Politics* (Allen and Unwin, Sydney).

Buchanan, W. (1986). 'Election Predictions: An Empirical Assessment', *Public Opinion Quarterly*, 50: 222–7.

Budge, I., Crewe, I., and Farlie, D., eds. (1976). *Party Identification and Beyond: Representations of Voting and Party Competition*, (Wiley, London).

Burch, M., and Moran, M. (1985). 'The Changing British Political Elite', *Parliamentary Affairs*, 38: 1–15.

Burnham, W. D. (1970). *Critical Elections and the Mainsprings of American Politics* (Norton, New York).

Butler, D (1952). *The British General Election of 1951* (Macmillan, London).

—— (1973). 'By-elections and Their Interpretation', in Cook and Ramsden (1973).

—— (1986). 'Brecon's Three-Way Signpost', *The Times*, 6 July.

—— (1987). 'The Lessons for the Marginals', *The Times*, 28 February.

—— and Kavanagh, D. (1974). *The British General Election of February 1974* (Macmillan, London).

———— (1985). *The British General Election of 1983* (Macmillan, London).

———— (1988). *The British General Election of 1987* (Macmillan, London).

—— and King, A. (1965). *The British General Election of 1964* (Macmillan, London).

—— and Pinto-Duschinski, M. (1971). *The British General Election of 1971* (Macmillan, London).

—— and Rose, R. (1960). *The British General Election of 1959* (Macmillan, London).

—— and Stokes, D. (1974). *Political Change in Britain* (2nd edn.; Macmillan, London).

Cain, B., Ferejohn, J., and Fiorina, M. (1987). *The Personal Vote: Constituency Service and Electoral Independence* (Harvard University Press, Cambridge, Mass.).

Cairns, A. (1968). 'The Electoral System and the Party System in Canada, 1921–1965', *Canadian Journal of Political Science*, 1: 55–80.

Campbell, A. (1966). 'Surge and Decline: A Study of Electoral Change', in Campbell, A., Converse, P. E., Miller, W. E., and Stokes, D. E., *Elections and the Political Order* (Wiley, New York).

——, Converse, P., Miller, W., and Stokes, D. (1960) *The American Voter* (Wiley, New York).

Citrin, J. (1974). 'Comment: The Political Relevance of Trust in Government', *American Political Science Review*, 68: 973–88.

—— and Green, D. P. (1986). 'Presidential Leadership and the Resurgence of Trust in Government', *British Journal of Political Science*, 16: 431–53.

——, McClosky, H., Merrill Shanks, J., and Sniderman, P. M. (1975). 'Personal and Political Sources of Political Alienation', *British Journal of Political Science*, 5: 1–31.

Clarke, H. D., and Stewart, M. (1985). 'Short-Term Forces and Partisan Change in Canada: 1974–80', *Electoral Studies*, 4: 15–35.

——, ——, and Zuk, G. (1986). 'Politics, Economics and Party Popularity in Britain, 1979–83', *Electoral Studies*, 5: 123–41.

Clemens, J. (1983). *Polls, Politics and Populism* (Gower, London).

Cocks, M. (1987). 'Labour after Greenwich; Alibis Won't Do', *Sunday Times* 1 March.

Conover, P., Feldman, S., and Knight, K. (1986). 'Judging Inflation and Unemployment: The Origins of Retrospective Evaluations', *Journal of Politics*, 48: 565–88.

Converse, P., and Pierce R. (1985). 'Measuring Partisanship', *Political methodology*, 11: 143–66.

Cook, C., and Ramsden, J., eds (1973). *By-elections in British Politics* (Macmillan, London).

Craig, F. W. S. (1980). *Britain Votes, 2: British Parliamentary Election Results 1974–1979* (Parliamentary Research Services, Chichester, West Sussex).

—— (1981). *British Electoral Facts 1832–1980* (Parliamentary Research Services, Chichester, West Sussex).

—— (1987). *Chronology of British Parliamentary By-Elections 1833–1987* (Parliamentary Research Services, Chichester, West Sussex).

Crewe, I. (1981). 'SDP Proves It Can Capture the Heavy Industrial Vote', *The Times*, 17 July.

—— (1982*a*). 'Improving but Could Do Better: The Media and the Polls in the 1979 General Election', in Harrop and Worcester (1982).

—— (1982*b*). 'Is Britain's Two Party System Really about to Crumble?' *Electoral Studies*, 1: 275–313.

—— (1983). 'Surveys of British Elections: Problems of Design, Response and Bias', in *Essex Papers in Politics and Government* (University of Essex, Colchester).

—— (1984). 'The Electorate: Partisan Dealignment Ten Years On', in Berrington, H. (ed.), *Change in British Politics* (Frank Cross, London).

—— (1985). 'Great Britain', in Crewe and Denver (1985).

—— (1986*a*). 'On the Death and Resurrection of Class Voting: Some Comments on How Britain Votes', *Political Studies*, 34: 620–38.

—— (1986*b*). 'Saturation Polling, the Media and the 1983 Election', in Crewe, I., and Harrop, M. (eds.), *Political Communications: The General Election Campaign of 1983* (Cambridge University Press).

——, Alt, J., and Fox, A. (1977). 'Non-Voting in British General Elections 1966–October 1974', in Crouch, C. (ed.), *British Political Sociology Yearbook III (Political Participation)* (Croom Helm, London).

——, ——, and Sarlvik, B. (1977*a*). 'Angels in Plastic: Liberal Support in 1974', *Political Studies*, 15: 343–68.

——, ——, —— (1977*b*). 'Partisan Dealignment in Britain 1964–1974', *British Journal of Political Science*, 7: 129–90.

—— and Denver, D. (1985) *Electoral Change in Western Democracies: Patterns and Sources of Electoral Volatility* (Croom Helm, London)

—— and Harrop, M. (1989). *Political Communications: The General Election Campaign of 1987* (Cambridge University Press).

Criddle, Byron (1988). 'Candidates', ch. 9 in Butler and Kavanagh (1988).

Curtice, J. and Steed, M. (1982). 'Electoral Change and the Production of Government: The Changing Operation of the Electoral System in the United Kingdom since 1955', *British Journal of Political Science*, 12: 249–98.

—— —— (1986). 'Proportionality and Exaggeration in the British Electoral System', *Electoral Studies*, 5: 209–28.

—— —— (1988). 'Appendix 2: An Analysis of the Vote', in Butler and Kavanagh (1988).

Denver, D. (1985). 'Scotland', Crewe and Denver (1985).

Downs, A. (1959). *An Economic Theory of Democracy* (Harper and Row, New York).

Drucker, H. and Brown, G. (1980). *The Politics of Nationalism and Devolution* (Longman, London).

—— *et al.* (1982*a*). 'Do Party Workers Matter? The Evidence from Crosby', *Parliamentary Affairs*, 143–59.

——, —— (1982*b*). 'Learning to Fight Multi-Party Elections: The Lessons of Hillhead', *Parliamentary Affairs*, 252–66.

Dunleavy, P. (1987). 'Class Dealignment in Britain Revisited', *West European Politics*, 10 (July): 400–19.

—— and Husbands, C. (1985). *British Democracy at the Crossroads* (Allen and Unwin, London).

Edwards, M. (1985). 'The Australian Democrats', in Woodward, D., Parkin, A., and Summers, J., *Government, Politics and Power in Australia* (3rd edn; Longman, Melbourne).

Eulau, H., and Lewis-Beck, M. (1985). *Economic Conditions and Electoral Outcomes: The United States and Western Europe* (Agathon, New York).

Feigert, F. B. (1989). *Canada Votes: 1935–1988* (Duke University Press, Durham, NC).

Fiorina, M. (1981). *Retrospective Voting in American National Elections* (Yale University Press, New Haven, Conn.).

Flanagan, S., Dalton, R. J., and Beck, P. A. (1985). *Electoral Change in Advanced Industrial Democracies* (Princeton University Press).

Franklin, M. (1985). *The Decline of Class Voting in Britain* (Clarendon Press, Oxford).

Frey, B. S., and Schneider, F. (1981). 'Recent Research on Empirical Politico-Economic Models', in Hibbs, D. A., and Fassbender, H. (eds.), *Contemporary Political Economy* (North-Holland, Amsterdam).

Gilmour, R. S., and Lamb, R. B. (1986). *Political Alienation in Contemporary America* (St Martin's Press, New York).

Goodhart, C. A. E., and Bhansali, R. J. (1970). 'Political Economy', *Political Studies*, 18.

Gopoian J. D., and Yantek, T. (1988). 'Cross-Pressured Economic Voting in America: The 1984 Election', *Political Behaviour*, 10: 37–51.

Harrop, M. and Worcester, R., eds. (1982). *Political Communications: The General Election Campaign of 1979* (Allen and Unwin, London).

Heath, A., Jowell, R., and Curtice, J. (1985). *How Britain Votes* (Pergamon Press, Oxford).

——,——,—— (1987). 'Trendless Fluctuation: A Reply to Crewe', *Political Studies*, 35: 256–77.

——, ——, —— (1988). 'Partisan Dealignment Revisited', Paper at the Political Studies Association Annual Conference, Plymouth (April).

Hibbs, D. A. and Fassbender, H., eds. (1981). *Contemporary Political Economy* (North Holland, Amsterdam).

Himmelweit, H., Humphreys, P., and Jaeger, M. (1985). *How Voters Decide* (revised edn.; Open University Press, Milton Keynes).

——, Jaeger, M., and Stockdale, J. (1978). 'Memory of Past Vote: Implications of a Study of Bias in Recall', *British Journal of Political Science*, 13: 545–65.

Hinckley, B. (1981). *Congressional Elections* (Congressional Quarterly Press, Washington, DC).

Hodder-Williams, R. (1970). *Public Opinion Polls and British Politics* (Routledge and Kegan Paul, London).

Hudson, J. (1984). 'Prime Ministerial Popularity in the UK: 1960–81', *Political Studies*, 32: 86–97.

—— (1985). 'The Relationship between Government Popularity and Approval for the Government's Record in the United Kingdom', *British Journal of Political Science*, 15: 165–86.

Ingle, S. (1987). *The British Party System* Blackwell, Oxford).

Irvine, W. P. (1981). 'The Canadian Voter', in Penniman, H. R., *Canada at the Polls, 1979 and 1980* (American Enterprise Institute, Washington, DC).

Jupp, J. (1982). *Party Politics: Australia 1966–1981* (Allen and Unwin, Sydney).

Kavanagh, D. (1970). *Constituency Electioneering in Britain* (Longman, London).

—— (1982). 'Election Campaigns and Opinion Polls: British Political Parties and the Use of Private Polls', in Harrop and Worcester (1982).

Kay, B. J. (1981). 'By-Elections as Indicators of Canadian Voting', *Canadian Journal of Political Science*, 14: 37–52.

Kellas, J. G. (1984). *The Scottish Political System* (Cambridge University Press).

Kellner, P. (1985). 'How to Judge Polls and By-Elections: A Case Study', *New Statesman*, 13 December, 9.

—— (1987). 'Polls, Damned Polls and the Battle for Greenwich', *New Statesman*, 20 February, 7.

Kemp, D. A. (1978). *Society and Electoral Behaviour in Australia* (University of Queensland Press, St Lucia).

Kernell, S. (1977). 'Presidential Popularity and Negative Voting', *American Political Science Review*, 71: pp. 44–66.

Key, V. O. (1966). *The Responsible Electorate* (Vintage, New York).

Kiewiet, D. R. (1983). *Macroeconomics and Micropolitics* (University of Chicago Press).

—— and Rivers, D. (1984). 'A Retrospective on Retrospective Voting', *Political Behavior*, 6: 369–93.

Kinder, D. R., and Kiewiet, D. R. (1979). 'Economic Discontent and Political Behavior: The Role of Personal Grievances and Collective Economic Judgements in Congressional Voting', *American Journal of Political Science*, 23: 495–527.

——, —— (1981). 'Sociotropic Politics: The American Case', *British Journal of Political Science*, 11: 129–62.

—— and Mebane, W. R. (1983). 'Politics and Economics in Everyday Life', in Monroe, K. (1983). *The Political Process and Economic Change* (Agathon, New York).

King, A. (1968). 'Why All Governments Lose By-Elections', *New Society*, 21 March, 413–15.

—— (1982). 'Whatever is Happening to the British Party System?', *Political Studies*, Winter: 10–17.

Kramer, G. H. (1983). 'The Ecological Fallacy Revisited: Aggregate- versus Individual-level findings on Economics and Elections, and Sociotropic Voting', *American Political Science Review*, 77: 92–107.

Lewis, E. G. (1943). *British By-Elections as a Reflection of Public Opinion* University of California Publications in Political Science, 1, Berkeley, Calif.).

Lewis-Beck, M. S. (1988). 'Economics and the American Voter: Past, Present, Future', *Political Behavior*, 10: 5–21.

Lovenduski, J., and Norris, P. (1989). 'Selecting Women Candidates: Obstacles to the Feminisation of the House of Commons', *European Journal of Political Research*, 17: 533–62.

MacIver, D. N. (1982). 'The Paradox of Nationalism in Scotland', in Williams (1982).

McKie, D. (1973). 'By-Elections under the Wilson Government', in Cook and Ramsden (1973).

Mendelsohn, G. H. and Crespi, I. (1970). *Polls, Television and the New Politics* (Chandler, Pa).

Milbrath, L. W. (1966). *Political Participation* (Rand McNally, Chicago).

Miller, A. H. (1974*a*). 'Political Issues and Trust in Government: 1964–70', *American Political Science Review*, 68: 951–72.

—— (1974*b*). 'Rejoinder to "Comment" by Jack Citrin: Political Discontent or Ritualism?', *American Political Science Review*, 68: 989–1001.

—— (1983). 'Is Confidence Rebounding', *Public Opinion*, 6 (June/July), 16–20.

—— and Wattenberg, M. P. (1984). 'Throwing the Rascals out: Policy and Performance Evaluations of Presidential Candidates, 1952–1980', *American Political Science Review*, 78: 359–72.

Miller, W. L. (1981). *The End of British Politics* (Clarendon Press, Oxford).

——, Broughton, D., Sontag, N., and McLean, D. (1989). 'Political Change in Britain during the 1987 Campaign', in

——, Crewe, I. and Harrop, M., *Political Communications: The General Election Campaign of 1987* (Cambridge University Press).

——, Clarke, H., Harrop, M., Le Duc, L., and Whiteley, P. (1990). *How Voters Change: The 1987 British General Election Campaign in Perspective* (Clarendon Press, Oxford, forthcoming).

—— and Mackie, M. (1973). 'The Electoral Cycle and the Asymmetry of Government and Opposition Popularity: An Alternative Model of the Relationship between Economic Conditions and Political Popularity', *Political Studies*, 21: 263–79.

Monroe, K. (1979). 'Econometric Analysis of Political Behaviour: A Critical Review', *Political Behavior*, 1: 137–74.

—— ed. (1983). *The Political Process and Economic Change* (Agathon, New York).

—— (1984), *Presidential Popularity and the Economy* (Praeger, New York).

Mughan, A. (1986*a*). *Party and Participation in British Elections* (Frances Pinter, London).

—— (1986*b*). 'Towards a Political Explanation of Government Vote Losses in Midterm By-Elections', *American Political Science Review*, 80: 761–75.

—— (1988). 'On the By-Election Vote of Governments in Britain', *Legislative Studies Quarterly*, 13 (1 Feb.): 29–43.

Mullin, W. A. R. (1979). 'The Scottish Nationalist Party', in Drucker, H. (ed.), *Multi-Party Politics* (Macmillan, London).

Nicholas, H. G. (1951). *The British General Election of 1950* (Macmillan, London).

Norpath, H. (1987). 'The Falklands War and Government Popularity in Britain: Rally without Consequence or Surge without Decline', *Electoral Studies*, 6: 3–16.

Norris, P. (1987*a*). 'Four Weeks of Sound and Fury: The 1987 British Election Campaign', *Parliamentary Affairs*, 40: 458–67.

—— (1987*b*). 'The 1987 British General Election: The Hidden Agenda', *Teaching Politics*, 16: 311–23.

—— (1987*c*). 'Retrospective Voting in the 1984 Presidential Elections: Peace, Prosperity and Patriotism', *Political Studies*, 35: 289–300.

—— (1989). 'Marginal Polls: Their Role and Record', in Crewe, I., and Harrop, M., *Political Communications: The General Election Campaign of 1987* (Cambridge University Press).

—— (1990). 'Thatcher's Enterprise Society and Electoral Change', *West European Politics*, 13: 63–78.

—— and Lovenduski, J. (1989). 'Women Candidates for Parliament: Transforming the Agenda?', *British Journal of Political Science*, 106–115.

Oakeshott, M. (1973). 'Towards an Economic Theory of By-Elections since the War', in Cook and Ramsden (1973), ch. 11: 316–29.

Paldam, M. (1981). 'A Preliminary Survey of European Theories and Findings on Vote and Popularity Functions', *European Journal of Political Research*, 9: 181–99.

Patterson, P. (1967). *The Selectorate* (MacGibbon and Kee, London).

Pedersen, M. (1980). 'On Measuring Party System Change: A Methodological Critique and a Suggestion', *Comparative Political Studies*, 12: 387–403.

Penniman, H. R., ed. (1977). *Australia at the Polls: The National Elections of 1975* (American Enterprise Institute, Washington, DC).

Perry, P. (1979). 'Certain Problems in Election Survey Methodology', *Public Opinion Quarterly*, 43; 312–25.

Pissarides, C. A. (1980). 'British Government Popularity and Economic Performance', *Economic Journal*, 90: 569–81.

Pollock, J. K. (1941). 'British By-Elections since the War', *American Political Science Review*, 35: 607–19.

Rallings, C., and Thrasher, M. (1987). 'Using Local By-Elections as Surrogate Indicators of National Party Support', *Local Government Chronicle*.

Ranney, A. (1965). *Pathways to Parliament* (Macmillan, London).

Rasmussen, J. (1965). *The Liberal Party* (Constable, London).

—— (1981*a*). 'The Electoral Costs of Being a Woman in the 1979 British General Election', *Comparative Politics*, July, 461–75.

—— (1981*b*). 'Women Candidates in British By-Elections: A Rational Choice Interpretation of Electoral Behaviour', *Political Studies*, 29: 265–74.

Reynolds, P. (1977). 'The Role of the Minor Parties', in Penniman (1977).

Robertson, D. (1984). *Class and the British Electorate* (Blackwell, Oxford).

Robinson, W. S. (1950). 'Ecological Correlation and the Behavior of Individuals', *American Sociological Review*, 15: 351–7.

Roper, B. W. (1983). 'Some Things that Concern Me', *Public Opinion Quarterly*, 47: 303–9.

Rose, R. (1984). 'Opinion Polls as Feedback Mechanism', in A. Ranney (ed.), *Britain at the Polls, 1983* (American Enterprise Institute, Washington, DC).

—— (1986). 'Brecon's Three-Way Signpost', *The Times*, 6 July.

—— and McAllister, I. (1986). *Voters Begin to Choose* (Sage Publications, London)

Rush, M. (1969). *The Selection of Parliamentary Candidates* (Nelson, London).

—— (1986). 'The Selectorate Revisited: Selecting Parliamentary Candidates in the 1980s', *Teaching Politics*, 15: 99–113.

Sarlvik, B., and Crewe, I. (1983). *Decade of Dealignment* (Cambridge University Press).

Saunders, D., Ward, H., and Marsh, D. (with Fletcher, T.) (1987). 'Government Popularity and the Falklands War: A Reassessment', *British Journal of Political Science*, 17: 281–313.

Scarrow, H. A. (1961). 'By-Elections and Public Opinion in Canada', *Public Opinion Quarterly*, 25: 79–91.

Sigelman, L. (1981). 'Special Elections to the US House: Some Descriptive Generalizations', *Legislative Studies Quarterly*, 6: 577–88.

Silver, B. D., Anderson, B. A., and Abramson, P. R. (1986). 'Who Overreports Voting?', *American Political Science Review*, 80: Part 2.

Starr, G., Richmond, K., and Madox, G. (1978). *Political Parties in Australia* (Heinemann Educational Australia, Richmond).

Steed, M. (1983). 'The Electoral Strategy of the Liberal Party', in Bogdanor (1983).

Stephenson, H. (1982). *Claret and Chips: The Rise of the SDP* (Joseph, London).

Stovall, J. G., and Solomon, J. H. (1984). 'The Polls as News Event in the 1980 Presidential Campaign', *Public Opinion Quarterly*, 48: 615–23.

Stray, S. J., and Beaumont, C. D. (1987). 'Government Popularity and Attitude toward the Government's Record Revisited', *British Journal of Political Science*, 17: 122–8.

—— and Silver, M. (1979). 'Do By-Elections Demonstrate a Government's Unpopularity?', *Parliamentary Affairs*, 32: 264–70.

—— —— (1983). 'Government Popularity, By-Elections and Cycles', *Parliamentary Affairs*, 36: 49–55.

Studlar, D. (1984). 'By-Elections and the Liberal-SDP Alliance', *Teaching Politics*, 13: 85–94.

—— and Sigelman, L. (1987). 'Special Elections: A Comparative Perspective', *British Journal of Political Science*, 17: 247–56.

Swaddle, K. (1988). 'Doorstep Electioneering in Britain: An Exploration of the Constituency Canvass', *Electoral Studies*, 7: 41–66.

Tatchell, P. (1983). *The Battle for Bermondsey* (Heretic Books, London).

Taylor, S., and Payne, C. (1973). 'Features of Electoral Behaviour at By-Elections', in Cook and Ramsden (1973).

Teer, F., and Spence, S. D. (1973). *Political Opinion Polls* (Hutchinson, London).

The Times Guide to the House of Commons, June 1987 (1987). (Times Publications, London).

Tufte, E. R. (1975). 'Determinants of the Outcomes of Midterm Congressional Elections', *American Political Science Review*, 69: 812–26.

Tyler, R. (1987). *Campaign: The Selling of the Prime Minster* (Grafton, London).

Vallance, E. (1988). 'Two Cheers for Democracy', *Parliamentary Affairs*, 41.

Verba, S., and Nie, N. (1972). *Participation in America: Political Democracy and Social Equality* (Harper and Row, New York).

Wallace, W. (1983). 'Survival and Revival', in Bogdanor (1983).

Weatherford, M. (1983). 'Economic Voting and the "Symbolic Politics" argument: A Reinterpretation and Synthesis', *American Political Science Review*, 77: 158–74.

Whitley, P. (1983). *The Labour Party in Crisis* (Methuen, London).

—— (1984). 'Inflation, Unemployment and Government Popularity', *Electoral Studies*, 3: 3–25.

Williams, C. H. (1982). *National Separatism* (University of Wales Press, Cardiff).

Wilson, D. (1987). *Battle for Power* (Sphere Books, London).

Wolfinger, R. E., and Rosenstone, S. J. (1980). *Who Votes?* (Yale University Press, New Haven, Conn.).

Worcester, R. M. (1980). 'Pollster, the Press and Political Polling in Britain', *Public Opinion Quarterly*, 44: 548–66.

—— (1983). 'Political Opinion Polling in Great Britain', ch. 4 in Worcester, R. M. (ed.), *Political Opinion Polling* (Macmillan, London).

—— (1984). 'The Polls: Britain at the Polls 1945–1983', *Public Opinion Quarterly*, 48: 824–33.

Young, H. (1986). 'Pessimism Will Call in the Votes', *Guardian*, 6 November.

Young, K. (1973). 'Orpington and the "Liberal Revival"', in Cook and Ramsden (1973).

Zentner, P. (1982). *Social Democracy in Britain* (John Martin, London).

Index

Index compiled by Peva Keane